p142 n2
p.7 objective

JON BALSERAK 07771-467-774

The Judaizing Calvin

OXFORD STUDIES IN HISTORICAL THEOLOGY

The Judaizing Calvin

*Sixteenth-Century Debates over
the Messianic Psalms*

G. SUJIN PAK

OXFORD
UNIVERSITY PRESS
2010

OXFORD
UNIVERSITY PRESS

Oxford University Press, Inc., publishes works that further
Oxford University's objective of excellence
in research, scholarship, and education.

Oxford   New York
Auckland   Cape Town   Dar es Salaam   Hong Kong   Karachi
Kuala Lumpur   Madrid   Melbourne   Mexico City   Nairobi
New Delhi   Shanghai   Taipei   Toronto

With offices in
Argentina   Austria   Brazil   Chile   Czech Republic   France   Greece
Guatemala   Hungary   Italy   Japan   Poland   Portugal   Singapore
South Korea   Switzerland   Thailand   Turkey   Ukraine   Vietnam

Copyright © 2010 by Oxford University Press, Inc.

Published by Oxford University Press, Inc.
198 Madison Avenue, New York, New York 10016

www.oup.com

Oxford is a registered trademark of Oxford University Press.

Library of Congress Cataloging-in-Publication Data
Pak, G. Sujin, 1971–
The judaizing Calvin : sixteenth-century debates
over the Messianic Psalms / by G. Sujin Pak.
       p.   cm.
Includes bibliographical references and index.
ISBN 978-0-19-537192-5
1. Messianic Psalms.   2. Calvin, Jean, 1509–1564.
3. Bible. O.T. Psalms—Criticism, interpretation, etc.—History—16th century.   I. Title.
BS1445.M4P35 2009
223'.20609—dc22   2009009643

9 8 7 6 5 4 3 2 1

Printed in the United States of America
on acid-free paper

For Ken, my beloved Presbyterian

Acknowledgments

This project began as a doctoral dissertation submitted to the Religion Department at Duke University. Not only for his role as serving as the advisor of this study but even more for the matchless model he provides for research in the history of biblical interpretation, I owe a deep debt of gratitude to David C. Steinmetz, former Amos Ragan Kearns Professor of the History of Christianity and now professor emeritus. For his examples of mentoring, scholarship, and teaching, I am eternally grateful. These are gifts that go on giving and guiding me in my own development as a scholar and teacher. I also offer my sincerest thanks to the other members of my committee, Elizabeth Clark, Kalman Bland, and Warren Smith, for their support and helpful feedback.

I am ever so grateful to my reviewers in the manuscript submission process to Oxford University Press. I appreciate the time, care, and detail with which they responded to my work and their encouragement and enthusiasm for it. The specific insights provided in these reviews truly enabled me to strengthen and improve the final product. Of course, any remaining shortcomings are solely my own. In addition, I want to thank Cynthia Read, Christine Dahlin, and Mariana Templin for their excellent work in seeing the manuscript through the review and production process.

The journey of bringing this work to publication has been longer than I had hoped, and along the way, there have been true friends and colleagues who have offered me profound encouragement in my research and career. They include Mickey Mattox, Susan Schreiner, Esther Chung-Kim, Edwin Tait, Deborah Marcuse, Andrew Yang, Brent Laytham, George Kalantzis, K. K. Yeo, and Steve Long. I also owe a huge debt of gratitude to the Perilman Scholarship from Judaic Studies at Duke University for their financial support of my doctoral studies, as well as A Foundation for Theological Education for a yearly stipend and for connecting me to many significant Methodist scholars, many of whom have become close friends.

My parents, David and Sue Pak, have been and continue to be my most enthusiastic supporters. I would not be who I am today without their love, guidance, discipline, and praise. Though I have dedicated this work to my husband, they should know that it is in so many ways equally theirs. I also want to thank other friends who have inquired about the project and awaited its publication. Here I especially mention my best friend, Ashley; my sister, Minna; my pastor, Kevin; and my godmothers, Betty and Priscilla. Though my two daughters, Amelie and Anika, are too young to understand what has been preoccupying their mother, I also want to thank them for their patience with me. To my husband, Ken, I dedicate this work. He knows better than anyone else what this project entailed in its daily journey. You are the joy and love of my life, the truest of partners, my most cherished companion, my beloved Presbyterian.

Contents

Abbreviations

CO   Ioannis Calvini Opera Quae Supersunt Omnia. 59 vols. Corpus Reformatorum, vols. 29–88. Ed. G. Baum, E. Cunitz, E. Reuss. Brunswick and Berlin, 1863–1900.

CR   Corpus Reformatorum. Braunschweig, 1834–.

PL   Patrologia Latina. 221 vols. Ed. J.-P. Migne. Paris, 1844–55.

WA   D. Martin Luthers Werke. Kritische Gesamtausgabe. 72 vols. Weimar: H. Böhlau, 1883–2007.

WABr D. Martin Luthers Werke. Kritische Gesamtausgabe. Breifwechsel. 18 vols. Weimar: H. Böhlau, 1930–85.

WATr D. Martin Luthers Werke. Kritische Gesamtausgabe. Tischreden. 6 vols. Weimar: H. Böhlau, 1912–21.

NRSV New Revised Standard Version

The Judaizing Calvin

Introduction

Since David C. Steinmetz's hallmark essay "The Superiority of
Pre-Critical Exegesis," the importance of the history of exegesis has
been rediscovered and revitalized in both medieval and Reformation
scholarship.[1] Particularly in the area of Reformation research, works
from such scholars as John Thompson, Susan Schreiner, Timothy
Wengert, Craig Farmer, Barbara Pitkin, Irena Backus, Mickey Mattox,
Beth Kreitzer, and Raymond Blacketer have provided careful and
splendid studies of the significance of biblical exegesis in the theology
and work of the Protestant reformers.[2] Other significant volumes of
compiled essays on this topic have also contributed to the ongoing
understanding of the importance of sixteenth-century biblical
interpretation for the processes of reform, confessional formation,
and shifts in the practices of reading and preaching Scripture.[3]
John Calvin's exegesis, in particular, has been the subject of
several important books and articles, both among historians of the
sixteenth-century and even among modern theologians and biblical
scholars.[4] Although some modern scholars like Hans Frei recognize,
affirm, and exalt Calvin's premodern presuppositions and practices,
others such as Frederic Farrar and Philip Schaff have found in him the
precursor to principles of modern historical criticism.[5] This book
offers a very concentrated and, I think, very interesting piece of this
puzzle of Calvin's role and place in the history of biblical exegesis; for
by contextualizing Calvin's exegesis of a particular set of Psalms
within his larger sixteenth-century setting, one can discover many of

the reasons that several insist upon his precritical status while others hail him as the first modern exegete.

Not enough can be said about the crucial importance of the views and practices of reading and interpreting Scripture for the Protestant Reformation. All of the excellent books written in the last three decades still cannot capture the magnitude and breadth of this subject in any single volume, and by no means, do I claim even to come close to such a feat. Indeed, the statement of the problem by Richard Muller in the introduction to the essays compiled in *Biblical Interpretation in the Era of the Reformation* still remains true: "There are at present no studies of the history of biblical interpretation in the sixteenth century comparable in their scope and detail to the work of Margerie on the patristic period or to the works of Spicq, Smalley, and de Lubac on the Middle Ages."[6] Yet, I hope in this book to make a modest contribution not only to the subject of Calvin's place in the history of biblical exegesis but also to studies concerning Protestant debates about their relationship to the prior exegetical tradition, suitable christological interpretations of the Old Testament, and proper Christian views and uses of Jewish exegesis.

As many readers already know, one of the focal points of the Protestant challenge to the Roman Catholic theology and practices of their day was the call for the church to return to Scripture and the forms and practices of the early apostolic church as laid out in Scripture (particularly the Book of Acts). This brought about significant changes in the life and worship of the church, including, most notably for our purposes here, the shift from the Mass to the preaching of God's Word as the centerpiece of the worship service, more vernacular translations of the Bible, and an emphasis on the education of laypersons, especially in the domain of biblical knowledge. The call of *prima scriptura* for some (i.e., a more correct description of Luther and Calvin) and *sola scriptura* for others (e.g., Anabaptists) voiced the challenge of various Protestant reformers to Roman Catholic understandings of the authority of tradition and the power of the pope especially. While Roman Catholics tended to give equal voice to Scripture and the tradition vested in ordained persons, Protestants wanted Scripture to be the unquestioningly chief authority on all issues, if not the sole authority.

Yet, Protestants' appeals to Scripture as a clear and decisive authority soon became problematized as they increasingly realized that such appeals are first and foremost to their various *interpretations* of Scripture—interpretations that very often exhibited numerous levels of disagreement. Disagreements over the proper interpretation of Scripture on such matters as the theology and practices of justification, Eucharist, and baptism became immediately evident in the early years of reform and are at the heart of the development of separate confessions of faith, in addition to important other political, economic, and social factors. The history of the exegesis of a set of significant Psalms examined in this particular study portrays in miniature form how Protestants used the biblical commentary to set forth specifically Protestant programs of theology and practice. In other words, Luther, Calvin, and Bucer—each in their own particular ways—used the Psalms to teach key Protestant doctrines and Protestant understandings of piety and worship. Despite many significant agreements among them, noteworthy shades of difference or outright disagreements are equally illuminating.

Moreover, a study of a piece of the history of Christian Old Testament exegesis, and Psalms exegesis in particular, contains important implications for the history of Christian-Jewish relations. Within the bounds of this particular study, issues of the views of Jews and Judaism that emerge from various Christian readings of the Psalms, as well as Christian practices of christological interpretation and suitable Christian uses of Jewish exegesis, arise as critically debated matters. Thus, in this introduction, I first set forth the scope, framework, and thesis of this book and close with a modest account of the significant role biblical exegesis has played in the history of Christian-Jewish relations.

The Scope, Framework, and Thesis of This Study

The Book of Psalms has had a long-standing central place in the worship life and theological formation of the Christian church. The Protestant reformers knew this just as well as, or perhaps better than, anyone else. Martin Luther, John Calvin, and Martin Bucer equally emphasized the vitally formative role the Psalms play in the Christian life and the life of the church. Martin Luther turned to the Psalms time and again throughout the crucial stages of his theological development and emergent reforming program. Both Luther and Calvin looked upon the Psalms as a Christian handbook or "miniature Bible" that provided a mirror to teach and reflect the true content and practice of Christianity.[7] Bucer chose to write a commentary on the Psalms under a pseudonym in hopes of reaching a wider audience and for the purposes of encouraging the persecuted Protestant churches of France and Lower Germany.[8] Both Bucer and Calvin explicitly used the Psalms for the theological and spiritual formation of their communities in Strasbourg and Geneva; indeed, the liturgical life of these communities centered upon the use of metrical Psalms and the practice of Psalm singing in worship.[9] Equally, they both appealed to the Psalms as the key source by which to teach the character and practice of Protestant piety—the very piety that is the heart of their reforming programs.

As has been already noted, the era of the Protestant reformations was a time when the sources of authority for the Christian life and for the life of the church were questioned and redefined in significant ways. Luther, Bucer, and Calvin equally, and in their own distinctive ways, called for the primacy of Scripture over and against the authority of the pope, the Roman Catholic Church, and an uncritical adoption of the patristic tradition. In their advancement of the superior authority of Scripture, they also held to an optimism about its perspicuity. Indeed, such clarity of Scripture was often elusive, and such was true for their readings of the Psalms as well. The proper interpretation of the Psalms became an area of debate among the Protestant reformers— a debate in which I believe they each had a deep investment precisely because of the central place of the Psalms in the theological and spiritual formation and worship of Christians.

This project aims to explore the history of the interpretation of Psalms 2, 8, 16, 22, 45, 72, 110, and 118. I focus on these because they are the Psalms that are quoted in the New Testament as literal prophecies of Christ's incarnation, passion, resurrection, ascension, and kingdom.[10] Thus, this is simply what I mean by referring to these eight Psalms as "messianic Psalms." Of course, among many Christian interpreters, many more Psalms have been read as literal prophecies of Christ. Yet, Christian interpreters have understood these eight Psalms as *particularly* clear in their teachings concerning Christ and Trinity.[11] The first chapter demonstrates that although patristic, medieval, and late-medieval interpreters of these Psalms do have their own nuances, their overwhelming consensus is that the literal sense of these eight Psalms is their prophecies of Christ and their teachings concerning Trinity and the two natures of Christ.

Because within the scope of a study like this, choices are necessary to make it a feasible project, the first chapter explores the commentaries of the Gloss, Denis the Carthusian, Nicholas of Lyra, and Jacques Lefèvre d'Étaples in order to give a representation of trends and consensus in the antecedent Christian tradition's interpretation of these eight Psalms. I have chosen the Gloss because it provides the readings of Augustine (354–430 CE) and Cassiodorus (490–585 CE) on the Psalms—both of which had widespread impact on Psalms reading in the medieval church. I include Nicholas of Lyra and Jacques Lefèvred' Étaples because we know that Martin Luther consulted their Psalms commentaries; thus, they serve as clear and important backdrops for his exegesis of the Psalms.[12] Finally, Denis the Carthusian is a good representative of the general consensus on the late-medieval reading of these Psalms, as seen in the prominence and frequency of his commentaries in monastic libraries and schools. Of course, scholars will recognize that one particular line of exegesis is lacking—namely, those with a kind of Antiochene emphasis on history, such as may be found in the Victorine School. This type is omitted specifically because there is little evidence that the Protestant reformers consulted these sources and more generally because, as Beryl Smalley states, "[m]uch of the Antiochene material was irretrievably lost to the medieval Latin student."[13] Moreover, Smalley points out that exactly these eight Psalms comprise a particularly special case, for Andrew of St. Victor and Herbert of Bosham maintain the christological readings of these Psalms as their chief sense. Indeed, Herbert of Bosham gives primacy to the christological meaning of ten of the first twenty-five Psalms, which include Psalms 2, 8, 16, and 22.[14]

After setting up this medieval and late-medieval backdrop, I then turn to analyze in separate chapters the interpretations of these eight Psalms by Martin Luther, Martin Bucer, and John Calvin. These three exegetes are chosen for their obvious prominent leadership in the Protestant Reformation and particularly concerning the emergence of Protestant biblical commentaries, but they are also chosen because of their intimate relationship with one another. Specifically, Martin Bucer is shown to be a significant mediating figure between the exegeses of Luther and Calvin. Thus correspondences are most clear between Luther's and Bucer's interpretations and between Bucer's and Calvin's interpretations of these Psalms. Each chapter underscores the theological content that the exegete finds in these Psalms, as well as their exegetical strategies and principles. The overriding objective is to demonstrate a significant shift that John Calvin introduces into the history of the exegesis of these eight Psalms. In the midst of doing so, however, I also portray some shared uses of these Psalms among these three Protestant reformers while highlighting the unique contributions of each. Key issues that arise among Luther's, Bucer's, and Calvin's readings of these Psalms include the identification of their "literal sense," proper principles of christological exegesis, the correct doctrine contained and taught therein, the uses of these Psalms to provide comfort, their polemical uses, the views of Jews and Judaism extracted from them, the appropriate Christian uses of Jewish exegesis, and the proper role that the human author and his history should play in the interpretations of these Psalms.

The study culminates in a debate over Calvin's exegesis between a Lutheran named Aegidius Hunnius (1550–1603) and a Reformed theologian named David Pareus (1548–1622) in which these eight Psalms figure prominently.[15] In 1589 (twenty-five years after Calvin's death), Hunnius wrote a treatise on the doctrine of Trinity in which he accuses Calvin of undermining the exegetical foundations of this central Christian doctrine. Four years later, Hunnius launched an even more in-depth and widespread attack on Calvin's biblical exegesis. The heart of Hunnius's allegations against Calvin concerns his lack of christological exegesis of biblical passages traditionally read first and foremost as literal prophecies of Christ's incarnation, passion, resurrection, ascension, exaltation, and kingdom. Equally and intimately related, Hunnius also rebuked Calvin for not reading in these same scriptural texts the central doctrines of Trinity and the two natures of Christ. By not rendering the christological reading as the primary sense and by denying the teachings of Trinity and the two natures of Christ found in these Psalms, Hunnius believes Calvin covers these most clear prophecies with "Jewish perversions." Hence, this treatise against Calvin is precisely named the "Judaizing Calvin," from which this book receives its title.[16]

In many ways, the debate between Hunnius and Pareus lays bare the central argument of this book. By using the debate between Hunnius and Pareus as the culminating piece of the history of the exegesis of these eight Psalms, I intend, principally, to argue a particular thesis concerning Calvin's place in this exegetical history and, secondarily, to suggest some possibilities for the significant role of biblical exegesis in the formation of emerging Protestant confessional identities in the sixteenth century. The culminations of both of these arguments are the subject of the book's conclusion, yet a few words should be said here at the start. This book reveals that Calvin introduces a significant shift in the history of the interpretation of these Psalms first and foremost concerning his identification of their "literal sense." Rather than identifying the literal sense with the christological reading, in which the majority of Christian interpreters prior to Calvin see in these Psalms prophecies literally fulfilled by Christ, Calvin identifies their literal sense in reference to the human author's intention and, thus, concerning their meaning in the life and experiences of David (or, in some cases, Solomon). In this way, Calvin very effectively narrows the suitable christological readings of these Psalms through his exegetical principles of maintaining human authorial intention, focusing on the author's historical context, and keeping the "plain and simple" sense of the text. Such exegetical emphases upon human authorial intention, the decisive role of the original historical context, and the grammatical reading of the text are precisely prominent among proponents of the modern historical critical method. Hence, the book concludes with an analysis of Calvin's place in the history of exegesis with exactly the crucial questions of his relationships to precritical exegesis and modern principles of exegesis in mind. Although I firmly locate Calvin in the realm of precritical exegesis and do not envisage him as a father of modern exegesis, I also suggest that Calvin cannot be so easily distanced from modern principles of exegesis either. One could understand some elements of modern exegesis as taking up precisely such emphases of Calvin's—yet doing so in wholly other contexts with considerably dissimilar exegetical assumptions and principles and thus leading to notably different exegetical outcomes that Calvin would probably never have imagined.

I also offer some suggestions concerning the role of sixteenth-century Psalms reading and the accusation of "judaizing" in the emergence of Protestant confessional identities. Though admittedly, the scope of this study cannot adequately prove these two points, I do believe it makes some stimulating inroads into these topics.[17] More generally, I hope that this book can contribute to the emerging focus on the role of biblical interpretation in confessional identity formation.[18] In doing so, I hope to begin to portray that Psalms reading is not only about meaning making but also about the advancement of particular theological, doctrinal, and ethical programs—indeed, it makes clear contributions to the process of confessional formation.[19]

The Significance of the History of Exegesis in Christian-Jewish Relations

The impact of biblical exegesis—particularly disputes over the correct interpretation of the prophecies in the Hebrew Bible—for the history of the relationship between Christians and Jews cannot be overstated, nor can it be adequately described here.[20] Yet, some things should be said by way of introduction so that the significance of this study's contribution to this topic can be made clearer. Much of Christian anti-Judaism from the earliest times up until the present comes in some considerable fashion from particular ways and kinds of readings of the Christian Bible.[21] There are at least four basic ways that Christians have used exegesis that have direct impact on their views of and relations with Jews and Judaism, and all four of these ways have tended to have far more of a negative impact than a positive one, although I argue that this does not necessarily have to be the case. The first concerns the interpretations and applications of prophecies in the Hebrew Bible or, as many Christians would name it, Old Testament prophecy. In precritical exegesis, with which this book is primarily concerned, the vast majority of Christian exegetes argued and aimed to prove that Jesus Christ fulfills the Old Testament prophecies of the Messiah. This was the central assertion of the early Christian faith that led to the separation of Christianity from its Jewish roots. Though I would maintain that such an assertion does not necessarily have to have a negative impact on Christian views of and relations with Jews and Judaism, sadly, more often than not, this is the case.[22] From the intensity and even nastiness of the early disputes over the Hebrew scriptures that appear in the New Testament texts themselves, to forced conversions of Jews that occurred all too frequently in the first fifteen hundred years of the church, to medieval sermons Jews were compelled to hear to try to convince them of the truth of Christianity, one can see just a few of the negative impacts of this claim.

In the sixteenth-century debate over the proper reading of these eight Psalms, Hunnius saw precisely this Christian assertion of the fulfillment of Old Testament prophecy by Jesus Christ as being weakened. This particular set of Psalms was understood as containing especially clear and strong prophecies of Christ as the promised Messiah; they were part of the exegetical mainstay of Christian claims about Jesus Christ. Thus, Calvin was performing no small feat when he made the christological content of these texts secondary to their reading concerning David. On the other hand, I want to suggest that perhaps Christians can see in Calvin's reading of these texts one possible way of reading them that still maintains a kind of christological center while also avoiding much of the anti-Judaism that has tended to accompany many premodern Christian readings of these Psalms.[23]

A second way that biblical exegesis has affected Christian-Jewish relations over the centuries is the use of the biblical text by Christians to disinherit Jews and Judaism. This is saying something more than simply the fulfillment of Old Testament prophecy by Jesus Christ, for it proceeds from this point to argue that the promises of God now no longer belong to the Israel Jews and Judaism embody but to the Israel now embodied by the church. This includes seeing the prophecy of Matt 24:1–2,[24] as well as various Old Testament prophecies about the coming judgment of Judah and Israel, as being fulfilled in the destruction of Jerusalem and the second temple by the Roman army under the Emperor Titus in 70 CE in order to argue that these events represent the punishment of Jews and their abandonment by God. Classic studies that highlight this development within Christian theology include James W. Parkes's *The Conflict of the Church and the Synagogue*, Rosemary Radford Ruether's *Faith and Fratricide*, and Jeffrey Siker's *Disinheriting the Jews.*[25] While I might want to still argue that Christian claims to scriptural promises again do not necessitate the disinheriting of Jews and Judaism (for one could claim the promises and not also make the additional move that they can no longer belong to Jews and Judaism), the fact of the matter is that such claims historically, more often than not, have had exactly that adjacent purpose. Exegetically, this might be expressed both in a pervasive prophecy-fulfillment schema, where Old Testament prophecy is fulfilled in Jesus Christ and in the experience of the Christian church, and in typological readings of Scripture, where what is foreshadowed in the Old Testament finds its fulfillment in the New Testament.

A third way that biblical interpretation has had a bearing on Christian-Jewish relations involves the use of scriptural passages to depict particular negative images of Jews and Judaism. Biblical passages from both the Old and New Testaments have been used to portray Judaism as a dead religion that is concerned merely with ceremony and law or as a religion of "works righteous-ness." Indeed, we will see that this is one of Luther's uses of these eight Psalms. Texts such as Ps 78:8 and Is 48:4 have been used by Christian exegetes to depict Jews as a stubborn, obstinate people, and Is 42:19–20 and particular verses in Exodus have been employed to represent Jews and Judaism as blind, deaf, stiff-necked, and resolutely unbelieving.[26] Harsh New Testament texts such as Jn 8:39–47 that describe the Jews as liars and children of the devil have been the basis of treatises such as Martin Luther's *On the Jews and Their Lies.*[27]

Several Christian exegetes of the eight Psalms considered in this study have conjured such images of Jews and Judaism already mentioned here, but even more common is the depiction of Jews as the crucifiers of Christ and, more generally, as the enemies of Christ and the church. These eight messian-ic Psalms in particular evoke from the Christian antecedent tradition the portrayal of Jews as the enemies and crucifiers of Christ, for such is the consequence of reading them as pure prophecies of Christ's passion and resurrection, especially. Luther retains this tradition and redeploys it in a reading strategy whereby he uses Jewish attributes and practices as the proto-typical definition of the "enemy" of Christ and the church and thereby aligns Roman Catholicism with these attributes and practices to recast Roman Catho-lics as the contemporary enemies of Christ and the church. John Calvin, on the other hand, in not reading these as pure prophecies of Christ's passion, resurrection, and ascension, does not retain this delineation of Jews as the enemies of Christ and the church. On the contrary, Calvin elevates biblical Jews, such as David, as supremely positive examples for the church's imitation. Though I by no means mean to argue that Calvin fully escapes the anti-Judaism of his time (for he certainly does not), I do find in his exegesis of these eight Psalms a powerful alternative nonetheless.

Fourth, biblical exegesis itself has been an important point of contact between Christians and Jews. At several moments in this history, Christian exegetes have sought out Jewish rabbis for the purposes of learning or improv-ing Hebrew language skills, acquiring better knowledge of the historical context of a passage, and/or gaining a clearer understanding of the *peshat*, or "plain sense," of the biblical text. We see such points of contact in the works of Origen, Jerome, Nicholas of Lyra, Andrew of St. Victor, and Martin Bucer in particular. The questions of the usefulness of knowing the Hebrew language and the usefulness of Jewish exegesis are both key issues that arise in the interpretive history of these eight Psalms. Luther affirms the usefulness of Hebrew but condemns Christian consultation with Jewish exegesis. Bucer explicitly uses Jewish exegesis and finds great value in it as a tool for Christian exegesis, for he contends that such a tool helps to anchor Christian readings in the historical sense and makes Christian readings more defensible before the Jews.[28] I argue and demonstrate that although Calvin does not use Jewish exegesis overtly in the manner of Martin Bucer, he is very much using Jewish exegesis and much of it quite positively.

Fifth, I should at least note that exegesis was also one of the crucial arenas in which Judaism defended itself and expressed strong polemic against Christianity. The Psalms commentaries, in particular, are a good source of Jewish polemic against Christianity, particularly against Christian interpretations of them in reference to Jesus Christ.[29] Among the Jewish interpreters considered in this study, David Kimhi rises to prominence, for his exegeses of Psalms 2, 7, 15, 19, 22, 72, and 110 all contain significant anti-Christian polemic—particularly polemic against Christian uses of these Psalms to teach Trinity, the two natures of Christ, and the claim of Jesus as the Messiah.[30] Martin Bucer was clearly aware of this polemic, as the study of his commentary shows. Hence, it is my hope that this book will not only contribute to the field of Reformation studies, and to Calvin studies in particular, but also be seen as having some input concerning the long-standing place that biblical exegesis has inhabited in the history of Christian-Jewish relations.

I

Medieval and Late-Medieval Interpreters

The Legacy of Literal Prophecies of Christ

A significant part of the weight of Aegidius Hunnius's charges against Calvin is precisely the fact that Hunnius has the Christian interpretive tradition of the Psalms behind him. Concerning these eight Psalms in particular, Hunnius time and again asserts that they are rightly interpreted only as literal prophecies of Christ's incarnation, passion, resurrection, ascension, exaltation, and kingdom.[1] Second, Hunnius points out that past interpreters repeatedly used these Psalms to teach the doctrines of Trinity and the two natures of Christ—teachings he finds lacking in John Calvin's exegesis of these Psalms.[2] I provide a representational piece of the medieval and late-medieval interpretation of the eight messianic Psalms considered in this study by looking at the commentaries of the *Glossa Ordinaria*, Nicholas of Lyra (1270–1349), Denis the Carthusian (1402–1471), and Jacques Lefèvre d'Étaples (1455–1536). Indeed, there are strikingly consistent agreements between these exegetes concerning the primary content of these Psalms as prophecies of Christ and teachings of Trinity and the two natures of Christ, plus interest in the descriptions these Psalms provide concerning the virgin birth of Christ and the sacrament of Eucharist. In truth, there does appear to be a shared Christian interpretive tradition of these eight Psalms, to which Hunnius has every good reason to appeal.

Although each of the sources considered here has its own particular features, the agreement among them is considerable. Therefore, this chapter is arranged according to their common

themes, while also pointing out the various nuances and distinctions between the authors along the way. First and foremost are their common
readings of these eight Psalms as literal prophecies of Christ. The
overriding consensus is that the primary, literal sense of these Psalms is
their christological meaning. There is also a discernible increasingly emphatic insistence on reading these Psalms as prophecies of Christ over and
against Jewish readings of them.

Literal Prophecies of Christ

The primary reading of the messianic Psalms by the interpreters in the *Glossa
Ordinaria*, Nicholas of Lyra, Denis the Carthusian, and Jacques Lefèvre d'Étaples is to see them as literal prophecies of Christ's incarnation, suffering,
crucifixion, resurrection, exaltation, and future kingdom. Indeed, the Gloss,
Denis the Carthusian, and Lefèvre give no reading of any of these Psalms
within the history of David at all; instead, the historical context is literally the
history of Christ's earthly life and future kingdom. Thus, Denis the Carthusian
states explicitly that the literal sense of all of these Psalms is their meaning concerning Christ,[3] and he writes on the second Psalm, "No Christian
interpretation to explain the literal sense of this psalm is suitable or allowed
unless it is interpreted concerning Christ."[4] Even Nicholas of Lyra—despite
all the emphasis on his readings of Old Testament books in their original
historical settings—clearly states in his exegesis of these eight messianic
Psalms that they speak of Christ *ad litteram*.[5] Indeed, while Lyra acknowledges
the possibility of referring the Psalm to David (or Solomon), in every case
except one, he rejects these readings in favor of the christological interpretation.[6] Jacques Lefèvre, on the other hand, gives a reading of them *solely*
as prophecies of Christ's suffering, crucifixion, resurrection, ascension, and
future kingdom, and he explicitly argues against any reading that is not
christological.[7] Hence, the literal sense for these interpreters is its reading
as a literal prophecy of Christ. Any mention of David concerns his role as a
prophet who foresees Christ, with a particular emphasis on the clarity of David's
foresight.[8]

Thus, time and again, the Gloss, Lyra, Denis, and Lefèvre read these
eight messianic Psalms as prophecies of Christ's incarnation, suffering, crucifixion, resurrection, exaltation, and kingdom. In this way, Psalm 2 is a prophecy of the rebellion against Christ that leads to his crucifixion and eventual
triumph in his resurrection. The kings and princes who "take counsel together
against the Lord and his anointed" (Ps 2:2) are Herod, Pilate, and the Jewish

leaders rising up against Christ in his passion (Ps 2:1–2), and the latter half of the Psalm speaks of the promise of Christ's resurrection (Ps 2:4, 6) and eventual triumph over his enemies (Ps 2:7–9).[9] Psalm 8 for these commentators speaks of Christ's incarnation and passion, triumphal entry into Jerusalem, ascension, and the eventual triumph and dominion of his kingdom, so that "you have made him a little lower" (Ps 8:5a) indicates Christ's passion, and the crowning with glory and honor (Ps 8:5b) designates his resurrection and ascension. Furthermore, "babes and sucklings" (Ps 8:2) are the children who honored Christ upon his entry into Jerusalem, the "enemy and avenger" (Ps 8:2) are the Jewish chief priests and scribes who rebuked these children, and the remainder (Ps 8:6–8) portrays Christ's kingdom and dominion.[10]

Similarly, the Gloss, Lyra, Denis, and Lefèvre read Psalm 16 as containing prophecies of Christ's passion and resurrection, and they view this Psalm as Christ's prayer for protection during his passion. Lyra argues that "I will say to the Lord, 'You are my Lord'" (Ps 16:2) is fulfilled when Christ calls out to God, "My God, my God" on the cross; the Gloss teaches that "I will bless the Lord" (Ps 16:7) designates Christ's thanksgiving to the Father for the resurrection. All four apply the assurances of Ps 16:9–10—that his body will rest secure and that he will not be given up to Sheol or see corruption—to the promise of the resurrection.[11] In addition, Lyra and Denis identify the "kidneys" that rebuke in Ps 16:7 with the Jews who mock Christ.[12]

Not surprisingly, the Gloss, Lyra, Denis, and Lefèvre also interpret Psalm 22 as a testimony of Christ's crucifixion. The Gloss quotes the statement by Cassiodorus—and Denis repeats it—that the passion "is described in such apt terms that it is expressed not so much as prophecy but as history."[13] Hence, Ps 22:12–21 describes the various sufferings of Christ, such as the encircling of the bulls or the dogs, feeling like he is poured out like water or his strength has dried up, the piercing of his hands and feet, and the bartering over his clothes. The Jews, for these interpreters, appear as the persecutors of Christ, so that they are identified as the "strong bulls" that surround him (Ps 22:12), the ones who mock him (Ps 22:13, 17), the "dogs" and the "company of evildoers" (Ps 22:16), and the ravening and roaring lion that seeks to devour him (Ps 22:13, 21). Other figures in Psalm 22, such as the melting wax (Ps 22:14) and the bones that are counted (Ps 22:17), refer to the disciples who fled Christ's trial and crucifixion. The last half of the Psalm, however, predicts the resurrection and triumph of Christ. Thus, the request "deliver my soul from the sword" (Ps 22:20) points to Christ's resurrection.[14]

These interpreters commonly read Psalm 45 as an allegory of Christ and the church through the figures of the bride and bridegroom, and they find therein prophecies concerning Christ's incarnation, passion, and resurrection. For example, according to the Gloss and Lyra, the "myrrh, aloes and cassia" (Ps 45:8) indicate the perfumes and spices that the women brought with them to anoint Christ's body in the tomb, and the gladness "from houses of ivory" (Ps 45:8) points to the gladness with which these women departed upon hearing the news that Christ had risen. Furthermore, they understand the exhortation to the "daughter" to "forget her people" (Ps 45:10) as the call of the church to turn away from a Jewish emphasis on legal rites and ceremonies.[15]

While Psalm 45 is a prophecy of Christ the Bridegroom and his bride the church, Psalm 72, according to the Gloss, Lyra, Denis, and Lefèvre, contains prophecies of Christ's kingdom and incarnation. This Psalm describes the breadth and power of Christ's kingdom, along with its wealth and reign of peace and righteousness. It also speaks of Christ's dominion over his foes, of which these interpreters specifically identify the "oppressor" in verse four with the Jews who killed Christ. Furthermore, the "rain that falls on the mown grass" (Ps 72:6) foretells the incarnation of Christ.[16]

Likewise, Psalm 110 prophesies Christ's incarnation, passion, ascension, priesthood, and kingdom. Thus, Ps 110:2 indicates that Christ's reign commences from Zion, while "from the womb of the morning" (Ps 110:3) designates his incarnation. In addition, "sit at my right hand" (Ps 110:1) indicates Christ's ascension, and "you are a priest forever" (Ps 110:4) designates Christ's priesthood. Furthermore, "he will drink from the stream" (Ps 110: 7) alludes to Christ's passion, and "he will shatter kings" (Ps 110:5) prophesies Christ's triumph over Herod, Pilate, and the Jewish princes who persecuted him. The Jews, then, are identified as the enemies who are placed under Christ's feet (Ps 110:1). Moreover, phrases such as "rule in the midst of your foes" (Ps 110:2), "he will execute judgment among the nations" (Ps 110:6), and "he will lift up his head" (Ps 110:7) denote Christ's kingdom.[17]

Like Psalms 16 and 22, the Gloss, Lyra, Denis, and Lefèvre read Psalm 118 as Christ's prayer during his passion, but also as a Psalm of praise of God's goodness and salvation given through Christ, because Jesus is not only the cornerstone of the twenty-second verse but also the only "gate of righteousness" (Ps 118:19) through whom one can obtain salvation.[18] Thus, the Psalm describes a number of Christ's sufferings (Ps 118:10–13), gives the promise of his resurrection and ascension (Ps 118:15–19), demonstrates Christ as the cornerstone who unites the church (Ps 118:22), and announces the time of the New Testament (Ps 118:24) and the festivals of the church (Ps 118:26–27). As in the other Psalms already covered, the Jews are consistently identified as the persecutors of Christ, for they are the bees that surround him (Ps 118:12) and the builders who reject him (Ps 118:22).[19]

Increasing Emphasis on These Psalms as Literal Prophecies of Christ

Not only are these eight Psalms consistently read as literal prophecies of Christ but also one can discern over time an increasingly emphatic insistence upon reading them as such. This begins with Nicholas of Lyra's arguments for the primacy of the christological reading and moves to Denis the Carthusian's goal to make these christological readings defensible before the Jews. This growing emphasis culminates in Jacques Lefèvre's insistence that these Psalms be read solely as literal prophecies of Christ.

Lyra's Arguments for the Primacy of Christological Readings

Nicholas of Lyra is the only commentator among those considered here who gives any attention to the original historical context of these Psalms. Indeed, he is known for advocating a double literal sense. Hence, it is particularly noteworthy that Lyra gives an extensive defense of reading these Psalms as literal prophecies of Christ. While he affirms that each of these Psalms may be understood within their original historical context, he contends that the true history to be found in them is the history of Christ. For example, on Psalm 2, although Lyra first gives a Jewish interpretation in reference to David and his triumph over the Philistines, more than three-fourths of his exposition refers the Psalm to Christ's suffering, eventual triumph, and kingdom.[20] Lyra resolutely argues that Psalm 2 speaks of Christ *ad litteram* and appeals to the New Testament uses of this Psalm, as well as to a statement made by Rashi that the ancient Hebrew doctors interpreted the Second Psalm concerning the Messiah.[21] Employing Rashi for his purposes, Lyra argues:

> *Because* he [Rashi] confesses that the ancient doctors of the Hebrews expounded this psalm as referring to Christ . . . and *because* he [Rashi] confesses that the exposition of this psalm as referring to David is for providing a response to the heretics, from which it seems fabricated, evidently for evading the arguments of the heretics, I therefore wishing to follow the doctrine of the Apostles and the statements of the ancient Hebrew doctors will expound this psalm *ad litteram* [of Christ].[22]

Similarly, Lyra argues for the reading of Psalm 110 concerning Christ *ad litteram* based on the New Testament use of the Psalm and the fact that the ancient Jewish expositors also interpreted it concerning the Messiah.[23]

More pointedly, Lyra gives no reference to the original historical context of Psalm 8 and barely mentions the original historical contexts of Psalms 16, 22, 45, and 72. Instead, he interprets these Psalms solely concerning Christ, and the figure of David appears only as a prophet who foresees Christ.[24] Although he acknowledges that Psalm 16 may be understood of David's persecutions under Saul and then Absalom, it is better understood as David foreseeing the resurrection of Christ. Lyra emphatically argues that the whole of Psalm 72 describes the dignity and authority of Christ's kingdom, for the Psalm is not fulfilled in the reign of Solomon. On Psalm 45, on the other hand, he attends more to the original historical context of Solomon's reign and his marriage to pharaoh's daughter. However, he prefers to read the Psalm as pertaining to the marriage of Christ and the church. Lyra also points out that certain verses, such as verse six ("Your throne, O God, endures forever and ever"), apply *only* to the kingdom of Christ.[25] Thus, Nicholas of Lyra pointedly insists that the literal sense of these particular Psalms is the christological prophecies that they contain. He argues for the primacy of the christological reading as the literal sense of these Psalms by appealing to the New Testament uses of these Psalms, the exegesis of the ancient Hebrew doctors who read these Psalms concerning the Messiah, and the conviction that aspects of these Psalms are fulfilled only by Christ.

Denis's Defense of Christological Readings before Jews

Denis the Carthusian refers to Lyra's defense of the primacy of the christological reading in his comments on Psalms 2 and 118. Denis, however, more strongly demonstrates a concern to give christological readings that are defensible before the Jews. He emphatically insists that their literal sense must be Christ, because only the literal sense is suitable as a proof of faith. Thus, on Psalm 2, Denis reiterates Lyra's point that the early rabbis read this Psalm concerning the Messiah and that it was only later interpreted concerning David in order to refute the Christian readings. He contends, with Lyra, that the original rabbinic use of Psalm 2, along with its use in Acts 4:25–26 and Heb 1:5 by the apostles, demonstrates that its literal sense concerns Christ. Thus, Denis insists that the literal sense of Psalm 2 is Christ, with a particular concern to buttress this reading in the face of Jewish criticisms.[26]

Likewise, in his opening comments on Psalm 118, he argues that its literal sense is its christological reading and that this must be so in order to use it as a biblical text as a proof of faith against the Jews. He writes, "But a proof is not strong unless it is from the literal sense, especially for the Jews who do not receive [an interpretation] unless it is the literal sense."[27] Thus, Denis not only argues resolutely that these Psalms must be interpreted *ad litteram* of Christ but also does so specifically to sustain and substantiate Christian readings of these Psalms over and against Jewish ones. Should one see the christological reading of these Psalms as their *figural* reading, then they would be less defensible before the Jews, because everyone knows that only the literal sense is suitable as a proof of faith.[28]

Lefèvre's Profound Emphasis on the Psalms as Literal Prophecies of Christ

Lefèvre's particular contribution to the exegetical history of these eight Psalms is his *single-minded* interpretation of them as literal prophecies of Christ. In Lefèvre's exegesis, one sees a thorough conflation of the literal-historical and the prophetic-historical so as to render these Psalms as literal, historical prophecies of Christ and the church. He drops the previous anagogical, tropological, and allegorical senses of Scripture—found in the readings of the Gloss, Lyra, and Denis before him—in favor of the one literal, historical, christological, prophetic sense. This is seen in not only his verse-by-verse expositions of these Psalms but also in his setting apart a section of his interpretation for the harmony of each Psalm with the rest of Scripture to emphasize even more profoundly the fulfillment of the prophecies therein.[29] Although the three previous expositors also related these Psalms to their New Testament usage, Lefèvre goes beyond even this to adjoin them to similar Old Testament prophecies and the evidence of their fulfillment in the New Testament.

For example, he sees the fulfillment of Psalm 2's prophecies not only in the explicit use of the text in Acts 4:24–27 but also in the Gospel accounts of those who rose up against Christ (Matt 12:14 and Jn 11:47–48). Thus, the defeat of Christ's enemies, particularly the Jews, is already foretold in other Old Testament prophecies (Prov 1:24–27 and Jer 12:14). Likewise, the prophecies of Christ's kingdom contained in Psalm 2 match those expressed elsewhere (Jer 23:5, Ps 72:8, Lk 13:29, Rev 2:26–28, and Lam 3:66). Finally, for Lefèvre, the prophecies of Christ's divine nature and relationship to God the Father in the Trinity (Ps 2:7) parallels those of other verses (Ps 110:3, Heb 1:5, and Acts 13:32–33).[30] Lefèvre also accentuates the correspondences between Psalm 8 and the New Testament hymn of Christ's kenosis and subsequent exaltation in Phil 2:6–11.[31] Thus, he matches the descriptions of Christ's humiliation and exaltation (Ps 8:4–5) and the prophecy of salvation through Christ (Ps 8:6–8) with prophecies found in Mal 1:11, Ps 19:6, and Ps 138:2 and the expressions of the fulfillment of these prophecies in Phil 2:7–10, Eph 1:20–21, Heb 2:5, and Acts 4:12. Moreover, he parallels Christ's cry for protection in Ps 16:1 with other such declarations and promises of help and eventual triumph in Ps 71:1, Is

2:17–18, Mal 1:11, Ps 142:5, Ps 26:12, and Ps 26:3 and their fulfillment as seen in such passages as Lk 10:19 and Lk 10:22.[32] Finally, Lefèvre's harmony of Psalm 22 with the rest of Scripture is packed full of parallels with the Gospel narrative accounts of Christ's suffering and crucifixion and other Old Testament prophecies of the passion.[33]

Just as significant as Lefèvre's profound emphasis on reading these Psalms as purely prophecies of Christ is his even more unyielding insistence that any interpretation of these Psalms concerning David and his time cannot be their proper reading. Coupled with this is Lefèvre's ardent claim that Christians cannot ever rely on Jewish interpreters to teach the true literal sense of a text, particularly the Psalms. In the preface to his Psalms commentary, he writes that the Jews are blind interpreters of Scripture, which can be especially seen when they apply the Psalms to David himself.[34] Lefèvre avers, concerning Jews and Jewish exegesis,

> How, therefore, can we rely on the interpretation of those whom God has stricken with blindness and terror, and not fear that when a blind man offers us guidance we will fall into a ditch together? It is impossible for us to believe this one to be the literal sense which they call the literal sense, that which makes David a historian rather than a prophet. Instead, let us call that the literal sense which is in accord with the Spirit and is pointed out by the Spirit.... Therefore, the literal sense and the spiritual sense coincide. This true sense is ... the sense the Holy Spirit intends as He speaks through the prophet.[35]

Finally, Lefèvre also argues that his commentary more succinctly and accurately uncovers the simple, literal sense intended by the divine author than the commentaries of the church fathers before him. Whereas previous church fathers have worked with multiple senses, Lefèvre believes that he has clearly demonstrated the one true sense intended by the Holy Spirit.[36]

One can observe a trend toward an increasing emphasis not only upon the proper, singular, literal sense of these Psalms as pure prophecies of Christ but also upon a concern to protect Christian christological readings of these Psalms over and against Jewish readings and criticisms. Nicholas of Lyra demonstrates the positive use of Jewish exegesis to serve Christian purposes; indeed, he appeals to Jewish exegesis to support christological readings. Denis follows this but adds a more explicit concern to defend Christian readings against Jewish criticisms. Lefèvre goes beyond Lyra and Denis in both his resolute interpretation of these Psalms as literal prophecies of Christ and his insistence that Jewish interpreters and exegesis cannot reveal the Spirit's true intention of a passage and thus should never be used by Christian exegetes.

Ecclesial Readings of the Messianic Psalms

Although the primary, literal reading of these eight Psalms for the Gloss, Lyra, Denis, and Lefèvre is as a literal prophecy of Christ, for all of these interpreters the prophecies in these Psalms not only apply to Christ but also often to the church as Christ's body. These readings—which I will call *ecclesial* readings—include not only prophecies concerning the church but also pastoral messages of comfort and exhortations. The importance placed on these ecclesial readings demonstrates the understanding of these commentators that christological readings are intimately tied to ecclesial readings, for the body of Christ is the church, where Christ is the head and those in the church are members of his body.[37]

Prophecies of the Church

The Gloss, Lyra, Denis, and Lefèvre unearth in these eight Psalms prophecies concerning Christ's body, the church. More specifically, these Psalms portray the restorative and saving work of Christ to accomplish reconciliation between humankind and God, in which the gifts of God are mediated to the members of the church through its head, Christ. Thus, these commentators read Psalm 2 to refer to the tribulations of the church. The nations conspiring in Ps 2:1–2 can be applied, then, to the Jews and Gentiles who rose up and persecuted the church after Christ's resurrection and ascension. God's laughter in Ps 2:4, as well, belongs to the church as a promise that its enemies plot in vain, for one day the church will reign with Christ.[38] Likewise, they read Psalms 16, 22, and 118 as not only Christ's prayer in the passion but also as Christ's prayer for the church in its times of tribulation. Thus, Lyra and Denis interpret Psalm 16 as a prayer to God for protection for the church or for any individual Christian. Hence, the promise of resurrection with which this Psalm ends is also a promise given to the church.[39] Psalm 22 describes the future persecutions of the church and provides a model of praying to God for deliverance from tribulations.[40] Just as much as Psalm 22, Psalm 118 is also a model prayer for the church during times of trial and persecution. Furthermore, according to the Gloss and Lefèvre, Psalm 118 speaks of the gifts given to the church through Christ.[41]

For the Gloss, Lyra, and Denis, Psalms 8 and 118 provide descriptions of the church militant and the church triumphant,[42] while Psalms 16 and 110 portray God's election of the church. Thus, in Psalm 16, the "saints who are in the land" (Ps 16:3) are the elect who receive God's goodness through Christ. In this same way, the "boundary lines have fallen for me in pleasant places" (Ps 16:6) means that God's election has fallen among the saints of the church, while the "delights" in God's right hand (Ps 16:11) are God's favors shown to the church.[43] Similarly, Lyra and Denis read Psalm 110 in reference to the elect and the promise of a church triumphant in the rule of Christ.[44] Psalms 45 and 72, in particular, provide vivid depictions of the church, according to our commentators. Psalm 45, for all our interpreters, is a description of the marriage of Christ with the church. Thus, the royal scepter of equity (Ps 45:6) is not only the scepter by which Christ rules but also the scepter by which the church rules. The church is the "queen" (Ps 45:9) who is adorned with charity and diverse gifts and graces of the Holy Spirit.[45] Psalm 72 depicts, for them all, the founding of the kingdom of Christ, the church. Thus, the "mountains" of Ps 72:3 are the leaders of the church, and the "moon" that endures throughout all generations represents the perpetuity of Christ's church on earth.[46] Hence, for the Gloss, Lyra, Denis, and occasionally Lefèvre, these eight Psalms not only contain prophecies of Christ's passion, resurrection, ascension, and future kingdom but also give the church several models of faithful prayer in times of tribulation (i.e., the church militant) and prophesy the institution and practices of the church that will reign with Christ (i.e., the church triumphant). Moreover, these Psalms provide depictions of the gifts bestowed on the church through Christ.

Messages of Comfort and Exhortation

The Gloss particularly finds messages of comfort and exhortation for the church in these Psalms, as do Lyra and Denis. In the Gloss, for example, Psalm 2 encourages the church to take comfort in the laughter of God (Ps 2:4) and know that their enemies plot in vain. Likewise, Psalm 22 comforts the church in its suffering by demonstrating how to pray and trust in God during adversity. In this same way, the promises of Psalm 118 provide messages of comfort for the church that God is its helper and that it will eventually triumph over its enemies.[47] Denis, too, offers a message of comfort and exhortation to the church through the example of Christ's prayer in the Twenty-second Psalm. He writes that this Psalm is written "for our instruction, namely, that we not become weary or despair when we are not immediately heard or seen by God, but from the example of Christ we will submit and entrust ourselves to the pleasant goodwill of the Creator because he cares for us." Likewise, Denis sees in the account of Christ's sufferings a moral teaching that the church should ponder Christ on the cross as a means of overcoming temptations.[48]

For the Gloss, and for Lyra as well, these Psalms also give exhortations to the church to call and instruct it toward faithful and righteous living. Thus, the statement "I have established my king" teaches that one should not be blindly ruled by oneself but be instructed by the Lord. Similarly, Psalm 16 teaches the church through the example of Christ how to avoid sin by "setting the Lord always in [one's] sight" (verse 8). Moreover, the Gloss finds in Psalm 110 instruction concerning the true nature of faith—that faith is believing in things not yet seen. Finally, Psalm 118 instructs the church to trust in God alone and to practice the true praise of God.[49]

Doctrinal Readings of the Messianic Psalms

Even more pronounced than the ecclesial readings of the messianic Psalms, the Gloss, Lyra, Lefèvre, and Denis emphasize the doctrinal teachings contained in them concerning the two natures of Christ, Trinity, the virgin birth and the significance of Eucharist. All of these commentators especially accentuate the doctrines of the two natures of Christ and the Trinity in their readings of these Psalms. Although all four of these sources stress the doctrine of the virgin birth, this doctrine displays distinctive prominence in the exegesis of Denis the Carthusian. Eucharistic echoes found in certain verses of these Psalms are particularly stressed in the readings of Lyra and Denis.

Two Natures of Christ

The Gloss, Lyra, Denis, and Lefèvre apply many of the descriptions in these Psalms to expound on the two natures of Christ. For example, on Psalm 2, Denis asserts that God the Father speaks to the human nature of Christ in such phrases as "I have set my king" (Ps 2:6) and "ask of me" (Ps 2:8). On the other hand, the statement to Christ by God the Father, "You are my son" (Ps 2:7), speaks of Christ's divinity.[50] All of our commentators also find clear teachings of Christ's human and divine natures in Psalm 8. The phrases "you have set your glory above the heavens" (Ps 8:1) and "who is man that you are mindful of him" (Ps 8:4) indicate Christ's divinity, whereas the phrases "the son of man" (Ps 8:4) and "you have made him lower" (Ps 8:5) indicate Christ's humanity, as does the dominion that is given to Christ's humanity (Ps 8:6–8).[51]

Though our four sources do not exactly agree on what portions of Psalm 16 signify Christ's divine and human natures, they do all agree that such teaching is present therein. The Gloss interprets the requests for protection in Psalm 16 (Ps 16:1, 7) as proceeding from Christ's human nature, while the promise of the resurrection (Ps 16:9–10) indicates his divinity.[52] Nicholas of Lyra sees the teaching of the inseparability of Christ's divine and human natures in the phrase "because he is at my right hand" (Ps 16:8).[53] According to Denis, Christ in his human nature says, "You are my God" (Ps 16:2) and "my chosen portion and cup" (Ps 16:5), whereas God as always before him and at his right hand (Ps 16:8) depicts Christ in his divine nature, united to God as one.[54] Lefèvre, on the other hand, points to "my flesh" (Ps 16:9) as indicating Christ's humanity.[55]

For all our interpreters, it is Christ's human nature that cries out in the Twenty-second Psalm. They all view the "deer" in the title of this Psalm, "according to the deer of the dawn," as an image of Christ's humanity.[56] Although their readings of Psalm 22 tend to highlight Christ's human nature,[57] their interpretations of Psalm 110 contain a clear emphasis on Christ's divine nature. According to the Gloss, "sit at my right hand" (Ps 110:1) indicates the glory of Christ's humanity, and "the scepter of power" (Ps 110:2) and "with you is the beginning" (Ps 110:3) designate Christ's divinity.[58] For Lyra, Christ is called "Lord" (Ps 110:1) and "rules" (Ps 110:2) and "judges" (Ps 110:6) by virtue of his divinity.[59] For Denis, "The Lord says to my lord" (Ps 110:1) are the words of God the Father to God the Son, who is "Lord" according to his divinity and "son" according to his humanity. Likewise, Denis understands "sit at my right hand" (Ps 110:1) as indicating Christ's equality with God the Father.[60] For Lefèvre, Psalm 110 predominantly speaks of the divine nature of Christ, though his human nature may be seen in the allusions to his virgin birth (Ps 110:3, "from the womb of the morning") and to his passion (Ps 110:7, "he will drink from the stream"). Psalm 118 also contains a few depictions of Christ's humanity and divinity for the Gloss and Lyra. For both the Gloss and Lyra, the expression "you are my God" (Ps 118:28) points to the deity of Christ, and for Lyra Ps 118:20 also speaks of Christ's two natures.[61]

Psalms 45 and 72 explode with imagery of the two natures of Christ, according to these interpreters. The doubled description of the bridegroom in Psalm 45 designates the two natures of Christ. The Gloss teaches that in the phrase "your comeliness and beauty" (Ps 45:3), "comeliness" refers to Christ's humanity and "beauty" refers to his divinity.[62] For Lyra and Denis, the eternity of Christ's throne (Ps 45:6) indicates his divine nature, and the anointing by God (Ps 45:7) indicates Christ's humanity.[63] In Psalm 72, the Gloss, Lyra, and Denis all read the requests Christ makes as indicating his human nature, whereas the descriptions of the authority, dominion, eternity, and power of his kingdom indicate his divine nature.[64] Moreover, these same three interpret the "sun" and "moon" in Ps 72:5 as depicting Christ's divinity and humanity, respectively.[65]

Trinity

The Gloss, Lyra, Denis, and Lefèvre also find clear descriptions of the persons and workings of the Trinity within these Psalms. For example, the declaration

of Ps 2:7, "You are my son; today I have begotten you," describes the cosubstantiality of the Son and the Father and the eternal generation of the Son by
the Father.[66] Likewise, our commentators use portions of Psalm 8 to depict the
Trinity. The Gloss and Lefèvre find the action of the Trinity in "the work of your
fingers" (Ps 8:3), which expresses the cooperation of the Father, Son, and Holy
Spirit. Similarly, Denis understands in Ps 8:1 ("you have set your glory above
the heavens") a depiction of the workings of the Trinity, where Christ ascends
to God the Father and sends the Holy Spirit to the apostles and the church.[67]
For Denis, "because he is at my right hand" (Ps 16:8) depicts not only Christ's
divinity but also the unity of the persons of the Trinity; for Lefèvre, the
dominion of Ps 8:6–8 and the inheritance of Ps 16:5–6 indicate that the Son
receives all things from the Father.[68]

On Psalm 22, several of our commentators specifically argue that Christ is
speaking to the Father in this Psalm,[69] whereas on Psalm 45, the Gloss, Denis,
and Lefèvre all underscore the Trinitarian meaning of the phrases in Ps 45:1 of
the "good word," "I speak," and the "pen writing swiftly" by applying them to
Christ the Word, through whom the Father speaks and begets the Word.[70]
Furthermore, all four understand the justice and righteousness given to the
king's son (Ps 72:1) as the authority to judge that God the Father gives to Christ
the Son. Likewise, they all give Trinitarian readings to Ps 72:5 ("May he live
while the sun endures") and Ps 72:17 ("May his name endure forever, his fame
continue as long as the sun"), where these demonstrate Christ's coeternity with
the Father, his eternal generation, and his preexistence before creation.[71]

Finally, all of these interpreters see Psalm 110 as full of Trinitarian teachings. God the Father speaks to God the Son in the first verse of this Psalm, "The
Lord says to my Lord." Furthermore, the act of sitting at God's right hand (Ps
110:1) depicts Christ's equality and coeternity with the Father. They all argue
that Ps 110:3—regardless of its proper translation (whether it is "with you is the
beginning" or "from the womb of the morning")—points to the coeternity,
unity, coexistence, and inseparability of God the Father and God the Son.[72]

Virgin Birth and the Perpetual Virginity of Mary

These Psalms not only teach the doctrines of the two natures of Christ and the
Trinity for our exegetes considered here, they also affirm the virgin birth of
Christ. Specifically, the mentions of the womb contained in these Psalms (Ps
22:9–10 and Ps 110:3) evoke the image of Christ's virgin birth.[73] The Gloss cites
Cassiodorus's interpretation of Ps 45:4 as "Come forth from the womb of the
virgin"—an interpretation that Denis the Carthusian also maintains.[74] Furthermore, the "rain that falls on the mown grass" and the "showers that water the

earth" (Ps 72:6) are figures pointing to the virgin birth, according to the Gloss, Lyra, Denis, and Lefèvre.[75] As the Gloss states:

> Christ, who cannot in any sense be endured when he chooses to be recognized in his full power, sought to descend gently into the womb of a virgin without any sound, like rain upon the fleece of a lamb so that he may show his virtue all the more by restraining his indescribable power. Wool takes in water in such a way that it does not split or tear, so also God was in the womb of the Virgin. Another of the same likeness can be compared: "And as showers falling gently upon the earth," that is, they fall most gently like dew. Thus, therefore, without doubt the likeness to the virgin birth is revealed.[76]

Hence, the Gloss's reading upholds not only the doctrine of the virgin birth of Christ but also Mary's perpetual virginity—an emphasis that Denis later takes up more fully.

Indeed, Denis highlights the depictions of Christ's virgin birth found in these Psalms far more frequently than our other commentators. Moreover, he uses these passages to emphasize teachings concerning the Virgin Mary herself. Thus, he interprets Ps 22:9–10 not simply about the virgin birth but more pointedly to accentuate the enduring nature of Mary's virginity and intact womb.[77] Likewise, Denis finds an allusion to Mary's perpetual virginity in the word *until* of Ps 110:1 ("Sit at my right hand until I make your enemies your footstool"). He argues that this "until" does not mean that Christ ceases to sit at God's right hand once the enemies are placed under his feet, for Christ is eternally seated at the right hand of God; rather, says Denis, this "until" is a customary use in Scripture that "points to and includes all times." Such an understanding of "until" applies, then, also to Mary's perpetual virginity:

> Just as Matthew affirms that Joseph did not know Mary *until* Christ was born, it is certain that afterwards he did not know her. For if in this manner the mother of the only begotten Son of God was understood to cohabit, that would mean that she knows unworthiness. Thus, even while Mary was living with Joseph, still she did not come near to unworthiness.[78]

Hence, Denis parallels the perpetuity of Christ's sitting at the right hand of God with the perpetuity of Mary's virginity.

Furthermore, Denis interprets Psalm 45 not only as an allegory of Christ's marriage to the church or the faithful soul but also concerning the connection between Christ and the Virgin Mary. He argues that the "queen" described in Ps 45:9–15 represents not only the church or the faithful soul but also the divine virgin. Therefore, this text concerns Queen Mary, who sits at Christ's right hand in golden robes. Indeed, he asserts that this is the better reading of this passage, "for she is the only and highest Queen, always standing at the right hand of the Son himself." Hence, Denis upholds not only the perpetual virginity of Mary but also her status as coredemptrix with Christ. Queen Mary, he writes, "most ardently chooses that the death and blood of Christ the Son be made fruitful" for the church.[79]

Sacrament of Eucharist

Certain phrases and images in these Psalms call forth references to the sacrament of Eucharist in the exegeses of the Gloss, Lyra, Denis, and Lefèvre. These references are more pronounced in the interpretations of Lyra and Denis, which is not surprising, given the intensified centrality of the Eucharist for medieval worship. For all the interpreters, the phrases "I will pay my vows" and "the poor shall eat" of Ps 22:25–26 elicit a Eucharistic interpretation.[80] The mention of Melchizedek in Ps 110:4 also evokes a connection to the Eucharist—just as Melchizedek brought out bread and wine (Gen 14:18), so Christ offers his body and blood. Finally, the altar in Ps 118:27 summons up for the Gloss and Lyra an association with the Eucharistic altar, and Lyra and Denis see an allusion to the sacrament in the "gates of righteousness" of Ps 118:19–20. Lefèvre, on the other hand, points out that the words of Ps 118:26 ("Blessed is the one who comes in the name of the Lord") are said over the elements during the celebration of the sacrament.[81]

Lyra, Denis, and Lefèvre find an indication of the Eucharist in Ps 72:16, though they disagree on the proper translation of this verse. Lyra prefers the translation of Ps 72:16 as "abundance of grain" and uses this to refer to the Eucharist. Thus, "may it wave on the tops of the mountains" refers to the elevation of the host above the heads of the priests. Denis provides the various translations of Ps 72:16 as "abundance of grain," "memorial wheat," or "cake of wheat" and understands, in all of these, depictions of the sacrament. Likewise, the rest of the verse ("may it wave on the tops of the mountains") is a description of the elevation of the host, and "may the people blossom in the cities" (Ps 72:16), says Denis, describes Christians who, after going out from receiving the sacrament, then "spiritually blossom in grace."[82]

Conclusions

Though there are some differences between the interpretations of Psalms 2, 8, 16, 22, 45, 72, 110, and 118 by the *Glossa Ordinaria*, Nicholas of Lyra, Denis the

Carthusian, and Jacques Lefèvre d'Étaples, their agreements emerge emphatically and profoundly. The claim that for hundreds of years these eight Psalms were viewed by Christian exegetes as truly *messianic* Psalms is not an exaggeration. There is a strong consensus among medieval and late-medieval interpreters that these Psalms speak literally about Christ, so that they must first and foremost be interpreted concerning Christ. More specifically, these Psalms prophesy the events of Christ's incarnation, suffering, death, resurrection, ascension, and kingdom. Hence, their literal sense according to the Gloss, Lyra, Denis, and Lefèvre is their meaning as literal prophecies of Christ.

None of these interpreters read the primary, literal sense of these Psalms in reference to their historical context in the life of David or Solomon—not even Nicholas of Lyra.[83] Instead, the Gloss, Lyra, Denis, and Lefèvre emphasize David's exceptional capacity as a prophet who foresees Christ and speaks in the person of Christ. Moreover, the lack of any substantial historical referent to David or Solomon means that none of these interpreters gives a typological reading of these Psalms, in which David or Solomon acts as a type of Christ and in which their kingdoms and life events foreshadow the kingdom and life of Christ.

In addition, all of the interpreters considered here also read these Psalms as concerning the mystical body of Christ, the church. For some, this entails seeing portions of these Psalms as prophecies of the church's birth, which is Lefèvre's particular emphasis. For others, these Psalms provide moral instruction and messages of pastoral comfort to the church or the individual faithful soul by reading the Psalm as a prayer in its time of struggle, persecution, or temptation. Yet, even more than these ecclesial readings, they give readings for the church that teach about particular doctrines—namely, the doctrines of the two natures of Christ, Trinity, and the virgin birth of Christ—and portray the sacrament of Eucharist. Hence, the Gloss, Lyra, Denis, and Lefèvre use these eight Psalms to set forth assertions concerning God as Trinity and the proper relationships and workings of the persons of the Trinity. They also use these eight Psalms to reaffirm that Christ is fully divine and fully human and to describe the nature and powers of Christ's divinity and humanity, such as the hypostatic union of his two natures and clarification of those things that are said concerning Christ in his humanity from those things that are said concerning Christ in his divinity. Moreover, teachings concerning Christ's virgin birth and the perpetual virginity of Mary also emerge from the pens of these writers. Finally, all of these exegetes see portions of these Psalms as containing prophecies and descriptions of the sacrament of Eucharist.

This rather consistent interpretation of the medieval and late-medieval readings of these eight Psalms is an extremely important backdrop to later Reformation readings and debates over the proper interpretation of them.

Although there are clear, shared christological, doctrinal, and ecclesial emphases, I have also tried to point to some important trends in this exegetical history. Especially crucial to keep in mind is the growing emphasis on reading these Psalms as pure prophecies of Christ over and against Jewish historical readings of them. Such a trend can be traced from Lyra's positive use of Jewish exegesis to support Christian christological readings, to Denis's emphasis that the christological sense must be the literal sense in order for it to be more defensible before the Jews, and then to Lefèvre's sharp rejection of the usefulness of Jewish exegesis for Christian interpretation. These trends toward an insistence on the christological sense and a more negative view of the usefulness of Jewish exegesis are both crucial backdrops to Reformation readings of these eight Psalms.

Moreover, one must ask which aspects of the Christian tradition's interpretation of these Psalms a Protestant reformer might be maintaining, reinterpreting, or even disregarding. We will find that Luther preserves the predominant voice of this tradition in his readings of these Psalms as literal prophecies of Christ's incarnation, passion, resurrection, ascension, and kingdom and in his use of these Psalms to teach the doctrines of Trinity and the two natures of Christ. Bucer, while he maintains many of these readings as prophecies of Christ, equally or more so emphasizes the ecclesial readings of these Psalms. Calvin's exegesis of these Psalms, on the other hand, will demonstrate some very significant and revealing departures from the interpretations of the medieval and late-medieval Christian tradition and even from his own sixteenth-century contemporaries.

2

Martin Luther

Literal Prophecies Redeployed

The vital importance of the Book of Psalms to Martin Luther may
be seen throughout his lifetime in both his written works and his
teaching. He turned to the Book of Psalms time and time again in
the crucial stages of his theological development and the emergent
understanding of his reforming movement. In the first years as
a lecturer at Wittenberg, he began his lectures with the Book of
Psalms (*Dictata super psalterium*, 1513–1515), commented on the
seven penitential Psalms in 1517, and returned to a second set of
lectures on the first twenty-two Psalms (*Operationes in Psalmos*)
from 1518 to 1521. In 1521, while at the Wartburg, Luther wrote
a commentary on Psalm 68. He preached on Psalm 26 in 1525 and
on Psalm 112 in 1526. Also in 1526, Luther wrote a commentary,
Four Psalms of Comfort, dedicated to Queen Mary of Hungary, who
supported the cause of the Reformation. After several revised
editions of his translation of the Old Testament in the 1520s, by
1531 Luther endeavored to write a new revision of the Psalter in
order to express faithfully the message of the Psalms in the
German tongue. As he states it, he undertook this amendment of
his previous version of the Psalter "so that David might sound
purely German."[1] Furthermore, in 1532, Luther wrote the *Summaries
of the Psalms*, which were to accompany this new revision of the
Psalter.

His return to the Book of Psalms in the 1530s brought forth several
commentaries and sermons on individual Psalms as well. He

commented on Psalms 82, 111, 117, and 118 in 1530 and on Psalm 101 in 1534. Luther gave lectures on Psalms 2, 51, and 45 in the spring and summer of 1532, on Psalm 90 in 1534–1535, and on Psalm 23 in 1535, and he preached on Psalms 8 and 110 in 1535. As Heinrich Bornkamm has noted, the majority of Luther's career as a lecturer was devoted to the Old Testament, and the majority of his sermon texts came from the books of Psalms and Genesis, for Luther believed that among the Old Testament books, these most clearly witnessed to the gospel.[2]

Martin Luther frequently proclaimed that the Book of Psalms is like a Christian handbook, containing all the necessary principles and examples to guide Christian living. In his *Preface to the Psalter* (1531), he writes that Psalms "might very well be called a little Bible," for everything contained in the Bible may be found in the Psalter. He praises the Book of Psalms for the clarity with which it prophesies the death and resurrection of Christ, presents the human condition of sinner in need of grace, and exemplifies saintly words and actions in every situation of life. He concludes, "In sum, if you wish to see a picture of the holy Christian Church, presented in miniature and set forth with vivid colors and in lively figures, take the Psalter; there you will have a bright, clear, excellent mirror that will show you what Christianity is."[3] For Luther, the Psalms provide a gaze into the hearts of saints, in which Christians could find a pattern for how they should conduct themselves toward God, friends, and foes. Moreover, the Psalms teach the central doctrines of the gospel.

Martin Luther especially affirmed the clarity and beauty of certain Psalms in particular, those often identified as the messianic Psalms. He describes Psalm 2 as an "extraordinary psalm" because of its teaching of Christ as king and priest and because it was the first prayer of the church (Acts 4:25–26). Similarly, Psalms 8 and 45 are two of the most beautiful Psalms because of their outstanding descriptions of Christ's person and kingdom.[4] Concerning Psalm 110, Luther proclaims: "Here, as nowhere else in the Old Testament Scriptures, we find a clear and powerful description of His [Christ's] person . . . and His resurrection, ascension, and entire kingdom."[5] Moreover, Luther called Psalm 118 his "own beloved psalm," for he writes that it "proved a friend" to him in the midst of many great troubles.[6]

Given the vital importance of the Psalms for his life and theology, I focus on Luther's contribution to the history of exegesis of our eight selected messianic Psalms. I analyze the chronological development of Luther's thought by studying Luther's exegeses of these Psalms, first in his lectures in the *Dictata super Psalterium* (1513–1515), second in his treatment of the selected Psalms in his *Operationes in Psalmos* (1518–1521), and third in his exposition of individual messianic Psalms in the 1530s.[7] This examination indicates the importance of Luther's historical context to his exposition of the messianic Psalms, especially in regard to those he identifies as the enemies to be punished and overthrown in each Psalm.

A second purpose of this chapter is to demonstrate Luther's relationship to the previous exegetical tradition. An overview of the consistent elements of Luther's interpretations of these selected Psalms over time reveals that they are in striking agreement with the chief emphases of the antecedent exegetical tradition outlined in the previous chapter. Namely, Luther retains the readings of these Psalms as literal prophecies of Christ, the readings of these Psalms in reference to the church, the identification of the Jews as the enemies of Christ and the church, and the use of these Psalms to teach the doctrines of Trinity and the two natures of Christ.

A third purpose is to unpack Luther's attitudes toward Jews, the Hebrew language, and rabbinic exegesis as they appear in his expositions of the messianic Psalms. What kinds of references does Luther make to Jews or rabbinic exegesis in his interpretations? What role does the Hebrew language or rabbinic exegesis play in Luther's interpretation of these Psalms? Ultimately, consideration of these matters provides one of the important backdrops for John Calvin's own distinctive exegesis of the messianic Psalms and for the later Lutheran accusations of judaizing against Calvin.

Luther's Agreement with the Antecedent Tradition

Luther's interpretations of these eight messianic Psalms are first and foremost as literal prophecies of Christ. In addition, he does not interpret them in reference to the historical life of David—not even with David as a type of Christ.[8] Much like the previous exegetical tradition, he refers to David as a prophet who foresees Christ.[9] For Luther, all of these Psalms prophesy Christ and contain New Testament insight and teachings of the gospel. For example, Luther interprets Ps 2:7, "You are my Son; today I have begotten You," as the decree of the gospel. Psalm 2, then, tells of those who gather against Christ in vain (Ps 2:3), Christ's ultimate victory over them in the resurrection (Ps 2:4–5), Christ's anointing as king and the receiving of his kingdom (Ps 2:6–8), Christ's alien work of judgment to accomplish his proper work of salvation (Ps 2:9), and the honor and homage due Christ (Ps 2:10–11). Psalms 8 and 110 are both prophecies that teach the Trinity and the two natures of Christ and foresee Christ's crucifixion, resurrection, and coronation. They demonstrate that Christ's kingdom is not temporal but spiritual. Furthermore, Psalm 110:4 ("Thou art a priest forever after the order of Melchizedek") prophesies that Christ is the promised king of righteousness and the true priest. Psalm 22 teaches about the suffering and crucifixion of Christ (Ps 22:1–2, 7–8, 12–18), the two natures of Christ (Ps 22:6, 9–10, 27–28), the virgin birth (Ps 22:9–10), his resurrection and triumph over his enemies (Ps 22:24), and his kingdom (Ps 22:27–29) and people (Ps 22:30–31). Psalm 16, says Luther, is about the suffering, crucifixion, descent to hell, and resurrection of Christ (especially Ps 16:10), and Psalm 45 is an allegory of the wedding of the bridegroom Christ to his bride, the church.[10] All of these readings are very much in keeping with the antecedent tradition as set forth in the previous chapter.

Luther also consistently finds particular doctrinal teachings in these eight Psalms. Again much like the medieval interpreters, he time and again finds key teachings concerning the Trinity and the two natures of Christ. In the *Dictata*, the sun and the moon in Ps 72:5 depict for him the two natures of Christ, and the phrase "from the womb of the morning" in Ps 110:3 indicates the coeternity of the Father and Son.[11] The doctrinal teaching Luther high-lights most in his *Operationes* is the Trinity. Thus, the "Lord and his anointed" in Ps 2:2 indicates the Sender and the One sent, just as verses 8 and 11 portray that Christ's rule is established and guided by the will of the Father.[12] He parallels Ps 8:1 ("You have set your glory above the heavens") with Jn 7:39 ("For as yet the Spirit had not been given because Jesus was not yet glorified") to set forth the Trinitarian teaching that only when Jesus ascends to the heavens can the Holy Spirit be sent. Furthermore, he uses the phrase "you have made him a little lower than God" in Ps 8:5 to explain how Christ may be correctly said to be lower than God the Father. Luther's interpretations of Ps 16:6 and Ps 16:11 in the *Operationes*, as well, teach that Christ receives everything from the Father.[13]

In his 1530s commentaries on these Psalms, Luther continues to find key teachings concerning the Trinity and the two natures of Christ. His 1532 commentary on Psalm 2 begins with an assertion of the two natures of Christ.[14] The commentary based on his 1537 sermon on Psalm 8 also reiterates instruction concerning the Trinity, the two natures of Christ, and the messianic kingdom.[15] He finds an expression of the two natures of Christ in the two different Hebrew words of Ps 8:1 ("O LORD [יהוה] our Ruler [אדון]") and interprets "the work of your fingers" of Ps 8:3 as a Trinitarian expression of the gifts of the Spirit.[16] Likewise, Luther consistently unearths in his 1530s expositions of Psalm 45, 110, and 118 depictions of the two natures of Christ in their descriptions of the messianic king.[17]

Much like the antecedent tradition as well, Luther frequently interprets these messianic Psalms in reference to the church. He understands in them specific reference to the church as the people belonging to Christ. Thus, "Zion" in Ps. 2:6 and "infants and sucklings" and "sheep and oxen" in Ps. 8:2 and 8:7 all signify the church. The "holy ones of the land" (Ps 16:3) are the saints of the church, and the church is the Lord's "chosen portion" and "heritage" (Ps 16:5, 6). Furthermore, the church is the bride of the royal wedding in Psalm 45. The church is the people of Christ the king of which Ps 110:3 speaks, and the latter part of this verse—"from the womb of the morning like dew your youth will come to you"—indicates, says Luther, the whole church, "who are born like dew through baptism from the virginal womb of the church alone." Finally, the victory described in Psalm 118 is not just that of Christ the king, but of his people, the church, as well.[18] All of these readings are notably present in the antecedent tradition.

Finally, Luther consistently sets forth the Jews as the enemies of Christ and the church and criticizes the Jews' inaccurate and vain expectations concerning the Messiah and his kingdom. Thus the "bonds" of Ps 2:3 are the bonds of the law to which the Jews cling in their denial of Christ. Furthermore, the Jews are the ones who "take counsel against the Lord and his anointed" (Ps 2:2) and who will "perish in the way" (Ps 2:11). Christ will "speak to them in his wrath" (Ps 2:5) and "break them with a rod of iron" (Ps 2:9). While Psalm 8 teaches that Christ's kingdom is a spiritual one and not a temporal one, Luther argues that the Jews continue to look for a messiah with physical and political power. Likewise, "those who choose another god" (Ps 16:4a), says Luther, are the Jews who cling to the law and their own righteousness, and Christ will not "take their names upon [his] lips" (Ps 16:4b). In Psalm 22, Luther specifically names the Jews as those who mock and shake their heads at Christ (Ps 22:7), and they are the "ferocious people" who are the "bulls," "ravenous lion," and "dogs" who encircle Christ and the church (Ps 22:12–13, 16). The "pen of a man writing swiftly" (Ps 45:1) is that of the Holy Spirit speaking the gospel, as opposed to the Jews (and specifically as opposed to Moses), whose pen is slow and weighed down by the law. Luther contends that Ps 45:10—"Hear, O daughter, look, and incline your ear; forget your people and your father's house"—is directly admonishing the Jews to recognize that Christ has abrogated their law, priesthood, and kingdom. He also maintains that Ps 110:1 ("until I make your enemies your footstool") has been literally fulfilled in the Jews, who have been dispersed and trampled. Luther writes that the Jews' carnal doctrine is like a reed compared with Christ's scepter described in Ps 110:2, and the kings shattered "on the day of his wrath" (Ps 110:5) indicates the destruction of the synagogue. He interprets "they surrounded me like bees" (Ps 118:12) as referring to the Jews who persecuted Christ and the church, but Christ and the church shall look with triumph upon them (Ps 118:7). Finally, he argues that Psalm 118 rebukes the Jews for their carnal trust and pride in their law, temple, sacrifices, and priesthood, for they do not know the gate of righteousness (Ps 118:20), nor do they recognize Christ as the cornerstone (Ps 118:22).[19] Indeed, these depictions of the Jews as the defeated enemies of Christ and the church and these various criticisms of Jews are very much in line with those of the medieval interpreters of these Psalms.[20]

Thematic and Emphatic Developments

Throughout his lifetime, Luther steadfastly locates Christ, the church, and the Jews as the main players in all of his interpretations of these selected messianic Psalms. He also consistently employs these Psalms to teach the doctrines of Trinity and the two natures of Christ. Such interpretations and emphases have been shown to be in solid agreement with the antecedent tradition. Yet, different emphases develop and new themes arise as Luther returned to these Psalms over the years. For one, he moves from an emphatic reading of these Psalms as literal prophecies of Christ to an increased use of these Psalms to provide instruction and encouragement to the church. This change in emphasis appears in two forms: a heightened theme of comfort and an increased use of these Psalms to teach the true nature of faith and the doctrine of justification by faith alone.

Increasing Comfort

The theme of comfort makes three explicit appearances in Luther's early lectures on the Psalms. He interprets the conclusion to Psalm 2 ("happy are those who take refuge in him") as an exhortation and comfort to those who are suffering. Likewise, Ps 118:5 ("Out of my distress I called on the Lord, and the Lord heard me") promises Christ's assistance and deliverance to those who are persecuted, and later in this same Psalm, the description of the persecutors as "bees" (Ps 118:12) urges the hearer to patience, for, Luther explains, these bees can only sting, not kill.[21] Yet, this theme of comfort appears with increasing frequency in his *Operationes in Psalmos* and becomes a dominant theme in his 1530s commentaries and sermons on these Psalms.

When Luther turns to the Psalms in his 1518 *Operationes in Psalmos*, every Psalm is used as a source of comfort and consolation. Moreover, the precise content of the comfort he offers through these Psalms is quite specific to his particular context. The first verses of Psalm 2 provide the assurance of Christ's ultimate victory (Ps 2:4) over the enemies. Psalm 8:5 ("Who is man that you are mindful of him, the Son of Man that you care for him?") is a consolation given not only to Christ but also to every Christian that just as God did not forget Christ in his suffering, so God does not forget the church. The promise of God's constant presence and guidance (Ps 16:7–8) and the promise of future joy (Ps 16:11) in Psalm 16 are also a source of solace for every Christian. Finally, Psalm 22 exhorts the church to remember God's past faithfulness in the midst of its present suffering (Ps 22:4–5) and to trust in God's deliverance, just as Christ did (Ps 22:24).[22]

The theme of comfort blooms in Luther's 1530s treatment of these eight Psalms and becomes more personal and specific in content. He exhorts Christians who follow the reformers' teachings not to be surprised if the whole world is in an uproar or if they are opposed. These Psalms prophesy these very things. Moreover, it is proof that they are truly following Christ, for the enemies, the devil, and the world will always rise up against Christ and the true church. Thus, they should be consoled by the fact that these enemies are in actuality the enemies of Christ, not of them per se, and, argues Luther, they can take comfort in the promises that Christ fights for them, sustains the church, and always triumphs in the end. In addition, these Psalms teach the powerful effects of prayer and the promise of eternal life, so that even death is not the last word. Finally, Luther frequently declares in his 1530s interpretations of these Psalms that Christ is a king who "rules over consciences" and that his priestly office is one of comfort.[23]

The burgeoning employment of the messianic Psalms to provide comfort in the 1530s comes as no surprise. As scholars have observed, Luther is a "contextual rather than a systematic theologian, a biblical scholar who felt constrained to relate his findings to concrete situations relating to the issues of his age."[24] Historically, the 1530s was a time of struggle to refine and preserve Reformation objectives in the midst of internal disputes among the reformers and external strife from the Roman Catholics. It was a time when consolation was a dire need. For example, Luther's commentary on Psalm 118 was written in the context of the Diet of Augsburg, when he was in hiding at the fortress in Coburg. One of the first things he did was have some verses from the Psalms written on the walls of his room, one of which was Ps 118:17: "I shall not die, but I shall live and recount the deeds of the Lord."[25]

The Doctrines of Faith and Justification by Faith Alone

There is also intensified use of these Psalms to give specific teaching on the nature of faith and the doctrine of justification by faith alone in Luther's *Operationes* and even more so in his 1530s expositions. Although the seedlings of these doctrines may be found in his first lectures on the Psalms, one does not find the emphasis on the *didactic* power of the Psalms until his later accounts. There is also an even greater accent on the *clarity* of the teachings expressed in these eight Psalms. In his later 1530s commentaries, new doctrinal teachings concerning faith and justification by faith alone surface as even more important than his consistent use of these Psalms to teach the doctrines of Trinity and the two natures of Christ.

Thus, in 1532, Luther affirms that Psalm 2:7 sets forth the decree of the gospel, which is justification by faith alone: "I will tell of the decree of the Lord: He said to me, 'You are my Son; today I have begotten you.'" This verse, he asserts, demonstrates what Christ does for us—justification by faith alone—and the abolishment of the law.[26] Psalm 45, too, gives instruction about the doctrines of faith and justification, for it is a "poem for teaching spiritual alertness and arousing to faith," because it educates the reader about a new and spiritual king, kingdom, righteousness, and people.[27] More specifically, the king in Psalm 45 (who represents Christ) teaches a life of righteousness based on promise and faith and not upon works of the law.[28] Psalm 118, as well, instructs the church about the nature of true faith, the proper relationship of the Christian to temporal kingdoms, and the difference between trust and use:

> Here [Ps 118:8–9] David teaches that we should not place our
> confidence in even pious princes. . . . We should use and enjoy the
> princely office and temporal government for food, protection, and
> peace on earth, as God instituted it. But we should not rely, trust, hope,
> and boast in them. . . . To trust and to use are two different things. The
> former is appropriate to God; the latter is appropriate to creatures.[29]

This emphasis on not putting one's trust in princes provides the context for Luther's comments to Melanchthon on the Augsburg Confession, which was drawn up just after Luther finished his commentary on Psalm 118. He tells Melanchthon that it pleases him, but Melanchthon's error is that he puts too much hope in gaining the support of princes, when his hope can be only in God alone.[30]

Thus, although Luther remains very much in tune with the antecedent interpretation of these selected messianic Psalms, he also makes some unique contributions to this exegetical tradition that are directly related to his specific context and theological concerns. First, he uses these Psalms to give comfort to downtrodden Reformation churches. Second, he employs these Psalms to teach the true nature of faith and the doctrine of justification by faith alone. Indeed, Luther's tone and style in his later interpretations are much more explicitly pastoral.

Reading Strategies Reassessed and Redeployed

The reading strategies Luther employs in his readings of these eight Psalms also demonstrate both consistency and some important changes over time.

Luther is well known for his use of certain dichotomies to illuminate the meaning of Scripture, such as flesh versus spirit, letter versus spirit, and law versus gospel. Yet, while Luther uses the trope of letter versus spirit continually in the *Dictata*, he drops it almost entirely in his later exegesis and replaces it with the dichotomy of law versus gospel (which he also uses in the *Dictata*). Likewise, the trope of flesh versus spirit gradually is replaced by the language of visible versus invisible or language about God working under contrary appearances. Rather consistently throughout, all of these reading strategies are deployed against Jews and Jewish readings of Scripture. Indeed, the central role of the Jews as an exegetical tool themselves may be seen in Luther's use of Jews as the archetype for the enemies of Christ and the church.

Spirit versus Letter and Law versus Gospel

In the *Dictata*, Luther uses the dichotomy of spirit versus letter to differentiate between the living Word of Scripture, which lifts the believer to spiritual things, and the sluggish, heavy, dead letter that weighs down the believer toward carnal things. Thus for Luther the word "heavens" in Ps 8:3 points to the spirit over and against the letter, for "the Lord has destroyed the letter and the defenders and zealots of the letter, so that the heavenly spirit and the new church might be established by the fingers of God."[31] Likewise, in the title of Psalm 45, the Hebrew term *maskil* for Luther expresses a rebuke to those who follow the letter, "since everything in the whole Psalm wants to be spiritually understood."[32] This negativity attached to the "letter" is also seen in its identification with the Jews. He denotes the Jews as the "zealots" and followers of the letter and frequently criticizes them for clinging to carnal readings of Scripture and carnal expectations of the Messiah. On Psalm 16, Luther writes that Scripture has a twofold sense: "the veil and clarity, the letter and the spirit, the figure and the truth, the shadow and the form."[33] Here he identifies the figure or shadow with the negative concept of the letter and argues for the clarity of the spiritual reading. For Luther, if one can have the spirit and truth and clarity, then why would one acquiesce to the letter?[34]

In his interpretations of the Psalms after the *Dictata*, however, Luther drops this interpretive lens of letter versus spirit in favor of the lens of law versus gospel. One possible reason for this change is his growing appreciation of the literal sense and the possibility of terminological confusion between "letter" and "literal sense."[35] Nevertheless, Luther clearly found that the same ideas understood in the *Dictata* under the tool of spirit versus letter could be preserved under the reading strategy of law versus gospel.[36] For instance, Luther uses both letter versus spirit and law versus gospel to explicate the title in Psalm 45 in the *Dictata*, but he later (1532) explains the title and the whole Psalm in terms of law versus gospel only. Likewise, in the *Dictata* on Ps 45:1, he elucidates the difference between "utter" and "pour out" as the distinction between being content with the letter versus seeking the spirit. He interprets this same verse in 1532 solely in terms of law versus gospel: the law is uttered, but the gospel is poured out. He then concludes his 1532 comments on Ps 45:1 by saying, "So throughout the psalm an antithesis is set up with Moses, or between the law and the gospel."[37]

One of the key similarities of Luther's use of the strategies of spirit versus letter and law versus gospel is that they are both deployed against the Jews in his interpretations of the messianic Psalms. Indeed, two of the central motivating factors in his use of these interpretive devices are demonstrations of the Jews' mistaken understanding of Scripture and their resulting rejection by God. Luther intends to show that the content of these Psalms is Christ and the gospel, as seen in the clear prophecy and teaching it provides. He often accomplishes this by contrasting this clarity with the errors of the Jews. Thus in the *Dictata*, he warns against being content with, caught in, and weighed down by the letter. By insisting time and time again that the true content of these Psalms is spiritual, Luther challenges Jewish interpretation of these Psalms, which he constantly refers to as carnal.[38] Subsequently, in his second lectures on the Psalms and in his 1530s expositions, he regularly admonishes the Jews for remaining in the law and failing to see that with Christ the gospel has come and the law is abolished.[39] Thus, the Jews cannot interpret these Psalms rightly, and they cannot see the true nature of the messianic king and his kingdom.[40] So although Luther's terminology of letter versus spirit is replaced by law versus gospel, Luther's basic purposes of demonstrating the clarity of the Psalm and the Jews' culpability in not seeing the true, intended meaning are retained under both strategies.

Flesh versus Spirit and Visible versus Invisible

Another interpretive lens appears consistently in all of Luther's interpretations of the messianic Psalms throughout his lifetime, though it, too, undergoes a slight terminological modification. In the *Dictata*, this reading strategy appears mostly under the dichotomy of flesh versus spirit, but in his later writings, it increasingly materializes as a contrast between things visible and invisible (i.e., between what is seen with physical eyes and what truly is). He employs these reading strategies against the Jews as well, but more so, they are used to encourage the church of Luther's day to stand firm in the midst of persecution. The use of the lens of flesh versus spirit against the Jews appears mostly in the *Dictata*, where one already hears the echoes of the lens of visible versus invisible that will eventually replace it. Luther writes that the Jews' concerns and hopes are only of the flesh (on Ps 16:4) and that the "grace poured on his lips" (Ps 45:2) is Christ's preaching of invisible things and not the temporal things the Jews anticipate. Furthermore, in his comments on Ps 16:7, he draws a contrast between the "manifest, public, and perceptible" synagogue and the splendid church, whose magnificence is not entirely visible but remains hidden. Likewise, the Jews are concerned only with perceptible things, such as the law, righteousness of the flesh, and the letter, while the law of Christ is spiritual.[41]

In the *Operationes*, the tool of visible versus invisible is used less explicitly against the Jews, while the criticism of the Jews for holding to visible things is still implied. Moreover, he adds a new aspect: that Christ and his gifts are revealed under contrary appearances (Ps 2:10). He sees Ps 2:10 as a call to the Christian to turn away from transitory things toward things eternal, for the life of faith is not about outward appearances but is "a life hidden in Christ" (Ps 16:3).[42] Likewise, in his 1530s treatments of the messianic Psalms, the use of the reading strategy of visible versus invisible is less polemical against the Jews. Yet, it is still implied in passages in which Luther expounds that Christ's kingdom is established in a way that is a stumbling block to the Jews and foolishness to the Greeks (1 Cor 1:23, comments on Ps 2:9, 8:2, 110:1), for the king is hidden under an opposite appearance (Ps 45:2).[43]

This theme of the revelation of Christ under contrary appearances, along with the exhortation to look not at what is visible but at what is invisible, rises to prominence in Luther's 1530s commentaries on these eight Psalms. In these works, the reading strategy of visible versus invisible becomes a tool to provide comfort. Luther exhorts the Christians following the Reformation cause not to despair. Though they may see tyranny and oppression, God is actually laughing at the enemy (Ps 2:4). Though the Protestant church appears small and its people few and weak, they are really strong, for this is not unlike the early Christians among the synagogue (Ps 2:9). Though outwardly the church may look like a band of beggars, Ps 45:8 teaches them to have spiritual eyes. In fact, these things above all require the eyes of faith; faith is necessary in order to see the hidden rule of Christ (Ps 110:1). Finally, Luther reminds his hearers that those who serve God must expect tribulation and that their blessings will not be visible or of this world, but they will receive eternal life (Ps 118:14).[44]

Jews-as-Enemies Reading Strategy

While Luther uses letter versus spirit, law versus gospel, flesh versus spirit, and visible versus invisible all in one way or another to criticize Jewish readings of

Scripture and expectations of the Messiah, he frequently employs the Jews themselves as an interpretive tool for identifying the key characteristics of the enemies of Christ and the church. In his interpretations of these eight Psalms, the Jews often operate as the prototype or archenemy by which to evaluate all enemies of Christ and the church—what I will call his "Jews-as-enemies" reading strategy. Luther emphasizes not only the mistaken messianic expectations of the Jews but also their deliberate rejection of Christ and continued resistance to the gospel.[45] Traits that characterize this archenemy include dependence on the law and works-righteousness, confidence in things of the flesh (such as their physical lineage, temple, priesthood, and ceremonies), the practice of idolatry, and ignorance of the nature of true worship.[46] In the end, Luther intends with this strategy to give a message of comfort to afflicted Christians, for he says that one can find in these Psalms the promise of victory for Christ and the church and the destruction of their enemies. Thus, Ps 2:5 ("he will speak to them in his wrath") and Ps 2:9 ("[he will] dash them in pieces") indicate the scattering of the Jews. Psalm 16:10 ("I will not remember their names") demonstrates the rejection of the Jews, and Ps 110:1 shows that they will be made the footstool of Christ. Finally, Luther writes that Christ and the church shall "look in triumph" (Ps 118:7) upon their enemies, as has already happened to the Jews.[47]

In Luther's early lectures on the Psalms, the emphasis is on the Jews as the *actual* enemies with which Christ and the church contend. However, in the *Operationes* and especially in his 1530s writings on these eight Psalms, Luther redeploys his Jews-as-enemy reading strategy to apply it to the Roman church of his day. In these expositions, the "Jews" operate as a rhetorical tool to describe the Roman Catholic enemies, so that Roman beliefs and practices are paralleled with those of Jews in order to identify the Roman Catholics as the contemporary enemies of Christ and the church. In the *Operationes*, Luther points out that just as the Jews do not recognize who are the "holy ones of the land" (Ps 16:3) and refuse to accept that God no longer shows partiality, so do the Roman Catholics fail to see this in their insistence that to be a Christian one must be subject to the pope. Likewise, just as the Jews are those "who choose another god" (Ps 16:4) by trusting in the wrong things, the Roman Catholics are also guilty of idolatry. The Jews trust in the wrong things: their physical lineage, the fact that most of the Jews did not believe in Christ, and the glory of their religion and law. Just the same, says Luther, today the Roman Catholics trust in their apostolic succession, the fact that they are more numerous than the Protestants, and their ceremonies.[48]

The parallels between Roman Catholics and Jews abound in Luther's 1530s works on the messianic Psalms. The parallels may be categorized as (1) dependence on the wrong things for righteousness, (2) ignorance of true worship, (3) historical parallels that align the Protestants with the apostolic church and the Roman Catholics with the Jews, and (4) the just punishments deserved. Just as Jews pursue their own righteousness through the law, monks depend on their works-righteousness. Just as the Jews claim their law, temple, and worship (and ignore the exhortation in Ps 45:10 to "forget your father's house"), the Roman Catholics cling to their monasteries and masses. Likewise, says Luther, just as the Jews boast of their physical heritage, the Roman Catholics rely on their good works. Not only do the Jews put their trust in carnal things, the Roman Catholics also twist the promises into carnal promises. Thus, just as the Jews do not know the "gate of righteousness" (in Ps 118:20), the Roman Catholics also do not know this gate. It is not only the Jews, decries Luther, who do not recognize Christ as the cornerstone (Ps 118:22); the Roman Catholics say they do, but they do not practice it.[49] In this way, Roman Catholic worship is paralleled with Jewish worship. Just as the worship of the Jews is composed of merely external practices, Roman Catholic worship emphasizes external works and sacrifices—both of which miss the true worship that consists in the adoration of Christ (i.e., "kiss the son" of Ps 2:12). Luther concludes with the exclamation that the Roman church in effect leads the people back to obedience to the law. Thus, on Ps 110:4, he asserts that the Roman church promotes law, not gospel.[50]

Furthermore, Luther uses the parallels between the Roman Catholics and the Jews not only to identify the enemies of Christ and the church but also to give a message of encouragement and comfort. The Protestants may understand themselves as being in the same situation as Jesus and the early church were amid the Jews of the synagogue. The Jews, writes Luther, did not think they were opposing God by rejecting Christ. Likewise, the Roman church does not realize that it is attacking Christ when it attacks the Protestants. Just as the Pharisees mocked Jesus, the Protestants experience the same opposition from the pope and Roman Catholics. The Jews accused the apostles of being seditious, and now the Roman Catholics charge the Protestants with the same thing. Just as the Jews argued that the gospel is contrary to the first commandment, so do the Roman Catholics claim that the reformers' teaching is against Christ and the church. Furthermore, argues Luther, Paul's words concerning the Jews in Rom 9:4–5 are relevant to the Roman church of Luther's day. Paul lists the many blessings given to the Jews by God, and these may be said of the Roman church as well. But, Luther avows, Paul points out that the Jews have not heard the Word of Christ, and so they no longer have it. In this same way, the pope lacks the true Word of God. Luther writes, "Therefore, if the pope teaches something that is in accordance with the Word, I will listen and do it.

But if he speaks contrary to the Word, I will not listen." Finally, just as the apostles' preaching "ran the synagogue into the ground," the reformers can expect the gospel to "mow down the system of priests, monks, nuns, [and] the whole papacy."[51]

A final message of comfort in these eight Psalms comes from seeing in the castigation of the Jews a promise of the coming punishment of the pope and the Roman church. As Christ overturned the kingdom of the Jews and Paul overturned the Romans, so will the Protestants overturn the papacy, proclaims Luther. Just as the Jews believed themselves secure and yet they perish, the papacy will totter just when it thinks it is most secure. In this same vein, Luther writes that the example of the Jews becoming Christ's footstool (Ps 110:1) offers to the Protestants a promise that the current persecutors of the gospel—the Roman Catholics—will be cast down.[52]

Therefore, as far as Luther is concerned, the Roman Catholics of his day are no better than Jews. In fact, more than that, he exclaims that in some ways they are worse than Jews. In his commentary on Psalm 45, he writes that Jews are actually less culpable than the Roman church. He reasons that if the Protestants are unable to change the minds of the Roman Catholics, who hold many of the same doctrines as the Protestants, it is even less probable that the Jews would give up their ancient traditions. More specifically, if the Protestants cannot get the Roman Catholics to repudiate their own righteousness and dependence on works, it is even less likely that the Jews will.[53]

Concerning Jewish Things

There is little positive to be found in Martin Luther's exegeses of these eight messianic Psalms concerning the Jews. The significant reading strategies that Luther employs—such as letter versus spirit, law versus gospel, flesh versus spirit, and visible versus invisible—are deployed directly against the Jews. Even when he uses these Psalms for the purposes of bringing comfort to the struggling Protestant churches, the effect is still at the expense of the Jews.[54] Likewise, although Luther's polemical emphasis in his later commentaries on the messianic Psalms is against the Roman Catholics, his Jews-as-enemy reading strategy is the very interpretive tool he redeploys so effectively to make his points.

Is there anything positive that can be said about Luther concerning things Jewish? Yes, there are at least two areas. One can find in the evolution of Luther's exegesis an increasing emphasis on the Jews of the Old Testament as supreme examples of faith. There is also a clear mounting appreciation for and use of Hebrew in the development of his exegesis over time. However, these two positive areas certainly do not extend for Luther into any support for Christian use of Jewish exegesis. It is to these topics that we now turn.

Old Testament Exemplars of Faith in the Psalms

James Preus has argued that significant changes can be detected in Luther's approach to the Old Testament during the course of his first lectures on the Psalms. Specifically, Preus contends that the notion of *promissio* plays an increasingly greater role in the later lectures of the *Dictata*. In addition, Preus asserts that during this time one can perceive a crucial shift in Luther's thought from the view of the Old Testament as mere shadow to an appreciation of the Old Testament itself as theologically relevant. A specific example of this, argues Preus, may be seen in the shift from David the prophet being merely a mouthpiece for Christ to David himself being an example of faith in the pre-Advent situation, an example of "faith as expectation, trust, and hope in the sheer promising Word." Thus the "faith of the Old Testament people begins to emerge as a model for *Christian* faith."[55]

My problem with the first part of Preus's thesis is that at least in his exegesis on these eight messianic Psalms, Luther does not use the language of shadow for the Old Testament, nor does he employ the typical reading tool of typology that usually accompanies the understanding of the Old Testament as shadow. Rather than the language of shadow or veil, Luther instead praises the messianic Psalms for their *clarity*.[56] Moreover, from the very start, Luther finds the Old Testament theologically relevant "on its own terms." Time and again, he exclaims over the Book of Psalms (and the messianic Psalms in particular) that it holds such clear and concise teaching about Christ, the church, and the saintly life that all of Scripture is contained within it. He writes, "In the Psalter everything that is contained in the entire Bible is comprehended so beautifully and so briefly that it constitutes an excellent '*Enchiridion*,' or handbook." Likewise, he affirms concerning the Psalter: "It seems to me that the Holy Spirit deliberately undertook the task of bringing together material for a small Bible and for a book of examples whose range is representative of all Christendom and includes the lives of all saints, so that anyone who cannot read the entire Bible would have here in one small book, a kind of summary of all Scripture."[57] Furthermore, the Old Testament is "theologically relevant" in and of itself precisely because Luther finds the gospel in the Old Testament.[58]

The second part of Preus's thesis makes a very good point, which my own study supports. One can detect in Luther's writings on the messianic Psalms a shift from David as mere prophetic mouthpiece of Christ to David as significant *exemplar* of faith, though—at least in these eight Psalms—this shift does not occur in the *Dictata* but appears in his later 1530s commentaries on the messianic Psalms.[59] His emphasis, though, still falls on the extreme intimacy and clarity of David's prophecy. It was not just that Christ and the Holy Spirit spoke through David, says Luther, but it is "as though he were seeing the event take place before his very eyes."[60] Indeed, in his 1537 comments on Ps 8:5, Luther writes that David *actually* sees Christ's passion: "There is no doubt that in the spirit David is here looking at Christ as He struggles with death in the garden and cries out on the cross, 'My God, my God, why hast Thou forsaken Me?'"[61] In his 1535 commentary on Psalm 110, Luther moves from David as mere prophetic mouthpiece to David as exemplar of faith. He sees in the first verse of this Psalm a confession of David's faith and praises David's example:

> It is quite clear that this verse consists not only of prophecy or doctrine
> concerning Christ, but that it is also a confession of the psalmist's
> faith. It serves as an example for us to see what kind of power such
> faith has, how it produces a daring and courage that enables one to
> hold anything on earth in contempt, to fear nothing at all, but in
> happy defiance to depend only on Christ, who rules eternally, a Lord
> over the temporal and eternal, death and life, sin and righteousness,
> evil and good.[62]

The appeal to David as exemplar of faith, however, is found only in Psalm 110 and not in any of Luther's other commentaries on the eight Psalms considered here. It is quite possible that this one text stands out for him as showing David as an example of faith because Jesus himself quoted this text for that very purpose (Mt 22:44, Mk 12:36, Lk 20:42).

There are, however, two other instances in Luther's interpretations of the messianic Psalms where Luther appeals to Old Testament persons as exemplars of faith. The first also appears in his 1535 commentary on Psalm 110. This in many ways is a much stronger affirmation of Old Testament faith, for Luther proclaims that Christians' faith today falls short of the faith exhibited by the Old Testament fathers:

> For we see how the dear, holy fathers of the Old Testament took hold of
> their doctrine of the coming Christ, joyously waiting for Him with all
> their hearts as though they knew no other joy or comfort on earth.
> They believed this with much greater certainty and power than we
> believe our glorious resurrection and eternal life. If our hearts were
> equally full of faith, so that we could wait in certainty and happiness,
> surely we, too, would be able to compose such beautiful and joyous

psalms! But our faith, unfortunately, does not compare with the faith of those people. We must give them credit; they remain our fathers, teachers, and masters.[63]

Finally, also in his 1535 comments on Ps 110:4, Luther emphasizes that Melchizedek is not merely a type of Christ but that he is *in actuality* a preacher of the gospel.[64] So although he makes some strong statements about the exemplary power of the faith of Old Testament persons, still, one must keep in perspective that by "Old Testament faith" Luther means Old Testament persons with certainty in the truth of the promises and teachings of the gospel.

Luther's Use of Hebrew

Luther's exegesis of the messianic Psalms exhibits as well a clear increasing appreciation for and use of the Hebrew language. During the years of writing the *Dictata*, Luther's Hebrew was self-admittedly poor. Yet, just a few years later, when he turned to his second lectures on the Psalms, he felt confident enough not only to refer to other scholars' study of the Hebrew but also to apply his own translations of the Hebrew text in his interpretations of the Psalms. Significant from the time of the *Operationes* forward is that he does not merely report a translation of the Hebrew to supplement his exegesis; he uses the Hebrew to anchor particular theological interpretations and to correct the Vulgate translation of certain verses.[65] For example, in the *Operationes*, Luther argues that the Hebrew word אַדִּיר can mean both praise and confession in order to reinforce his prominent theme in his interpretation of Psalm 8 that justification involves praise of God and confession of oneself as a sinner, both of which are needed to engender mutual praise between God and the justified person.[66]

In addition, Luther embarks on a long excursus over the different Hebrew terms used for "man" in Ps 8:4 to support particular theological readings. The text, with the relevant Hebrew words inserted, reads: "Who is אֱנוֹשׁ (*enosh*) that you are mindful of them, the son of אָדָם (*adam*) that you care for them?" He argues (supported by Jerome and Eusebius) that *enosh* properly signifies humanity according to the soul, whereas *adam* signifies humanity according to the body. Thus, these two words indicate the two natures of Christ. Furthermore, he laments that this etymology is lost through translations of the Hebrew and argues that from the Hebrew one may see that "*enosh* pertains to men who before God are miserable and afflicted and *adam* pertains to the Son who before men is vile and despised." In this way, he argues that this verse refers to Christ and his passion, when he was briefly forsaken by God but not forgotten, and it is also a consolation to believers that though they may forget God, God does not forget them. Luther writes, "Therefore, this is a great miracle that man who in himself with every eye forsakes, despairs of, and forgets God, and yet God remembers him...thus the heart of man may understand and believe God to be pleasant, benevolent, and friendly."[67] Moreover, Luther asserts that the Hebrew word מָה in Ps 8:5 can be translated not only as "who" or "what" but also as "how." In effect, the theological reading of this verse is the following: "Do you not perceive how marvelous is that man? Do you not perceive how marvelous is that Son of Man? That he is mindful of him and does not forget him but visits him and does not forsake him."[68]

In his interpretation of Psalm 16, Luther uses Hebrew grammar for emphatic effect. For example, he points out that the Hebrew verb in Ps 16:4 is in the active form to emphasize the perverse zeal with which they "increased their idols."[69] More important, he employs the Hebrew to uphold his theological reading of Ps 16:10: "You did not give up my soul to the pit." Luther says that the Hebrew word for "soul" (נֶפֶשׁ) always refers to a *physical* soul. Thus, this verse speaks of Christ's soul in regard to the body and indicates Christ's bodily resurrection.[70]

Luther dedicates an extensive digression in his 1532 introductory comments on Psalm 45 to expound on the benefits of knowing Hebrew. He urges people to learn it for a number of reasons. First, the knowledge of Hebrew enhances service to God, for he writes, "In it we hear God speak." Furthermore, there are things about religion and divine worship that can be known only through the knowledge of Hebrew. "Thus," Luther claims, "study directed toward learning this language might rightly be called a kind of mass or divine service."[71] Second, knowledge of Hebrew is eminently useful. Hebrew is a strong tool with which to arm oneself against the enemies, particularly the Roman Catholics, states Luther. All theological teachers need this armor to effectively resist the devil and his servants:

> [I]f we do not hold fast to the language, they will ridicule and abuse us
> as though we were asses. But if we also are fortified with a knowledge
> of the language, we shall be able to stop their impudent mouths.... I
> know how useful it has been to me against my enemies. For that
> reason I would not be without this knowledge—however small it is—
> for infinite sums of gold. You, too, as future teachers of religion,
> should apply yourselves to the task of learning this language, unless
> you want to be taken for dumb cattle and uninstructed rabble.[72]

Likewise, in his 1532 commentary on Psalm 2, he exclaims that knowledge of Hebrew "adds remarkably to the ability of explaining the Scriptures."[73]

Similar to his use of Hebrew in the *Operationes*, Luther also uses Hebrew to support particular theological readings of the messianic Psalms in his 1530s commentaries. He argues that מַשְׂכִּיל is a Hebrew word denoting *spiritual* wisdom, a spiritual instruction. From this, he contends that this Psalm teaches about a *spiritual* king and kingdom, a new righteousness, and a new people. In addition, he asserts that יָפְיָפִיתָ in Ps 45:2 has a dual meaning (i.e., beautiful in form and spirit), and he concludes that this verse indicates the two natures of Christ. Finally, in his 1537 commentary on Psalm 8, he sees the two natures of Christ signified in the dual names of verse 1—*yahweh* and *adonai*.[74] However, despite a growing use of Hebrew in his exegesis and a move to buttress theological interpretation with reference to the Hebrew, these do not mean that Luther let the Hebrew text *determine* his exegesis. More specifically, Luther approached the Psalms armed with the conviction that they prophesied Christ; thus, he sought in the Hebrew an affirmation of that truth. Any interpretation of the Hebrew that did not support the content of Christ in the text—or, even worse, that undermined such a reading—he rejected.[75]

Luther on Jewish Exegesis and Christian Hebraists

Despite his high appraisal of the Hebrew language, Luther denounced and ridiculed Christian use of Jewish exegesis. Censures of Jewish exegesis can be found in nearly all of his exegetical works and in many of his treatises.[76] Perhaps what is more surprising is that there is not *more* of these negative evaluations of Jewish exegesis on the messianic Psalms in particular, in that for centuries, Christians and Jews have disagreed on how to interpret these Psalms. Nevertheless, Luther does make a handful of statements against Jewish exegesis in his interpretations of these eight Psalms.

Although there are no direct statements against Jewish exegesis in Luther's accounts in the *Dictata* of our selected messianic Psalms, he clearly states his estimation of Jewish exegesis in his preface to the *Dictata*. He writes, "Some explain very many Psalms not prophetically but historically, following certain Hebrew rabbis who are falsifiers and inventors of Jewish vanities."[77] Several criticisms of Jewish exegesis do appear in his later 1530s expositions of these Psalms. He writes that Jews deny that Ps 2:11 ("kiss the Son," as Luther translates it) is about the Son of God, and thus they are idolaters. He criticizes Jewish interpretation of Psalm 45 as speaking of temporal goods and pleasures. He argues that though the rabbis themselves know that Ps 110:1 refers to the Messiah, they are blind to the meaning of this Psalm. Furthermore, they pervert the meaning of Ps 110:7 ("He will drink from the brook") "with strange and contradictory interpretations and glosses," and thus they fail to understand that this signifies the suffering of the Messiah.[78]

Luther's historical context gives insight into why these statements against Jewish exegesis arise in his 1530s commentaries on the messianic Psalms. The 1530s was a crucial decade in the growth of Christian Hebraica.[79] Martin Luther became increasingly critical of the Christian Hebraists during this time, especially of the kind of Christian Hebraists who turned to Jewish exegesis to aid them in their interpretation of the Old Testament and to provide historical contexts and historical readings of Old Testament texts. There was, however, a kind of Christian Hebraica that Luther was willing to condone, such as the work of Johannes Forster that focused on the uses of the Hebrew language for Christian study of the Bible but denied the usefulness of Jewish exegesis. Indeed, he had recruited Forster to occupy the Hebrew chair at Wittenberg University. Forster expresses the views of Luther when he writes in the preface of his Hebrew language dictionary:

> Often I have wondered about the feeblemindedness of my Christian colleagues who without any discernment have happily embraced the commentaries of the Jews in which there is no light, no knowledge of God, no spirit, no real solid knowledge of any discipline and art, no learning of any language, not even of Hebrew. . . . They [the Jews] do not discern and see that the end of the law is the Son of God. . . . Therefore their dictionaries and commentaries have brought more obscurity and error into the church of Christ than light and truth.[80]

Luther's own explicit statements about Christian Hebraists become more pronounced in his later years—in his lectures on Genesis and in his later anti-Jewish writings. He fumes in his comments on Gen 6:3: "But the Jews make fools of these modern Hebraists by convincing them that Holy Scripture cannot be understood except by means of grammatical rules and their minute system of pointing."[81] Indeed, Luther states that he wrote his anti-Jewish treatises as much against the Hebraists as against the Jews.[82] At the end of his anti-Jewish treatise Vom Schem Hamphoras und vom Geschlecht Christi, he addresses the Christian Hebraists directly, saying that it is fine and well to learn the Hebrew language from Jews, but they should not seek guidance in the subject matter from blind men. Luther then dedicates the whole treatise to the purpose of showing how completely incapable Jews are of understanding the true subject matter of Scripture—namely, Christ—and how Jews have deliberately set out to twist Scripture "with dots, distinctions, and conjugations" in order to render readings contrary to the gospel. And so he exclaims, "If a Christian seeks understanding in the scriptures from Jews despite such damnation and judgment, what else does he do but that he seeks the face of a blind man, cleverness from a madman, death from life, and grace and truth from the Devil?"[83]

Conclusions

Martin Luther's interpretation of these eight Psalms is very much in keeping with the emphases of the medieval and late-medieval interpreters covered in the previous chapter. He also reads these Psalms first and foremost as literal prophecies of Christ's incarnation, passion, resurrection, ascension, and kingdom. Like the antecedent tradition, Luther sustains the identification of the "enemies" in these Psalms with the Jews. Furthermore, he maintains their employment to teach the central Christian doctrines of Trinity and the two natures of Christ. Finally, he also applies these eight Psalms to the situation of the church and the individual believer in order to give messages of comfort and exhortation. The distinctive contributions Luther makes to the history of the interpretation of these Psalms are his emphasis on the teaching of justification by faith alone and his reading strategy of law versus gospel.

This study of Luther's interpretation of the messianic Psalms demonstrates that he does not use the language of "shadow" or "type," nor does he use the historical context of David to inform his reading of the text. Thus, like the expositors considered in the previous chapter, he does not use typology to interpret these Psalms. Luther makes clear that these Psalms are wholly prophetic; their literal sense is the prophecy of Christ they foretell. The "historical" reading of a messianic Psalm is precisely the *history of Christ* it contains concerning his passion, his persecution by Jews, his resurrection, and his coronation.

For Martin Luther, then, the messianic Psalms are about Christ, the church, and their enemies, who are exemplified by the Jews. Furthermore, he hears in these Psalms clear prophecies concerning the person and work of Christ, powerful teaching of the central doctrines of the Christian faith, and soothing messages of comfort for weary and downtrodden Protestant churches. None of this is surprising. But there are several important things to note as we set up Luther's exegesis of these eight Psalms as one of the backdrops for John Calvin's treatment of them.

The Jews occupy a pivotal *theological* place in Luther's interpretation of these Psalms, and they play a vital interpretive role in his exegesis. Theologically, the Jews define how the enemies of Christ and the church look and act. Theologically, the Jews represent the things that Christ has come to abolish— dependence on law, physical lineage, works, ceremonies, and sacrifices.

Theologically, the Jews are a key piece in these Psalms precisely as *prophetic* Psalms; they show that in their persecution and crucifixion of Christ and in their resulting demise, the prophecies of these Psalms have been fulfilled. Furthermore, Jews play a fundamental role in particular reading strategies Luther employs to explicate the messianic Psalms. At the heart of each one of his letter versus spirit, law versus gospel, flesh versus spirit, and visible versus invisible reading strategies, one finds the Jew as decisive in both the definition and the deployment of these devices. Even more considerable is his Jews-as-enemy reading strategy, which he redeploys to describe, measure, and castigate the current enemies of his day. Finally, Luther's conviction that Jews cannot interpret Scripture rightly determines his decidedly negative view of the usefulness of Jewish exegesis for the Christian expositor.

Even more to the point, Luther uses the Jews as a tool to depose Roman church authority and teachings in favor of Protestant ones. By intimately aligning the Roman Catholics with the beliefs and practices of the defeated Jews as they appear in these Psalms, he promotes Protestant confessional formation over and against the present-day Roman church. Through his implicit accusations of judaizing against the Roman church—in their maintenance of law rather than gospel, trust in carnal things rather than spiritual, and dependence on works rather than faith—Luther endorses the truth and purity of the Protestant cause and advances the strengthening of Protestant churches. It is no wonder, then, that Luther is concerned with the rising interest in Christian Hebraica in his day, not only because he insists that Jews cannot read Scripture properly but also because he has consistently used Jews and Jewish things as a negative foil to define and identify the enemies of Christ and the church.

Given the central negative role that Jews play in his use of the biblical commentary to promote the emerging program for Protestant—and later specifically Lutheran—confessional formation, would not biblical exegesis that lacks this anti-Jewish polemic (let alone contains positive uses of Jewish exegesis) undermine some of the very exegetical strategies Luther has devised for his promotion of Protestantism over and against Roman Catholicism? Lutherans following the pattern set by Martin Luther and the previous medieval tradition would expect that the exegete would maintain the primacy of reading these Psalms as literal prophecies of Christ and as teaching key Christians doctrines, particularly the doctrines of Trinity and the two natures of Christ. For Luther, this is simply the foundation of a *Christian* reading of these Psalms. They might also expect, if they are closely following Luther's reading strategies, a clear depiction of Jews as the enemies of Christ and the church and the use of the Jew as the model to define all other enemies, specifically the Roman Catholics of their day.

Thus, any reading that fails to comprehend these Psalms primarily as literal prophecies of Christ, lacks anti-Jewish rhetoric, and fails to employ these Psalms to teach the Christian doctrines of Trinity and the two natures of Christ would signify a substantial break from their prior exegetical treatment. Indeed, these deficiencies are blatantly evident in Calvin's readings of these eight Psalms, and they become central to the Lutherans' negative appraisal of Calvin's exegesis. I demonstrate in subsequent chapters how the absence of these emphases lays the foundation of the later Lutheran accusations of judaizing against Calvin. Before focusing upon Calvin, however, we turn to Martin Bucer's exegesis of these eight Psalms as a significant contribution to the interpretive history of the messianic Psalms and, particularly, as a crucial backdrop to Calvin's understanding of them. Bucer's distinctive contributions include a turn to typological exegesis and a confidence in the usefulness of Jewish exegesis for Christian readings of the Psalms. Furthermore, Martin Bucer's exegesis of these Psalms can be viewed as a critical mediating position between the Psalms readings of Luther and Calvin.

3

Martin Bucer

Christological Readings through Historical Exegesis

Martin Bucer's commentary on the Book of Psalms is recognized as his most admired commentary, as evidenced by its many editions despite its considerable size. Bucer first published his *Sacrorum Psalmorum Libri Quinque* in 1529, and it later underwent five editions and two French translations.[1] His 1529 Psalms commentary was also translated into English a year later and most likely provided significant textual material for the English Psalter of "Matthew's Bible" and "Marshall's Primer."[2] Important Psalms commentaries closely prior to Bucer's commentary include expositions and paraphrases of certain Psalms by Erasmus (1515) and commentaries by Jacques Lefèvre d'Étaples (1508), Felix Pratensis (1515), Martin Luther (*Operationes in Psalmos*, 1519–1521), Johannes Bugenhagen (1524), and Conrad Pellican (1527).[3] The significance of Bucer's commentary on the Psalms in relation and contrast to these contemporary authors lies in his skills as a Christian Hebraist.[4]

Martin Bucer lectured on the Book of Psalms to a small group in Heidelberg late in the year of 1519. Furthermore, he probably lectured publicly on the Psalms in Strasbourg in 1524–1525 and again in 1528–1529. In 1525, Bucer translated Johannes Bugenhagen's 1524 commentary on the Psalms into German. Indeed, he not only translated Bugenhagen's work but also had permission from the author to edit it, which Bucer did, but not all to the liking of the original author. He revised the translation of Bugenhagen's Psalter along the lines of Luther's Psalter, adapted it to the Hebrew numbering of the Psalms, divided the Psalms into four classifications, and gave a summary of each Psalm that presages the later *argumenta* that Bucer would use in his own commentary on the Psalms.[5] In addition, he inserted his Zwinglian understanding of the Lord's Supper into Bugenhagen's comments on Psalm 111, much to the dismay of Bugenhagen.[6]

Indeed, the Lutherans viewed this insertion of his pro-Zwinglian view of the Eucharist as a deceptive trick on the part of Bucer, and their opinion probably contributed to Bucer's decision to publish his Psalms commentary under the pseudonym of Aretius Felinus. In a letter to Zwingli, Bucer explains some of the reasons for the pseudonym:

> Moved by the brothers and sisters of France and Lower Germany,
> I have decided to issue a commentary on the Psalms using a different
> name so that the work may be purchased by booksellers there. For it is
> a capital offense to import volumes bearing our names into those
> regions. So I pretend to be a Frenchman and take pains to put across
> the truth in the various commonplaces under the authority of the
> Fathers. . . . I intend three things by this subterfuge: first of all, to
> encourage by this means a more genuine method of biblical
> interpretation among those sisters and brothers in captivity; secondly,
> to take away that inopportune sense of alienation they feel with
> respect to dogmas of our religion . . . and thirdly, that from this these
> folks may be the more surely confirmed by these sacred consolations
> in the persecution that they are undergoing.[7]

Under the guise of a French humanist, Bucer hoped to keep his commentary from being eschewed by both Lutherans and Roman Catholics alike, while also putting it in the hands of the persecuted Protestants of France and Lower Germany for their consolation and edification.[8] Indeed, the pseudonym worked for a short time, as seen in the praise it received from several Catholic cardinals and bishops.[9] Yet, within a month of the 1529 publication of Bucer's Psalms commentary, Erasmus discovered Bucer's authorship and attacked his artifice without explicitly naming Bucer; instead, he used an allusion that anyone would recognize who knew of the quarrels between Bucer and Luther and Bugenhagen over the revision of Bugenhagen's Psalms commentary. Luther also echoed Erasmus's attack, for he saw it as further proof of Bucer's intentions to deceive.[10]

Bucer was very upset by these attacks and defended himself by replying, "A deceit that hurts nobody and is useful to many is an act of piety."[11] Indeed, his purpose for the Psalms commentary was precisely to promote the cause of reform by setting forth Reformed doctrine with the support of the church fathers, while avoiding the doctrinal pedantry of the Lutherans. Furthermore, he hoped to do so by providing a reading and understanding of the Psalms based upon their "simple sense" that sets forth the types of Christ and the patterns for true piety contained in the Psalms.[12]

Thus, I begin with an analysis of Bucer's use of historical typology in order to give readings of these eight Psalms in reference to Christ and the church. It shows that at their heart, his historical interpretations remain in keeping with the antecedent tradition. Furthermore, I highlight Bucer's particular contributions to the exegetical history of these Psalms in both the specific theological themes he emphasizes and his uses of Jewish exegesis. Indeed, I demonstrate Bucer's positive employment of Jewish exegesis precisely to anchor his particular theological readings that emphasize the beneficence of God, the doctrine of election, and the cultivation of true piety. Finally, the chapter concludes with an analysis of Bucer's criticisms of Jewish exegesis and his anti-Jewish rhetoric in order to demarcate Bucer's own conception of the boundaries of the usefulness of Jewish exegesis for Christian biblical interpretation.

Bucer's Historical Exegesis and the Unity of the Two Testaments

Martin Bucer insists on the primacy of historical exegesis to attain the simple sense of a Psalm—namely, using a Psalm's historical context as the tool to unlock its meaning. For these eight messianic Psalms, he consistently employs the device of typology, in which he sees in the figure of David and his history a foreshadowing of Christ and the church.[13] This typological reading is intimately tied to his views on the profound unity of the two testaments. Indeed, more specifically, Bucer holds to a unity of the two peoples of the Old and New Testaments, so that the church is just as central a player in his interpretations of these Psalms as is Christ.

In his "Preface to the Pious Reader," he sets forth the reasons for his adherence to a historical exegesis of the Psalms:

> The reader may moreover wish to be acquainted with my goals in the
> commentary itself. I have endeavored to the best of my ability to give the
> right interpretation to each unit, in accordance above all with the
> historical context. In this way we leave no opportunity to the Jews of
> ridiculing these sacred things; nor will the academic quibblers amongst
> us find excuse to snub them, let alone to undermine their credibility.
> Finally, I am thus able to anchor more solidly in the historical foundation
> those things that are interpreted of our Savior Christ and the church.[14]

Thus, the superiority of historical exegesis for Bucer lies in the historical sense as the solid foundation of christological and ecclesial readings so that these readings are defensible against Jews and academic disputants.[15] Giving primacy to the historical sense also guides one to limit the use of allegorical interpretations and to follow the example of the apostles, who show that they also interpreted within the bounds of the historical sense, for, says Bucer, "indeed there is nothing pertaining to piety that the historical [sense] does not abundantly teach."[16]

Martin Bucer also holds strongly to an understanding of the profound and intimate unity of the two testaments. This is deeply tied to his historical exegesis and exhibited in his typological approach to the interpretation of the Old Testament, in which Old Testament figures serve as types of Christ and in which the people of the Old Covenant (Israel, the Jews) foreshadow the people of the New Covenant (the church). This unity of the Old and New Testament scriptures may be seen in the ways in which Bucer interweaves Old and New Testament passages together, not only in the expected places where an Old Testament passage is quoted in the New but also where he finds common doctrinal content.

At every place that verses of these eight Psalms are quoted by a New Testament author, Bucer positively follows the meaning the New Testament author gives them. Thus, following Acts 4:25–28 and 13:32–33, he interprets Psalm 2 as concerning the historical events of the passion and death of Christ. He applies Ps 2:7 to Christ as the mediator of salvation and Ps 8:4–5 to Christ's humiliation and exaltation, just as the author of Hebrews (Heb 1:5, 5:5, 2:6–8) did. He parallels Ps 2:7, "You are my son; today I have begotten you," with the accounts of Christ's baptism in the Gospels (Matt 3:17, Mk 1:9, Lk 3:22). Like Acts 2:25–31 and 13:34–27, he applies Ps 16:8–11 to Christ's death and resurrection. He parallels David's affection for the "holy ones" (Ps 16:3) with Paul's affection for the church in Philippi (Phil 4:1), and the superstitious and idolatrous cult described in Ps 16:4 is the same as that depicted by Paul in 1 Corinthians 8–10. Not surprisingly, like the Gospel writers and apostles, Bucer applies Psalm 22 to Christ's suffering and death on the cross. And he likens the example of David in setting forth true piety (Ps 22:22–25) to Christ as exemplar of true Christian piety. Furthermore, he cites the quotations of Ps 45:6–7 in Heb 1:8 to display Solomon as a type of Christ, Ps 110:1 in Matt 22:43–46 to show that the Psalm more properly applies to Christ than to David, Ps 110:4 in Heb 7:11–14 to describe the priesthood of Christ, and Ps 118:22 in Matt 21:42–44 to prophesy the Jews' rejection of Christ. Bucer also gives a Trinitarian reading of Psalm 72 based on verses in the Gospel of John, parallels the deliverance of the poor (Ps 72:12–14) with Christ's compassion on the crowds

(Matt 9:36), and corresponds the Eucharistic connotations of Ps 72:16 with Christ as the bread of heaven (Jn 6:32–33).[17] Thus, Bucer truly follows his own principle that the apostles set the example of good historical exegesis.[18]

Bucer's Christological Readings

Bucer's historical exegesis of these eight Psalms leads him to interpret them in one of three ways or in any combination of these three ways: (1) christological readings through historical typology, where the life and kingdom of David foreshadow Christ and Christ's kingdom, in whom the Psalm is more completely fulfilled; (2) as literal prophecies of Christ, where David is a prophet who foresees Christ and speaks of those things that do not so much apply to himself as to Christ alone; and (3) readings in which the Psalm is fulfilled in the experience of the *church*. Thus, although Bucer's historical exegesis does lead him to devote a fair amount of his comments to the history of David, his uses of David to provide readings in reference to Christ and the church remain in essential agreement with the readings found in the antecedent tradition.[19]

Bucer often applies the history of David or Solomon in these Psalms to foreshadow the history of Christ. His interpretation of Psalm 2 provides a good example of a christological reading through the tool of historical typology. Just as David was the anointed son of God (Ps 2:2), even more does this Psalm foreshadow Christ as the anointed Son of God. Just as David was the true king over Jerusalem (Ps 2:6), even more so is Christ the true king. Just as David triumphed over his enemies (Ps 2:3, 9), so will Christ triumph. Just as God's fatherly beneficence is shown to David (Ps 2:7–8), so through Christ, the church may embrace God's paternal benevolence, for the Spirit of Christ raises believers to the faith of being God's adopted children. Just as this Psalm expresses the expansion of David's kingdom (Ps 2:8), even more so Christ's kingdom extends to the ends of the earth. Finally, just as David restores true faith and piety to the kingdom of Israel (Ps 2:7, 10–11), even more so does Christ show the church the true path of piety and faith.[20]

Bucer gives christological readings through historical typology in a number of these eight Psalms, but a few more examples will suffice. For instance, David's persecutions under Saul (Ps 22:1–21) foreshadow the passion of Christ, and David's leadership in calling the people of God back to true religion and piety (Ps 22:22–31) again typifies this act even more fully accomplished by Christ. The splendor, dignity, and power of Solomon's kingdom in Psalms 45 and 72 describe a type of the kingdom of Christ, just as Psalm 110 portrays the defeat of David's enemies and the adoration of the king—both of which are more fully completed by Christ. Finally, just as Psalm 118 describes David's inauguration as a public day of salvation, so the inauguration of Christ brings forth the saving kingdom of Christ.[21]

Although Bucer's preferred method is to give christological readings through historical typology, at times he also argues that some verses pertain to Christ alone. In these cases, rather than David portraying Christ through the experiences of his own life, David is a prophet who foresees and foretells literal events in the life of Christ. Thus, Bucer argues that Ps 16:10 ("You did not let your faithful one see corruption") is rightly said of Christ alone, just as the severe suffering and mocking described in Psalm 22 more rightly apply to Christ than to David.[22] Likewise, certain verses of Psalms 45 and 72 refer to the eternal kingdom of Christ and are not fulfilled in the kingdoms of either David or Solomon—particularly those verses describing the perpetuity and extent of the kingdom (Ps 45:17; 72:8, 17). Finally, the descriptions of the king at God's right hand (Ps 110:1) and of the king as a priest according to the order of Melchizedek (Ps 110:4) are not completed by David, argues Bucer, but by Christ alone.[23]

Bucer's Doctrinal Readings

Bucer is also intent on using these Psalms to teach certain points of doctrine.[24] He finds in these Psalms doctrinal teachings concerning the two natures of Christ, Trinity, the beneficence of God, election, and the true nature of faith. The use of these Psalms to teach points of doctrine is part of his larger purpose: to give instruction and exhortation to the church concerning true Christian piety. Indeed, chapter 1 has shown that it was a medieval commonplace among Christian interpreters to use these Psalms to teach about the Trinity and the two natures of Christ, and Bucer retains this use of these Psalms. So, for example, on Ps 2:7 ("He said to me, 'You are my son; today I have begotten you'"), Bucer asserts the necessity for salvation that Christ is both truly human and truly divine and the same substance with the Father. His readings of Ps 8:4 and most of Psalm 22 also set forth the doctrine of the two natures of Christ, with emphasis on Christ's incarnation and redemption of human nature through his divine nature. For example, the "son of man" in Ps 8:4 indicates how Christ took on human wretchedness, except for sin, and by doing so, redeemed humanity.[25]

What is even more noteworthy in his exegesis of Psalm 2 is that Bucer's excursus on the two natures of Christ is clearly tied to a defense of the Christian doctrine of the Trinity over and against Jewish exegesis and, specifically, against the anti-Christian rhetoric of David Kimhi.[26] Furthermore, on Ps 2:7–8, he highlights the presence and workings of the Trinity at Christ's baptism. His intention to give Trinitarian teachings may also be seen in his discussions of the distinctions of the persons of Father, Son, and Holy Spirit. Finally, his emphases on the importance of the workings of the Holy Spirit for biblical interpretation and Christian sanctification also speak to the intrinsic significance of the Trinity for Bucer's theology and exegesis.[27]

In addition to teachings concerning Christ's two natures and Trinity, Bucer consistently finds in these Psalms examples of God's election and fatherly care of the elect. On Psalm 2, he remarks that just as God calls David his son and shows him fatherly beneficence, so does God elect believers through Christ and give them particular indulgence. Likewise, for Bucer, Psalm 8 praises God's benevolent tenderness toward the elect. God's goodness to God's children may also be seen in Ps 22:9–11 ("You took me from the womb; you kept me safe on my mother's breast..."), for God does not desert them but promises to be their help and hope. Similarly, Psalm 45 teaches that the elect are made heirs to the goodness and gifts of God.[28] Indeed, Bucer insists that the teachings contained in these Psalms are for the church—the saints of God, the elect—for they give instruction concerning the blessings God bestows on the elect and the pious life to which the elect are called. For example, Psalm 16 provides training for the saints of God in prayer, separation from impurity, and true Christian piety. Likewise, the last third of Psalm 22 instructs the elect toward a life of praise and gratitude toward God. Furthermore, Psalm 110 teaches about the distinctions between the elect and the reprobate.[29]

Finally, Bucer often finds in these Psalms opportunities to expound upon the doctrine of faith. He maintains that the statement "You are my son; today I have begotten you" (Ps 2:7) applies just as much to the believer's election as a child of God as it does to Christ. The Holy Spirit, argues Bucer, raises believers to this faith by *persuading* their hearts that they truly have been made children of God. His definition of faith as persuasion is developed at greater length in his comments on the last verse of Psalm 2, "Happy are all who take refuge in him," in which he finds an "exceptional maxim of faith" that teaches the name, nature, and virtue of faith.[30] Using his definition of faith as persuasion, he argues that the elect are justified when they are persuaded that God is the only author of goodness and are specifically persuaded of God's goodness toward them. Thus, for Bucer, the saying "The just shall live by faith" (Hab 2:4) means that one is persuaded of God's goodness and in response believes and loves nothing more than God. Although he argues for justification by faith alone and not by good works, he clearly maintains "righteousness flows from faith and proceeds from love of God." Citing the support of Bernard, Chrysostom, and Augustine, in particular, Bucer affirms that the good life is inseparable from faith. In this way, he aims to steer clear of a staunch sola fideism in order to set forth a more intimate and clear tie between faith and righteousness, between faith and good works.[31]

The Church as the Central Subject of the Messianic Psalms

Even more than locating Christ or certain doctrinal teachings, Bucer's primary purpose in his readings of these eight Psalms is to position the church as their central player and subject, and he does this in three ways. First, Bucer's doctrinal teaching concerning faith is part of a larger purpose: to exhort the church toward the cultivation of true Christian piety. Second, his doctrinal teachings concerning God's beneficence, election, and the work of the Spirit are part of the larger aim of setting forth the call of the church to increase the kingdom of Christ on earth. Third, his instruction concerning the two natures of Christ and the work of the Spirit in justification and sanctification is part of the greater goal to set forth what I would argue is for Bucer the central meaning of all of Scripture: the restoration of God's people through the saving act of Christ.[32]

Bucer makes the church the key player in these Psalms, first through his use of them to exhort the Christian church to cultivate true piety. This exhortation has three prongs: the cultivation of true faith, the advancement of the praise of God, and the establishment of the true Christian religion over and against superstitious cults. As his views on the nature of faith have already been addressed, we turn to the latter two. For Bucer, the right and proper responses of humanity to God's eternal power and grandeur are recognition of God's excellence and a life lived in praise to God. God is to be praised because of the salvation and restoration given in Christ and for the protection and deliverance God gives from enemies and oppressors. Thus, the true Christian religion, according to Bucer, is typified by a secure and persuaded faith, recognition and belief in the goodness of God, and a life lived in eternal praise to God.[33] Indeed, these Psalms provide instruction to help distinguish between true and false religion and true and false piety. Thus, Ps 8:2 teaches the distinction between the pious praise that comes "out of the mouths of babes and sucklings" and the impiety of the "enemy and avenger."[34] Similarly, according to Bucer, Ps 16:4 is a declaration that the faithful will not follow superstitious cults but will desire holiness and abhor idolatry. Thus the Psalmist sets the example of praying for protection from God, separating himself from impurity, and calling others to follow the true Christian religion. Likewise, Bucer maintains that Ps 118:26–28 clarifies the divergence between true and false piety and between false sacrifices of blood and true sacrifices of praise. For Bucer, all of Psalm 22, as well, describes the true religion of God, in which David is calling Israel back to true piety—a task more fully completed by Christ.[35]

Alongside his exhortations to the church to embrace true Christian piety, Bucer also finds in these Psalms expressions of God's election of the church and descriptions of the church as the kingdom of God. He lays out key aspects of his kingdom theology, which include the establishment of a Christian society, the coming of Christ's kingdom on earth through the saving act of Christ, and the continuing faithfulness of the elect. Bucer affirms that Psalms 2, 22, 45, 72, 110, and 118 all foreshadow the kingdom of Christ through the earthly expressions of David and Solomon's kingdoms. These Psalms demonstrate the defeat of Christ's enemies, the splendor and glory of Christ's kingdom, the righteousness and justice established by this kingdom, and its expansion, universality, and eternal character.[36]

In addition to providing a clear delineation of the kingdom of Christ, Bucer argues that these Psalms also urge the elect to seek this kingdom above all things and work to increase Christ's kingdom on earth. For him, the embodiment of Christ's kingdom on earth is the calling of the church and, specifically, of the elect. Indeed, the believers in the church, argues Bucer, "dwell bodily in the divine" through Christ. They are members of the body of Christ and, thus, participate in Christ's life and saving acts by embodying Christ's kingdom of righteousness in the world.[37] Furthermore, Bucer emphasizes that the church bears this responsibility specifically by performing acts of righteousness and charity, such as the care of the poor.[38]

Bucer also uses these Psalms to give instruction to earthly princes concerning how a true godly prince should rule. He quite literally applies Ps 2:10–11 ("O kings, be wise; be warned, O rulers of the earth; serve the Lord with fear and trembling") to his contemporary princes and magistrates to draw a contrast between wicked and pious princes.[39] For Bucer, Psalms 45 and 72 also demarcate the characteristics of the pious king, first and foremost of which are the love of righteousness, the hatred of wickedness, and the administration of equity, peace, and justice. In keeping with his vision of God's kingdom on earth, he not only mingles the earthly kingdom of the church with the heavenly kingdom and the divine body of Christ but sees an important role to be played by earthly princes to further the kingdom of God. For instance, Bucer argues that Psalm 22 "signifies how often the rules of a pious king are to be a benefit and a divine help." This leads him to affirm that earthly kingdoms can assist in ushering in Christ's kingdom by helping to fight sin in the world.[40]

In sum, according to Bucer, these Psalms edify the church by exhorting the elect to true faithfulness and piety and calling the church to embody Christ's kingdom in the world. Yet, the reading that is the very heart of Bucer's interpretation of these Psalms is his constant refrain that Christ has restored the saints of God (the elect) to the life-giving gifts of God. All of his doctrinal teachings and the placement of the church as the central player in these Psalms are established upon the restoration brought by Christ. The teaching concerning the two natures of Christ is in the context of the restoration Christ brings, for Christ renews human nature by taking on flesh. Likewise, Christ makes God's fatherly beneficence accessible to the elect, for Christ is the one through whom the elect are able to call God "father" and children of God.[41] Bucer defines faith as the persuaded conviction of God's goodness, a goodness that is first and foremost shown in the salvation and restoration given through Christ. True piety, then, is praise of this goodness of God given in Christ; furthermore, Christ is the one who restores true Christian religion and piety. Moreover, Bucer's vision of the kingdom of God on earth is rooted in Christ's restoration of the elect so that the elect are incorporated into the body of Christ and participate in Christ's saving actions in the world.[42]

Thus, the focal point of Bucer's christological readings of these Psalms is not so much the literal prophecies of Christ that they contain but, rather, the *body of Christ*, which is the *church*. The church becomes the central player in these Psalms by way of the salvific and restorative act of Christ so that it now participates in the life of Christ. Thus, Bucer's interpretation of these eight Psalms exhibits a profound envisioning of the church as the body of Christ, so that what may be said of Christ, the head, is also said of the church, the members of Christ's body. This placement of the church as central to his readings of these Psalms is intimately tied to their christological import.[43]

Bucer's Employment of Jewish Exegesis

One of the most distinctive characteristics of Bucer's interpretations of these eight Psalms is his extensive and explicit use of Jewish exegesis, specifically the commentaries of David Kimhi, Abraham Ibn Ezra, and Solomon ben Isaac (Rashi).[44] In fact, he makes very little explicit use of Christian commentaries on the Psalms.[45] Just after he states in his preface that the purpose of his Psalms commentary is to give a reading of each Psalm in its historical context in order to "anchor more solidly in the historical foundation those things that are interpreted of our Savior Christ and the church" so that the Jews may not undermine the credibility of these interpretations, Bucer then tells the reader that he will not be reciting Christian readings of the Psalms. Instead, he encourages his readers to examine these Christian authors directly for themselves.[46]

The significant lack of citations of Christian sources, as opposed to the frequent overt references to Jewish exegesis of the Psalms, leads to questions of why Bucer found Jewish commentaries so very useful. He finds Jewish exegesis supremely beneficial in three basic ways. First, he uses Jewish commentators to enhance and inform his historical exegesis. Second, he found the rabbis to be *theologically* helpful in buttressing his own particular theological emphases. Third, he employs the Jewish commentators to equip his Christian readers with knowledge that would enable them to defend their Christian readings of these Psalms over and against Jewish readings.

Bucer's Use of Jewish Exegesis to Enhance His Historical Exegesis

In the preface to his Psalms commentary, Bucer states that one of his main reasons for using Jewish sources is the information they provide for the historical context and the "plain sense" (*peshat*) of a Psalm.[47] For example, on Psalm 2, he not only reads the Psalm exactly as the rabbis do in reference to the life of David and the Philistine uprising against him but also utilizes several of the Old Testament references cited by the rabbis to fill in the historical context of the Psalm. Both Kimhi and Rashi begin by citing 2 Sam 5:17 and 1 Sam 28:4 as the context for Psalm 2, and Bucer cites exactly these passages.[48] Kimhi quotes Ps 59:8 to augment the meaning of God's laughter in verse 4; Bucer also quotes Ps 59:8 in his comments on this verse.[49] Kimhi quotes Deut 14:1, 2 Sam 7:14, 1 Sam 16:13, and Deut 32:18 to give context for Ps 2:7, and Bucer cites all of these passages.[50] Likewise, in his comments on the second half of verse 12, Kimhi cites Ps 1:6, Is 1:30, and 2 Sam 13:31 to inform the meaning of those who "perish in the way"; again, Bucer quotes these exact same passages in his comments on this verse.[51] The example of Psalm 2 alone demonstrates how rich Bucer finds Jewish resources to be for enhancing knowledge of the Psalm's historical and scriptural contexts.

Likewise, Kimhi, Rashi, and Ibn Ezra read Psalms 22, 45, 110, and 118 in reference to the life of David and Psalm 72 in the context of the reign of Solomon, and again, Bucer finds much usefulness in their comments to shed light on the historical contexts of these Psalms in his own exegesis.[52] Beyond all the historical details and biblical references that he excavates from these Jewish sources in all of these Psalms (which are many), the more important point here concerns the way Bucer provides readings in keeping with Jewish interpretive principles and at the same time facilitates their being read christologically. In his elucidation of these Psalms, Bucer's primary goal is not simply a historical reading pertaining to the life of David or Solomon but in addition a reading for the church in reference to Christ and his restoration of the elect. Thus, he not only attends to the rabbis' historical readings of these Psalms but also points to the places where they apply the Psalm as a promise and prophecy of the Messiah. Indeed, Rashi notes that the rabbis interpret Psalm 2 as concerning the Messiah.[53] Kimhi and Ibn Ezra both read Psalms 45, 72, and 118 as pertaining to the Messiah, the promised redemption of Israel, and the future messianic kingdom, where David and Solomon and their kingdoms serve as types of the Messiah and his reign.[54] In this way, Bucer appeals to the rabbis' messianic readings of these Psalms to buttress his own christological readings. Furthermore, Kimhi in particular uses the tool of typology in his exegesis of Psalms 72 and 118, where he first reads the Psalms concerning the historical figure (i.e., Solomon or David) and then applies them to the Messiah and his kingdom, in which the Psalms are more completely fulfilled.[55] Thus, in Kimhi, Bucer finds a model and predecessor for his typological method, by which he can defend his own Christian typological readings in reference to the fulfillment of these Psalms by Jesus Christ.

Bucer's Use of Jewish Exegesis to Buttress Particular Theological Readings

Bucer's positive employment of Jewish exegesis extends beyond its usefulness to inform the historical context of a Psalm and into the actual theology taught by a Psalm. Indeed, he finds in the commentaries of Kimhi, Rashi, and Ibn Ezra ample support for his particular theological emphases on the beneficence of God, the cultivation of true piety, and the doctrine of election. For example, the rabbis read Psalms 8, 16, and 118 as praise songs of God's loving-kindness or *hesed*, which Bucer translates as God's beneficence. Indeed, Kimhi summarizes all of Psalm 8 as a "recital of the loving-kindnesses which God shows towards man and the dominion God has given man over all."[56] Bucer, citing the rabbis in support, likewise summarizes the content of Psalm 8 as concerning the immensity of God's goodness to humanity and the honor and dignity God bestows on humankind.[57] He also uses Kimhi's interpretation of Ps 16:2 to support his emphasis on God as the source of all goodness and God's beneficence to humanity.[58] In addition, Bucer employs the rabbis' translations of certain Hebrew words to buttress his interpretive emphasis on God's beneficence. For example, on Ps 8:2, he provides great detail concerning Kimhi's and Ibn Ezra's interpretations of יִסַּדְתָּ in order to elaborate about the founding of God's praise from the beginning of human life (i.e., infants and sucklings) and speak of the immensity of God's fatherly goodness.[59] Likewise, Bucer uses Kimhi's and Ibn Ezra's translations of certain Hebrew words in Ps

16:5–6—גּוֹרָלִי and חֲבָלִים—to demonstrate the great benefits God bestows on God's people.[60]

Bucer also employs the rabbis to buttress his readings of Psalms 2, 8, 16, 22, and 118 as issuing a clear call to the cultivation of piety and, more specifically, the call for the pious to separate themselves from the superstitious cult. Just as Bucer defines true piety and true worship as praise of God and God's goodness and contrasts this to superstitious cults, so also Kimhi, Rashi, and Ibn Ezra exhibit similar definitions in their readings of these Psalms.[61] For example, Rashi reads Psalm 16 as David giving instruction to the congregation of Israel in order to establish true religion. More broadly, all three rabbis describe David as setting forth in this Psalm the example of true humility, obedience and worship of God, and rejection of idolatry.[62] On both Psalms 22 and 118, Bucer applies the readings of Kimhi and Ibn Ezra to buttress his use of David as an example of bringing God's people back to true piety and worship in contrast to the false religion of Saul.[63] In addition to utilizing these theological themes set forth by the rabbis, Bucer again explicitly uses the rabbis' translations of certain Hebrew words to support his contrast between true and false piety. For instance, he states a clear preference for Rashi's translations of the Hebrew noun עַצְּבוֹתָם and verb מָהֲרוּ in Ps 16:4 as "idols" and "they hasten" (after another god), respectively, in order to argue that the Psalmist is speaking against idolatry and superstitious cults.[64]

Besides the obvious parallel between the Jewish view of Israel's election and the Christian view of the church as the elect, Bucer uses the rabbis' comments on certain verses to support his own emphasis on God's special favor to the elect and the attributes that separate the elect from the reprobate. Concerning the "holy ones in the land" in Ps 16:4, Bucer writes, "Because God chose the people of Israel for himself, God has them as his property and they are taken care of by him alone, to whom he gives many and vast benefits and known signs."[65] Indeed, he applies Kimhi's emphasis on the elect to show that the elect receive help from God to do good to the saints (Ps 16:4) and to receive the inheritance God intends for them (Ps 16:5–6).[66] Furthermore, in his interpretations of Psalms 2 and 16, he employs the rabbis to reinforce his emphasis on the contrast between the pious elect and the impious reprobate. Bucer applies Kimhi's comments on Ps 2:12 ("lest he be angry and you perish in the way") to demarcate and emphasize the two paths: election and reprobation. He notes that Kimhi connects this verse to Psalm 1, where the way of the righteous and the way of the wicked are contrasted.[67] After using Rashi's translations of the Hebrew terms in Ps 16:4, Bucer proceeds to reiterate his point that the holy elect are instructed to flee the superstitions of the impious. Likewise, he cites Kimhi and Ibn Ezra in support of the application of Ps

22:22–25 to the establishment of piety and justice and the fleeing from impiety and unrighteousness first by David and then completed by the Messiah.[68]

Bucer's Criticisms of Jewish Exegesis

Although Bucer found much usefulness in Jewish exegesis to support his theological teachings about God's beneficence, election, and the cultivation of true piety and the methodological tool of historical typology, his criticisms of Jewish exegesis come to the forefront in his accentuations on the Christian doctrines of Trinity and the two natures of Christ. Indeed, these two doctrines were the target of anti-Christian polemic in David Kimhi's commentary on the Psalms. Kimhi concludes his comments on Psalms 2, 22, 72, and 110 with quite lengthy discourses on how Christians misread and distort these passages to read them concerning the divinity of Christ and the Trinity. Bucer, particularly on Psalms 2 and 22, directly quotes and rebukes Kimhi's attacks on Christian readings.[69]

Kimhi first launches his attack against Christian readings of Ps 2:7, "He [the Lord] said to me, 'You are my son; today I have begotten you.'" The heart of his attack is against the Christian doctrine of Trinity:

> For if they should say to you that he was the Son of God, answer that it is not proper to say "Son of God" in the manner of flesh and blood, for a son is the species of his father. . . . Say to them that of the Godhead it is unfitting to speak of father and son because the Godhead cannot be divided, for it is not a body that it should be divided; but God is one in every aspect of unity. He cannot be increased, decreased, or split up. And further say to them that a father is prior to a son in time, and the son issues from the father's vigor . . . for one is not called father until he has a son, and a son is not so called unless he has a father; nevertheless he who is called father when he has a son is prior in time without a doubt. And if this be so, the God whom you speak of and call "Father, Son, and Holy Spirit"—the portion you call Father existed before the other portion you call Son.[70]

Kimhi is clearly assailing the Christian beliefs in the unity of the persons of the Trinity and the preexistence of Christ. Also within this is an attack on the Christian doctrine of the two natures of Christ; indeed, this criticism figures more prominently in Kimhi's instruction on how Jews should respond to Christian readings of the next verse (Ps 2:8):

> And further say to them: Has the God whom you describe as "the Father" said to his Son, *Ask of Me and I will give the nations for your*

inheritance? How should the Son ask from the Father? Is he not God like Him?...And if they say to you that it is spoken in regard to the flesh, after the Godhead had taken on flesh, and to the Son in the flesh...this is not the case, for Jesus in the flesh had no kingdom or any authority over any nation.[71]

Bucer directly quotes a good portion of Kimhi's criticisms. He responds to those concerning the doctrine of Trinity by maintaining that such distinctions of persons is set forth by Scripture, so who is Kimhi to correct the tongue of God? Then he reaffirms the creedal formula that Christ is the same substance with the Father.[72] As to Kimhi's criticisms of the doctrine of the two natures of Christ, Bucer simply states that God subjected to Christ not only humanity but also spiritual things. Namely, he points out that one cannot separate Christ's divinity and humanity, which is exactly what he sees Kimhi's criticisms doing. Finally, throughout his comments on Psalm 2, Bucer consciously asserts Trinitarian language and specific teachings concerning Trinity and the two natures of Christ.[73]

David Kimhi also attacks the Christian reading of Psalm 22 as pertaining to the suffering and crucifixion of Jesus at the hands of the Jews. Particularly of concern is the Christian rendering of Ps 22:16, which Kimhi staunchly views as a corruption of the text.[74] Furthermore, he sees many contradictions in the Christian interpretation of this Psalm, such as why Jesus would speak of "our fathers" (Ps 22:4) when he has only one Father, how Jesus can say, "I will declare your name to my brethren" (Ps 22:22) when God has no brothers, and why Jesus could not save himself if he is truly God. Kimhi summarizes, "If he [Jesus] spoke of the human flesh, God did not deliver nor rescue him; and if of the Godhead, there was no need of rescue."[75] Again, the heart of Kimhi's attack is against the Christian doctrine of the two natures of Christ.

Bucer spends a considerable amount of time defending the Christian reading of Ps 22:16. After quoting Kimhi's translation of the verse as "they encircled me like a lion, my hands and feet" and citing Kimhi's interpretation of it in reference to the sufferings of Israel in exile, Bucer exclaims, "Truly I know these comments to be empty and worthless, that he asserts this Psalm sings concerning the present exile and all that he says concerning the lion!"[76] Bucer contends that "even if this passage was conceded to the Jews," there is proof enough in the Gospels to show that Psalm 22 prophesies Christ. Next, he appeals to a grammatical argument, citing other Old Testament passages where forms of ארי may be found,[77] and argues that whenever the Hebrew letter *cof* precedes this word, it always means "to pierce or dig." In the end, he appeals to the authority of Christian tradition: "Indeed, because I write as a Christian, along with the public consensus...for this reason it is better to be received as 'they pierce,' as the Christians receive it, than to assent to the contentious Jews."[78] Finally, Bucer responds to Kimhi's criticism of the Christian reading of Psalm 22 in reference to Christ's passion and Kimhi's attacks on the doctrine of the two natures of Christ. He does so through an in-depth excursus on the incarnation of Christ and the necessity of the incarnation for human redemption.[79] Through these citations of Kimhi's anti-Christian polemic, Bucer intends not merely a critique of Jewish exegesis on these points but also a defense of Christian Trinitarian and christological readings.

A second kind of criticism Bucer voices against Jewish exegesis arises when he believes the rabbi's reading is not in accordance with the simple sense of the text.[80] For example, on the second half of Ps 8:8, he recites Kimhi's interpretation that "whatever passes along the paths of the sea" refers to ships and the human ability to cross the sea by ships. Bucer argues that this is not in keeping with the simple sense of the text and its context, for in the previous verses, the Psalmist has enumerated the creatures over which God has given humanity dominion. Thus, this verse must refer to the diverse kinds of fish and sea creatures that God has made subject to human command.[81] Likewise, on Ps 2:7 ("You are my son"), he argues against Kimhi's interpretation that it is spoken concerning the first creation. He contends that it is more in keeping with the context of the Psalm to understand this verse in terms of a particular election.[82] Bucer also argues for the plain sense of Ps 110:7 in reference to Christ over and against Jewish readings: "In this clearly is seen Christ the Savior when all his enemies are doomed to Gehenna. Knowing the different meanings of the Hebrews, for us the meaning of this psalm is seen *more simply* as fitted to the great glory of Christ."[83]

Keeping the plain sense of a passage is often the criterion Bucer uses to favor one rabbi's interpretation over another's. For instance, he prefers Rashi's translation of the Hebrew word מָהֲרוּ as "they hasten" over Kimhi and Ibn Ezra's translation as "dowry" or "they endow" because the context of the passage, argues Bucer, concerns idolatry and the superstitious cult. Thus, the meaning "they hasten after other gods" is more fitting to the plain sense of the verse.[84] Likewise, on Ps 45:8, he prefers Ibn Ezra's translation of מֹר as "myrrh," rather than Kimhi's translation of "moss," because, again, Ibn Ezra's meaning is better suited to the context and plain sense of the passage. Then in the very next instance, he prefers Kimhi's translation of קְצִיעוֹת as some kind of aromatic spice over Ibn Ezra's translation of "folds or angles" for the very same reasons.[85] Finally, Bucer prefers Rashi's interpretation of Ps 72:15 ("Long may he live!") as "Long live King Solomon," rather than Kimhi and Ibn Ezra's interpretation of this phrase in reference to the poor. He notes that Rashi says his interpretation is the simple sense of the text, with which Bucer agrees and adds that this reading is in keeping with the history narrated in the tenth chapter of 1 Kings.[86]

Thus, while Bucer's criticisms of Jewish exegesis mostly focus around their attacks on the central Christian doctrines of Trinity and the two natures of Christ, they also revolve around maintaining what he believes to be the plain sense of the text.

Bucer's Anti-Jewish Rhetoric

Not only does Martin Bucer have clear criticisms of the Jewish sources he uses but also his commentary on the Psalms contains several instances of strong anti-Jewish rhetoric. This rhetoric follows the patterns of anti-Jewish rhetoric set by late-medieval commentators and retained in Martin Luther's commentaries on the Psalms; that is to say, there are two basic configurations of Bucer's anti-Jewish rhetoric. First, he maintains the identification of the enemies in these Psalms with the Jews. Second, he repeats statements concerning Jewish blindness and ignorance in their interpretations of certain biblical passages, particularly passages that Christians read as pertaining to Christ.[87]

As has been shown, Bucer positively recites the New Testament authors' use of these Psalms as literal prophecies of Christ's passion, death, resurrection, ascension, and exaltation. In these instances where he preserves the New Testament applications of these Psalms, he also repeats clear designations of Jews as the enemies of Christ and the church. For example, just as the disciples in Acts 2:25–28 interpret Ps 2:1–2 in reference to Herod, Pilate, and the Jewish rulers, Bucer does so through his method of typology:

> These enemies of David bear the type of the masses and the people—
> the Jewish princes, Herod, Pilate, the high priests and the experts of
> the law—they all pressed against the Lord Jesus for his destruction,
> but in vain. In this consideration, they were truly senseless and
> horrible and insane; they were not born of the Spirit of God. Nothing
> was less wise or sacred in the work of the nation of the Jews than this
> unspeakable madness . . . that the doctors of religion and scholars of
> Scripture arrogated themselves against the Lord.[88]

Likewise, Bucer notes the use of Ps 2:7–8 in Acts 13:27–33 to argue that Christ is the begotten Son of God who is given power and authority over his enemies to "break them with a rod of iron and dash them in pieces like a potter's vessel" (Ps 2:9). The context of Acts 13:27–33 implies that these enemies are the Jews. Even more clearly, in his comments on Ps 2:9, he narrates Josephus's account of the Jewish Wars to argue that the defeat of the Jews by the Romans is the fulfillment of this verse. He further supports the application of the shattering of the potter's vessel to the destruction of the Jews with references to Jer 19:11 and Is 30:14.[89]

Moreover, Bucer identifies the Jews as the "enemy and avenger" mentioned in Ps 8:2, though he first equates this description with "atheists who spread their impiety and dare to deny that God exists." By recounting the use of the first half of Ps 8:2 in Matt 21:16 as Jesus' response to the chief priests and scribes when they tried to silence the children who were welcoming Jesus into Jerusalem, Bucer concludes, "Truly this verse is the exact right response to them, the enemies of God who were silencing the beautiful voices of the children."[90] In addition, he interprets "deliver my only one from the hand of the dog" (Ps 22:20) typologically to refer first to Saul's persecution of David and then in reference to the assembly of the Jews who stood against Christ.[91] In his interpretation of Psalm 110, he recounts its application in Jesus' response to the Pharisees in Matt 22:41–46 to argue that Christ is prophesied in this Psalm contrary to "the accusations of the Jews." Therein, he specifically names the identity of the enemies in Ps 110:5–6 by writing, "At first [this is spoken of] the Jews; then it strikes down the head of the Romans, and then the heads all over the earth, including the destruction of the Turks." Finally, Bucer identifies the builders in Ps 118:22 ("the stone that the builders rejected has become the chief cornerstone") with the synagogue and any who inwardly reject Christ, who, therefore, are excluded and no longer have a place among the people of God.[92]

Though Bucer does retain the identification of the enemies in these Psalms with the Jews, he does not deploy this as a reading strategy, as Luther does, to align the pope and the Roman church with the Jews in order to reveal the Roman Catholics as the enemies of Christ and the church. In contrast, he has very little anti-Catholic rhetoric in his commentary on the Psalms. An obvious explanation for this absence is the fact that he wrote under a pseudonym in hopes of reaching a Roman Catholic readership. When he does give a more contemporary application of "enemy," it is in reference to atheists and the impious, which is in keeping with his aim to cultivate true piety and worship of God.

Bucer also repeats statements that disparage the Jews as blind and ignorant readers of certain biblical passages. For example, he criticizes the Jewish interpreters for their blindness in insisting that Ps 16:10 ("you did not give me up to the grave or let your faithful one see corruption") refers to David rather than to the resurrection of Christ. Likewise, in his reading of Ps 22:27 as "all the nations of the Gentiles," he emphasizes that God is now the God of the *Gentiles* (citing the support of Rom 3:29), to which he adds, "And rightly now before the whole world the blindness of the Jews is all the more evident." Finally, on Psalm 45, he criticizes the Jews for not having accepted Jesus as the Messiah, because they themselves interpret this Psalm in reference to the Messiah.[93]

Conclusions

Martin Bucer remains in keeping with the antecedent Christian exegesis of these eight Psalms on several points. He reads them as literal prophecies of Christ in keeping with the New Testament authors' applications of them. He finds in them clear doctrinal teaching concerning the two natures of Christ and Trinity. Yet, Bucer's exegesis of these Psalms is distinctive in significant ways. He argues for the primacy of historical exegesis and its ability to anchor christological readings. Specifically, he advocates the tool of typology to give christological readings that are rooted in the historical sense. Likewise, he brings in his own specific theological interests, such as praise of the beneficence of God, the doctrine of election, and the cultivation of piety. Thus, although Bucer maintains many traditional Christian elements in his interpretations of these Psalms, he also demonstrates the beginnings of a specifically Reformed reading of them. By this, I mean the turn to typological exegesis, the doctrinal emphases on election and the benefence of God, and the use of these Psalms to set forth a clear program for the cultivation of Christian piety.[94]

The other prominent distinctive in Bucer's exegesis of the Psalms is his recurrent use of Jewish exegesis. Bucer finds Jewish commentaries to be incredibly rich and beneficial resources for his own readings of these Psalms. The rabbis are not just helpful in the historical details and context they provide for the plain sense of each Psalm; he also affirms them to be valuable with regard to theological content. He garners support from Jewish exegesis for his particular Reformed emphases upon the benefence of God, the doctrine of election, the definition and cultivation of true piety, and the promised restoration of the people and kingdom of God. Indeed, it is striking how often Bucer's general reading of a Psalm matches the general meaning given to the Psalm by the rabbis. Yet, even with his rather extensive use of the rabbis, he preserves the heart of traditional Christian interpretations of these messianic Psalms, though he does so more through the method of historical typology than by reading them as pure prophecies of Christ. Furthermore, Bucer specifically maintains the use of certain passages to support the doctrines of Trinity and the two natures of Christ.

Thus, Bucer's criticisms of Jewish exegesis are determined by the principles of whether the reading keeps the plain, historical sense of the text and whether it preserves some form of the traditional Christian interpretation of these Psalms. When he finds that a rabbi's interpretation is not in keeping with what he believes to be the plain sense of the text, he rejects that reading. Likewise, when a rabbi's commentary expresses anti-Christian polemic, particularly against the doctrines of Trinity or the two natures of Christ or against the application of a verse to Christ, he responds negatively to such comments and launches a defense of these Christian readings. Hence, one could argue that Bucer achieves exactly his purpose concerning the defensibility of Christian readings vis-à-vis Jewish criticisms that he set out to attain, according to the preface to his Psalms commentary:

> The reader may moreover wish to be acquainted with my goals in the commentary itself. I have endeavored to the best of my ability to give the right interpretation to each unit, in accordance above all with the historical context. In this way we leave no opportunity to the Jews of ridiculing these sacred things; nor will the academic quibblers among us find excuse to snub them, let alone to undermine their credibility. Finally, I am thus able to anchor more solidly in the historical foundation those things that are interpreted of our Savior Christ and of our church.[95]

Indeed, Bucer gives readings of these Psalms that are in keeping with Jewish interpretations of them, and at the same time, these readings maintain their christological import and do so in a way that is in accordance with what he believes are Jewish exegetical principles of preserving their historical, plain sense.[96] He is convinced that he has succeeded in giving a Christian reading of these Psalms that would stand up to Jewish critique and still sustain a truly Christian reading in reference to Christ and the church.

One other element needs to be added to the list of distinctively Reformed contributions that Bucer has made to the exegetical history of these eight Psalms. In addition to the distinguishing characteristics of the turn to historical typology, the use of these Psalms to set forth a program for the cultivation of Christian piety, and his doctrinal emphases on election, the beneficence of God, and Christ's restorative work, one could add the belief in the usefulness of Jewish exegesis for Christian readings of Scripture.[97] Obviously, this is in precise conflict with the sentiments expressed by Martin Luther; that is to say, Luther has used the alignment with things Jewish to demarcate that which is false and to be avoided. Yet, while Bucer makes extensive positive use of Jewish exegesis, he does so within boundaries that Luther conceivably could approve (while still not condoning the use of Jewish exegesis)—namely, Bucer still maintains the christological import of these Psalms and their teachings concerning Trinity and the two natures of Christ, both of which cannot so easily be said of the exegesis of John Calvin. Indeed, I have spent a fair amount of time on Martin Bucer's exegesis of these eight Psalms because it serves as a vitally important backdrop to Calvin's interpretation of them. Calvin's exegesis shares with Bucer many significant exegetical methods, emphases, and concerns. On the other hand, the differences between Bucer and Calvin on these Psalms also reveal salient features of Calvin's exegesis that open him up to the accusation of judaizing.

4

John Calvin

The Sufficiency of David

Scholars of John Calvin have often noted the importance of the Book of Psalms for his life and thought. The preface to his commentary on the Psalms is one of the few places where he gives some insight into his conversion to Protestantism and his personal life experiences. This preface also indicates the ways in which Calvin deeply identifies with the experiences of David and finds in David an inspiring example of true faith and the practice of prayer.[1] Moreover, the Psalms occupy a central place in the worship life of sixteenth-century French Reformed churches, for Calvin emphasizes the use of the Psalter and the singing of Psalms in the public worship of the church.[2]

Calvin's commentary on the Psalms was published in Geneva in 1557. He writes in the preface to this commentary that he lectured on the Psalms in Geneva during the five years prior to its publication. Indeed, he states reservations about writing a commentary—the foremost being that Martin Bucer had already written on the Psalms—and the eventual reasons for his doing so, which include the continual urging of his colleagues, the satisfaction he found in expositing the Psalms, and his fear that others would publish his previous lectures on the Psalms, which he himself considered incomplete. Perhaps most of all, Calvin increasingly found that the Psalms resonated with his own personal experience, so that he came to believe he might very well have some particular insights into understanding the Psalms.[3]

In this same preface, Calvin sets forth all of the key theological emphases that he will highlight in his exegesis of the Psalms.[4] The Psalms provide supreme examples of true prayer, trust in God, faith that overcomes adversity, consolation and encouragement to believers, guidance in true worship, confidence in God's goodness and providential care, exercises of proper Christian piety, and the path of true salvation.[5] Furthermore, he asserts that these models are particularly found through the example of David, with whom Calvin deeply identifies his own life struggles. Just as David had to contend with the internal enemies of his kingdom, so Calvin finds encouragement and a model for his own toils with the internal afflictions of the church of his day. He writes,

> It has greatly aided me in understanding more fully the complaints
> made by him [David] of the internal afflictions that the church had to
> sustain through those who gave themselves out to be her members,
> that I had suffered the same or similar things from the domestic
> enemies of the church ... it has been of very great advantage to me to
> behold in him [David] as a mirror, both the commencement of my
> calling and the continued course of my function so that I know the
> more assuredly that whatever that most illustrious king and prophet
> suffered was exhibited to me by God as an example for imitation.[6]

Calvin likens himself to David, for just as David was taken from the humble position of a shepherd and elevated to be king, so God took Calvin from his "originally obscure and humble condition" and made him worthy of being a preacher and minister of the gospel. And just as David had to contend with not only internal enemies but also foreign enemies, so he finds in his own life that he has been "assailed on all sides" and had to "sustain some conflict from enemies without and within the church."[7] Finally, Calvin finds in David not only a teacher and model for his own life but also a teacher for the church overall. And indeed, his fundamental purpose in his Psalms commentary is to give a reading for the edification of the church through the person of David.

I demonstrate that above all Calvin reads these eight Psalms for the church through the example of David. Using David as a model of faith, prayer, trust in God's goodness and providence, true worship, and true Christian piety, Calvin instructs the church and provides a message of comfort to believers. Indeed, we find that often his readings of these Psalms through the person of David eclipse the traditional christological readings of them. Does Calvin read these Psalms as literal prophecies of Christ? Does he give any kind of christological reading of them, and if so, how? If not, why? Moreover, does he maintain other traditional uses of these Psalms to teach the doctrines of the Trinity and the two natures of Christ? Finally, I explore the various ways in which Jews or Jewish exegesis figures into his interpretation of these Psalms. Does Calvin, like those before him, retain the identification of the Jews as the enemies of Christ?

Calvin on Christological Exegesis of the Messianic Psalms

Calvin often does not follow the traditional christological readings of these eight Psalms—either in not giving a reading in reference to Christ or, more frequently, in the lack of prominence he gives to the christological reading. More specifically, he does not retain the primacy of reading these Psalms as literal prophecies of Christ's incarnation, crucifixion, resurrection, and ascension, though he does retain some of them as prophecies of Christ's kingship and kingdom. Most of the time, he mentions the christological application of a Psalm as a valid interpretation, but there are passages where he explicitly rejects the reading of the Psalm in reference to Christ. Furthermore, even on those Psalms that he agrees are more fully completed in Christ, the weight of his exegesis falls upon a reading for the church through the example of David. Through an analysis of his christological exegesis of these eight Psalms, one discovers that Calvin appears to be operating according to certain principles that guide him as to when a Psalm properly refers to Christ and when it does not. Furthermore, Calvin also lays out a number of the reasons for his more limited applications of these Psalms to Christ.[8]

Calvin has at least three general principles that regulate when he believes a Psalm can be properly applied to Christ. First, a Psalm may be read in reference to Christ when it is more fully completed by Christ or more appropriate to Christ. Circumstances such as these render a typological reading, in which David (or Solomon) acts as a type of Christ, where David foreshadows a reality that is more brightly set forth in Christ. Indeed, the vast majority of Calvin's christological readings of these eight Psalms are also typological— namely, they are grounded in the original historical person and context of the Psalm. Thus, he interprets those verses in reference to Christ that indicate some aspect that is not true of David or not fully completed in David and his kingdom, such as the descriptions of the eternity, vastness, invincibility, and unified peace of the messianic kingdom or the priestly function of the king.[9] In this way, the only time that Calvin retains a reading of these Psalms as literal prophecies of Christ is when the Psalm is a prophecy of Christ's kingship and kingdom—that is, the royal elements of a Psalm—which is a different emphasis than that of Luther or Bucer, who portray David as a prophet who foresees not only the kingdom of Christ but even more so the events of Christ's passion, crucifixion, and resurrection.[10]

Second, Calvin applies a Psalm to Christ when Christ himself utters the words of a Psalm in regard to himself. This is the case in Ps 22:1, which the Gospel of Matthew records as Christ's words from the cross (Matt 27:46): "My God, my God, why have you forsaken me?" Likewise, Christ uses Ps 110:1 to respond to a question about the Messiah and to demonstrate that the Messiah is not David's son but David's Lord.[11] Finally, Jesus applies Ps 118:22–23 to demonstrate that the kingdom of God will be given to the Gentiles. Although Calvin does retain the christological application of these verses, the *first* reading he gives for all of these passages is in reference to the life of David, and he often spends far more time and detail on the reading concerning David than on the one concerning Christ. For example, on Ps 22:1, he spends nearly three and a half times more space applying the verse to David than to Christ. Likewise, he first applies Ps 110:1 to David as especially anointed by God before arguing that it more properly applies to Christ.[12] On the other hand, he does not even address the christological application of Ps 118:22 until his discussion of the twenty-fifth and twenty-sixth verses. Instead, in his exposition of the twenty-second verse, he applies it only to David and argues that the stone is a similitude to represent David as being placed "by the purpose and power of God to sustain the whole building." Calvin introduces the application of Psalm 118 to Christ under the phrase in 118:26, "Blessed is the one who comes in the name of the Lord," where he uses David's election as king as a type of Christ's kingship.[13]

The third principle that guides Calvin in the proper application of a Psalm to Christ is when the christological reading retains the "simple and natural" sense of the passage and is in keeping with the author's intended meaning, and by "author," Calvin means both the Holy Spirit and the human author.[14] Hence, at the beginning of his exposition of Psalm 2, he states plainly that "those things that David declares concerning himself are not *violently, or even allegorically,* applied to Christ, but were truly predicted concerning him."[15] Likewise, concerning the Gospels' use of Ps 22:17–18 to describe the mockery Christ suffered on the cross, he comments,

> The Evangelists quote this place to the letter, as we say, and without figure—and there is no absurdity in their doing so—to teach us the more certainly that in this psalm Christ is described to us by the Spirit of prophecy. The heavenly Father intended that in the person of his Son those things should be visibly accomplished that were shadowed forth in David.[16]

Indeed, Calvin often specifies that the Holy Spirit speaks through David by the spirit of prophecy to indicate that a Psalm's christological application is in keeping with authorial intention. Hence, when he reads these Psalms as prophecies of Christ's kingship and kingdom, he begins with the statement that David prophesies through the Spirit.[17]

Perhaps more significantly, Calvin rejects several traditional christological readings of these Psalms on the basis that they do not retain this "simple and natural" sense of the passage and are in danger of allegorizing. Thus, on Ps 8:2, though this is quoted by Christ in reference to the children praising his entry into Jerusalem, Calvin believes that the more "clear and suitable" application of this verse is the praise of God's providence: "What need, then, is there to wrest the words of David, when their true meaning is so clear and suitable? He says that babes and sucklings are advocates sufficiently powerful to vindicate the providence of God."[18] Thus, Calvin concludes, "I have now discharged the duty of a faithful interpreter *in opening up the mind of the prophet*," by which he makes clear that the authorial intention of this passage is the praise of God's providence. Furthermore, he calls Christ's usage of this passage a "difficulty" that he then harmonizes with his reading in terms of God's providence.[19] On the next verses of Psalm 8, Calvin appeals to the "design of the Psalmist" to demarcate the contrast between humanity's lowliness and the goodness of God and therefore argues that the application of these verses to Christ's humiliation is not in keeping with authorial intention. Again, he contends directly against the apostle's application of these verses in Heb 2:7 as a prophecy of Christ's abasement and exaltation by insisting that the apostle "had not so much an eye to what David intended" but accommodates the text for his own purposes.[20] Likewise, Calvin does not follow the traditional Christian application of אַיֶּלֶת to Christ:

> The ancient interpreters thought that Christ would not be sufficiently dignified and honored unless, putting a mystical or allegorical sense upon the word "hind," they viewed it as pointing out the various things that are included in a sacrifice. . . . But as I find no solidity in these subtleties, it will be better to take that view of the title that is *more simple and natural*. I think it highly probable that it was the beginning of some common song; nor do I see how the inscription bears any relation to the subject matter of the psalm.[21]

At other points, Calvin does keep a christological reading but instead of the traditional christological reading he maintains one that he believes is more in keeping with the authorial intention and context of the passage. For example, the traditional Christian interpretation of Ps 110:7 ("he will drink from the stream by the path") is to apply this to Christ's passion, but Calvin prefers to interpret this as representing Christ's royal military prowess, which is more in keeping with the two previous verses that are also about military might.[22]

Another stated reason for Calvin's more limited christological readings of these Psalms is his concern for the defensibility of Christian interpretations before the Jews. For example, he writes that though the Book of Acts (2:27–28, 31; 13:35) uses Ps 16:10 as a prophecy of Christ's resurrection, "it is better to adhere to the *natural simplicity* of the interpretation that [he has] given that we may not make ourselves objects of ridicule to the Jews or that this *subtlety* [of applying it to Christ] may not involve us in a labyrinth."[23] Calvin also follows Jewish interpretation of certain Hebrew words when he believes it is more in keeping with the natural sense. This is the case in his argument for the translation of אֱלֹהִים in Ps 8:5 as "gods" rather than "angels."[24] Similarly, he sees a danger of Jewish ridicule in reading Psalm 72 solely in reference to Christ when the more natural sense is to read it in accordance with its historical reference to David:

> Those who would interpret it simply as a prophecy of the kingdom of Christ seem to *put a construction upon the words which does violence to them*; and then we must always beware of giving the Jews occasion of making an outcry, as if it were our purpose *sophistically* to apply to Christ those things which do not directly refer to him.[25]

In addition to the concern of Christians making themselves objects of Jewish scorn, these examples also continue to demonstrate Calvin's resolve to maintain the "simple and natural" sense of the passage.

Thus, Calvin limits the christological readings of these Psalms because he wants to preserve the simple and natural sense, follow authorial intention, and provide readings that are defensible before the Jews. I believe there is also one other compelling reason that he sees no problem with his more restricted christological applications of these Psalms. He finds that a reading in reference to the life of David renders a meaning sufficient and powerful for the church. In a word, when the simple sense concerning David and his historical context already gives a profoundly edifying reading, why need one "twist" the passage to refer it to Christ? This chapter demonstrates the compelling and inspiring readings for the church that Calvin offers through the example of David.[26]

Calvin's Break with Traditional Christian Readings of the Messianic Psalms

Calvin departs from the traditional Christian readings of these Psalms by not only the limitations he places upon reading them as literal prophecies of Christ's incarnation, crucifixion, resurrection, and ascension but also his restrictions upon their usefulness specifically to teach the doctrines of Trinity and the two natures of Christ. Christian interpreters have used a number of passages in these eight Psalms to teach the doctrines of Trinity and the two natures of Christ. Both Martin Luther and Martin Bucer continue to uphold these didactic traditions. Calvin, on the other hand, sees in these Psalms different teachings than those of Trinity and the two natures of Christ.

Calvin's concern for maintaining the "simple and natural" sense of these Psalms is one of the primary reasons we do not find him expounding upon their use to teach Trinitarian principles. Indeed, he explicitly argues against the Trinitarian readings of Ps 2:7 ("He said to me, 'You are my son; today I have begotten you'"):

> This passage, I am aware, has been explained by many as referring to the eternal generation of Christ; from the word "today" they have reasoned ingeniously as if it denoted an eternal act without relation to time.... Finally, this begetting ought not to be understood of the mutual love that exists between the Father and the Son.[27]

Instead, he contends that the correct reading of this verse concerns the time when the sonship of Christ was made manifest to the world, which was the time of Christ's resurrection. Furthermore, he makes no mention of the quotation of Ps 2:7 at Christ's baptism or the workings of the Trinity at Christ's baptism.[28]

Likewise, "you have set your glory above the heavens" in Ps 8:1 and "the work of your fingers" in Ps 8:3 raise no discussion of the Trinity for Calvin; rather, they demonstrate the glory and providence of God the Creator. Absent also in his account is the interpretation of "from the womb of the morning" (in Ps 110:3) as referring to Christ's coeternity and cosubstantiality with the Father. Instead, he reads this as David's prophecy of the people to be born to Christ. Although Ps 118:13–14 ("the Lord helped me; the Lord is my strength") has been interpreted by the antecedent Christian tradition as concerning the indivisibility of the Trinity, Calvin does not even refer these verses to Christ at all but instead interprets them concerning David's situation under the persecution of Saul.[29] He also does not apply certain passages to demonstrate the distinctions of the persons of the Trinity, where Luther does do so. For example, Luther uses "the Lord and his anointed" (Ps 2:2), "I have set my king" (Ps 2:6), and the dominion and gifts given to Christ by the Father expressed in Ps 8:6–8 and Ps 16:6–11 to demonstrate the distinctions between the Sender and the One sent and to indicate those things that Christ *receives* from the Father.[30] All such Trinitarian applications are missing in Calvin's expositions of these passages.

The previous chapter demonstrated how Martin Bucer not only upholds the Trinitarian teachings traditionally found in these Psalms but also explicitly contends against Jewish criticisms of the Christian use of these Psalms to teach the doctrine of the Trinity. Calvin, on the other hand, not only does not address these Jewish criticisms but also drops the Trinitarian readings altogether. Indeed, I mean to suggest that Calvin may very well drop these Trinitarian readings partly because he does not think that the Trinitarian readings of these Psalms can withstand such criticisms. Calvin maintains that the Trinitarian applications do not retain the simple sense of the passage.

Likewise, Calvin eclipses the use of these Psalms to teach about the two natures of Christ. Whereas over and over again, Luther uses these Psalms to teach the two natures of Christ and less frequently, but just as significantly, Bucer does so as well, there are only a few instances where Calvin employs these Psalms to discuss the divine and human natures of Christ. In these instances, he either briefly mentions the common application of a verse to the two natures of Christ or expounds upon the role of Christ as mediator, in which Christ's taking on human flesh is a central component of Christ's act of reconciling humanity with God. For example, on Ps 22:22, Calvin briefly cites the use of this verse by the author of Hebrews to refer to the two natures of Christ, but he expounds no further on this topic. He also talks about Christ taking on human nature in his discussion of Ps 22:14, but his main concern is to explain how it can be properly said that Christ suffered.[31]

The absences of such discussions on passages the antecedent Christian tradition explicitly used to teach about the two natures of Christ are much more striking. In Ps 8:4–5, the application of אֱנוֹשׁ (enosh) and אָדָם (adam) to the two natures of Christ is completely lacking; instead, Calvin says David is expounding on the infinite goodness of God to insignificant humanity. Furthermore, the beauty of the bridegroom in Ps 45:2 does not lead to a discussion of the two natures of Christ, nor does Ps 72:5–6 ("May he endure with the sun . . . . May he be like rain that falls on the mown grass"). Prior Christian exegetes interpret these verses in Psalm 72 to indicate Christ's divinity and virgin birth, but Calvin uses these verses to describe the establishment of true worship by Christ and his defense of the church. Whereas he does translate Ps 2:12 as "kiss the Son" and apply it to Christ, his exposition does not lead to a discussion of Christ's two natures, as it does for Christian medieval interpreters, Luther, and Bucer.[32]

David as Teacher and Example for the Church

Though Calvin does read most of these Psalms with some kind of reference to Christ, his christological applications are significantly more restricted and less frequent than those of Christian interpreters who have preceded him.

Moreover, he does not use these Psalms at all to teach the doctrine of the Trinity, and he applies them much less numerously to teach the two natures of Christ. Whereas Calvin operates with certain exegetical principles, another compelling reason that he does not apply verses of these Psalms or the whole Psalm itself to Christ is that he does not find it necessary for his purposes. When the "simple and natural" sense of the Psalm in reference to David already gives a reading that brings a message of consolation to the church, then he considers this reading not only sufficient but also powerful. Likewise, when a reading of the Psalm through the example of David teaches crucial Protestant doctrines, he considers such a reading thoroughly fitting and edifying.

David as a Teacher of God's Beneficence, Election, and Providence

Calvin sees David as a superlative teacher of theology and doctrine. Through the mouthpiece of David, he brings three related doctrinal teachings to the forefront in his readings of these Psalms. These are the teachings concerning the goodness of God, election, and divine providence. Much like Bucer, Calvin time and again finds in these Psalms clear and comforting expressions of God's fatherly goodness to humanity (and more specifically to the elect) and God's providential care of the church. For example, the whole of Psalm 8, according to Calvin, sets forth before the reader the theme of God's infinite goodness toward humankind. For him, the purpose of Psalm 8 is to stir the reader to the celebration and praise of this undeserved kindness of God.[33] Similarly, he summarizes the content of Psalm 16 as David's meditation "upon the benefits that he received from God." Hence, the comforts expressed in Ps 16:7–8 are expressions of the generosity and fatherly care of God to David in particular and to the church in general.[34] Indeed, Calvin applies Ps 16:11 to show that God's fatherly favor is the very source of election:

> The phrase, the countenance of God, may be understood either of our being beheld by him or of our beholding him; but I consider both these ideas included, for his fatherly favor that he displays in looking upon us with a serene countenance precedes this joy and is the first cause of it, and yet this does not cheer us until, on our part, we behold it shining upon us. By this clause David also intended distinctly to express to whom those pleasures belong, of which God has in his hand a full and an overflowing abundance. As there are with God pleasures sufficient to replenish and satisfy the whole world, how does it come to pass that a dismal and deadly darkness envelops the greater part of humankind but that God does not look upon all [humans] equally with his friendly and

> fatherly countenance, nor opens the eyes of all [humans] to seek the
> matter of their joy in him and nowhere else?[35]

God's fatherly countenance and kindness are specifically reserved for the
elect—a principle Calvin also sees demonstrated in Psalm 22. The cry of "my
God, my God" in Ps 22:1, he says, is the cry of faith that patiently trusts that God
will once again reveal God's fatherly countenance. Likewise, the continuation of
this cry in the second verse and the statement of trust in the fourth articulate the
hope the elect have in God's goodness. Although the third verse of Psalm 110
does not indicate the Trinity for Calvin, it does set forth for him David's teaching
concerning God's goodness in the promise that the elect will be born to Christ.
Finally, he sees in the statements of Ps 118:7 ("the Lord is on my side to help
me") and Ps 118:15 ("voices of shouting and salvation in the tents of the
righteous") David's expressions of public praise of God's infinite goodness.[36]

Even more so, Calvin finds David expounding upon the doctrine of providence in these Psalms. Most prominently, he unearths a marvelous expression
of God's providence in the verse, "Out of the mouths of babes and sucklings
you have founded your strength because of your foes" (Ps 8:2). Babes and
sucklings proclaim the providence of God, explains Calvin, because God's
provision may be seen in the nourishment of their mother's milk ready for
them right at birth and their innate instinct to suck. Likewise, divine providence is evident through God's beautiful order of creation (Ps 8:3–4) and the
dominion God gives to humanity (Ps 8:5–8).[37] In Psalm 16, David's words,
"I have set the Lord continually before me" (Ps 16:8), express his trust in God's
providence. Calvin writes, "The meaning therefore is that David kept his mind
so intently fixed upon the providence of God as to be fully persuaded that
whenever any difficulty or distress should befall him, God would be always at
hand to assist him." On Ps 22:9–10, he also identifies David's definition
of faith as trust in God's providence and again points to God's provision of
nurturing care right at birth as a powerful sign of this providence.[38]

Moreover, Calvin asserts that one sees God's providence in God's election
of David as a godly king and in the divine ordination and preservation of civil
governments. Thus, the anointing of the king above his companions (Ps 45:7)
is an indication of God's providence and election, for the anointing, he argues,
preceded any righteousness of the king; thus, the righteousness of the king is
not the cause of God's election but the fruit of it. Likewise, in his opening
comments of Psalm 72, Calvin exclaims that just as God sets up and maintains
rightful government in the world, how much more God will set up and
maintain the spiritual kingdom of his Son. Indeed, the providence of God
means that God's hand always preserves and protects God's people, the elect.[39]

David as Exemplar of Protestant Piety

Calvin finds in these Psalms time and time again an ample reading of comfort and consolation for the church in the example of David. Indeed, David arises from his exegesis of these eight Psalms as the exemplar of Protestant piety. David is the prototype of true faith and humility; he is the paradigm of supreme confidence in God and peace of mind. Furthermore, David serves as the model for preaching and prayer, and even more markedly, David exhibits the practice of true worship through his call to the praise of God's goodness and his fleeing from all idolatry, superstition, and impiety. In effect, David is the exemplar of the true life of piety for all believers.

Calvin repeatedly elevates David as a supreme example of true faith—faith as trust, confidence, and mental peace. In Psalm 2, David teaches that even when God seems slow to defend God's people, this is merely the time of God's laughter (Ps 2:4) and that in due time, God will overthrow the enemies (Ps 2:5, 9).[40] Similarly, in Psalm 16, David exhibits serene trust in God's protection and complete tranquility of mind. Thus, David's words in Ps 16:8 ("I have set the Lord always before me"), says Calvin, display the eyes of faith that believers should imitate:

> David set the Lord before him for the purpose of constantly looking to him in all his dangers.... David reckons himself secure against all dangers and promises himself certain safety because, with the eyes of faith, he beholds God as present with him.[41]

The gladness expressed in the next verse of Psalm 16 promises the fruits of this faith: such trust in God's protection gives the believer both mental tranquility and a life of happiness. Furthermore, the last verses of this Psalm (Ps 16:9–11) display David as an example of faith in God in the face of death, so that believers may see that they need not fear death but have the assurance of salvation.[42] Finally, Calvin finds in David's words of Psalm 22 an outstanding model of faithful and godly wrestling in times of despair and overwhelming adversity. David demonstrates for the church, says Calvin, how to wrestle faithfully with doubt and despair. Moreover, he gives an example for imitation of how believers should encourage themselves in such times of trial and suffering: to cry out to God, hope for deliverance, declare their own unworthiness, and recount the benefits and evidences of God's fatherly love that God has already bestowed upon them.[43]

David is also the exemplar of true humility for the church. For Calvin, Ps 2:10–11 ("O kings, be wise.... Serve the Lord with fear") is David's appeal to denounce confidence in one's own wisdom and to follow the fear of the Lord. More plainly, he interprets Ps 16:2–3 as expressing that the good one does is not for God but for the saints, so that in this way David teaches Christians to lay aside all presumption of merit. Furthermore, David's example of humility in Ps 22:6 ("But I am a worm") also points the believer to hope in God's relief. Likewise, in David's avowal that God is his "strength and song" (Ps 118:14), Calvin sees an acknowledgment of his weakness and an attribution of his safety exclusively to God—both of which are dispositions the church should emulate.[44] Hence, David serves as the exemplar of that humility that leads to complete surrender to God, attribution of all good things as coming from God, and the fear of the Lord that leads to true wisdom.

David is not only the supreme exemplar of faith and humility but also a preacher of the gospel and a model of true prayer. In Ps 2:7 ("I will tell of the decree of the Lord"), Calvin finds David assuming the office of preacher and later applies this to Christ and then more broadly to the apostles, pastors, and teachers of the church. The last verse of Psalm 22 ("and proclaim his deliverance to a people yet unborn") exhibits how the preaching of the gospel maintains the perpetuity of the church.[45] Moreover, Calvin lifts up David's prayers as models of authentic, devout prayer. Psalm 22 demonstrates David's perseverance in prayer through severe adversity and provides a rule for the church: "The true rule of praying is, therefore, this: that he who seems to have beaten the air to no purpose, or to have lost his labor in praying for a long time, should not on that account leave off or desist from that duty."[46] In addition, David's example of prayer gives instruction as to how to resist the deceptions of the devil through the practices of continual crying to God for help and enumeration of God's past benefits as evidence of God's continued goodness. Most of all, David prays with true, solid faith and believes without doubt that God will hear him and answer him. Calvin understands Psalm 72 as a prayer that David has offered as an example to the church of how to pray for the coming of the kingdom of God, and Psalm 118 exemplifies the power and efficacy of prayer. Finally, the example of David, along with the example of the Jews as a whole, gives powerful instruction to believers not to cease in praying for the restoration of the church.[47]

In Calvin's exposition of Psalm 8 especially, David models the right praise of God's beneficence to which all should be directed:

The Holy Spirit, who directed David's tongue, doubtless intended by his instrumentality to awaken [humans] from the torpor and indifference that is common to them so that they may not content themselves with celebrating the infinite love of God and the innumerable benefits that they receive at his hand in their sparing and frigid manner, but may rather apply their whole hearts to this holy exercise and put forth in it their highest efforts.[48]

David exemplifies not only the praise of God's infinite goodness but also the praise of God's providence (Ps 8:2). He contrasts God's liberality to humanity's lowliness (Ps 8:3–4) to further show forth God's fatherly beneficence. Proper praise of God's goodness, says Calvin, recognizes that all goodness has its source in God (Ps 16:2). In this way, Calvin views David as constantly setting before himself the remembrance of God's goodness and fatherly care in order to sustain himself through times of adversity (Ps 16:8 and 22:9–10). Likewise, David invites all believers to public praise of God through his example exhibited in Ps 22:22, "I will declare your name to my brethren; in the midst of the assembly I will praise you."[49] Thus, affirms Calvin, David's praise of God's fatherly goodness and providential care embodies for the church the proper attitude of praise that is part of the true worship of God.

David further exemplifies true worship and piety by setting himself apart from superstition and idolatry. By connecting himself to the society of the righteous (Ps 16:3) and separating himself from the pollutions of the world, he shows the true way to maintain unity with the saints of God. David's flight from impiety and idolatry may be seen in such statements as "I will not taste their drink offerings of blood" and "I will not take their names upon my lips" (Ps 16:4).[50] Likewise, the recognition of God as one's inheritance (Ps 16:5–6) offers an antidote against the false attractions of the world and sets forth the reason for the contentment Christians can have in God alone:

> [David] shows the reason why he separates himself from idolaters and resolves to continue in the church of God, why he shuns with abhorrence all participation in their errors and cleaves to the pure worship of God; namely, because he rests in the only true God as his portion. . . . This passage teaches us that none are taught aright in true godliness but those who reckon God alone sufficient for their happiness.[51]

Similarly, in Ps 22:25, David demonstrates that it is the duty of believers to desire the purity of the church, even if it is not fully in their power to cleanse the church completely of impiety. Calvin sees in Ps 118:19 ("Open unto me the gates of righteousness"), as well, an expression of David's elimination of impiety and his establishment of the true religion of God.[52] David illustrates the holy exercise of uniting himself to the society of the righteous, the saints, the true worshippers of God. Thus, David not only embodies the true worship of God through his proper disposition of a "sincere and pure affection of the heart" and reverent fear before God but also demonstrates that a truly righteous king upholds the true worship of God (Ps 72:5) and calls his people to prepare for the pure worship of God (Ps 118:19).[53]

The many facets that Calvin sees exemplified in David to furnish a powerful model for imitation by the church can be gathered together under the rubric of "Protestant piety." Through the example of David in these Psalms, Calvin essentially sets forth his many-faceted definition of the true piety that God requires from believers. Just as David looked at his situation with eyes of faith and saw not what the physical eyes see but what the spiritual eyes see—namely, that God is present and able to save—so also should the Protestant churches persevere and see with eyes of faith.[54] Hence, the faith of true Protestant piety is one that completely trusts in the protection of God, puts its confidence in God alone, and bears the mark of a tranquil mind.[55] True Protestant piety for Calvin also entails the proper dispositions before God of humility and acknowledgment that all good comes from God. Hence, one cannot rely upon one's own self, abilities, or works, but must render to God the due recognition that God is the beginning and end of the good life of faith.[56] Furthermore, Calvin argues through the example of David that the proper response to God is not only faith but also praise of God's goodness, liberality, and providential care. True piety, then, knows that all good comes from God and responds in praise of God's infinite goodness to humankind in general and to the elect in particular.

Finally, authentic Protestant piety requires proper practices of true worship as well. These include not only public praise of God but also preaching the gospel, the exercise of prayer, fleeing superstitions and idolatry, cleaving to the society of the righteous, and preserving the true religion of God. Indeed, David urges believers to be "stirred" to godliness, "inflamed" with the love of God, "aroused" from their lethargy, and "animated" in their praise of God. Calvin sees David as awakening people from their "torpor and indifference" in order that they celebrate God's goodness with their whole hearts, rather than in a "sparing and frigid manner."[57] In this way, David teaches the faith that trusts in God's eventual triumph over the enemies of the church:

> In a word, David here animates the hearts of the godly against being dispirited by the foolhardy attempts on the part of those who presume to introduce discord and disorder into the kingdom of Christ; for he shows them that God will put forth his invincible power for the maintaining of the glory of his sacred throne. When, then, our minds are agitated by various commotions, let us learn confidently to repose on this support, that however much the world may rage against Christ, it will never be able to hurl him from the right hand of the Father.[58]

These words of David demonstrate that the struggle of the Protestant churches in Calvin's day is not in vain. Calvin, then, intends through the powerful example of David's piety to arouse the Protestant churches to proper humility, fervent prayer, ardent love of God, exuberant praise of God's goodness, and faithful pursuit of godliness—all in all, to the exercises of true Protestant piety.

Calvin does not stop here, though. He sets the figure of David as the exemplar of true worship and piety in contrast to Roman Catholic impiety and false devotion as another means of setting forth the practices of true Protestant piety. Thus, Calvin uses David's example in Psalm 16 to call Christians to flee the "profane superstitions" of the Roman church.[59] Similarly, by setting forth the exercises of true godliness in his statement "I will pay my vows" (Ps 22:25), David, according to Calvin, expresses the holy desire for the purity of the church over and against Roman Catholic corruption of the church through their false and foolish vows. Likewise, Calvin contrasts David's confession of praise over and against Roman Catholic superstitions:

> The Papists, by wresting this passage to support their false and
> deceitful vows, show themselves so stupid and ridiculous. . . . What
> resemblance is there between these childish fooleries—with which
> according to their own imaginations they attempt to appease God—
> and this holy testimony of gratitude, which is not only a true sense of
> religion and fear of God suggested to the fathers, but which God
> himself has commanded and ratified in his law? Yea, how can they
> have the face to equal their foolish and infamous superstitions to the
> most precious of all sacrifices—the sacrifice of thanksgiving?[60]

Moreover, Calvin likens the Roman Catholics to Saul in David's day. While David aimed to purify the temple and establish the true religion of God, Saul profaned the temple and led the people astray. The Roman church today, decries Calvin, leads the people astray. Even more profoundly, Calvin equates the "builders" in Ps 118:22 with the Roman Catholics. Just as David had to oppose the religious rulers of Saul's regime in order to promote the true worship of God, so also in Calvin's day, the pope and the Roman Catholics are the illegitimate leaders who misguide the people. Indeed, says Calvin, they are the enemies of Christ. Hence, Calvin sets forth David as the exemplar of Protestant piety over and against Roman Catholic piety.[61]

Calvin on the Jews in the Messianic Psalms

Although Calvin does have a fair amount of anti-Catholic rhetoric in his interpretations of these eight Psalms, unlike Luther, he does not use the method of paralleling the Roman Catholics with the Jews as the previously established "enemy." Indeed, Calvin rarely identifies the "enemies" in these Psalms as the Jews. He usually first interprets the "enemies" within the historical context of David and his struggles against both domestic (e.g., Saul) and foreign (e.g., the Philistines) enemies. Thus, "all those who see me mock at me" (Ps 22:7) are the enemies of David who tell him that his prayers are in vain and that God has deserted him. Likewise, the description of the enemies found in Ps 22:12–13 indicate the cruelty of David's enemies. Similarly, "all the nations encompassed me" (Ps 118:10), explains Calvin, expresses David's feeling that the whole world is against him, while "you have sorely thrust at me" (Ps 118:13) is specifically directed at Saul.[62]

Even when Calvin applies the "enemies" in these Psalms to the enemies of Christ and the church, he does so in order to offer the comfort and promise of the future triumph of Christ's kingdom over its enemies. Thus, just as David's enemies did not think that they were rising up against God in Psalm 2, so also do Christ's enemies not realize that in raging against Christ, they are actually assailing God.[63] Likewise, Ps 110:1 ("until I make your enemies your footstool") is David's prophecy that all those who rise up against the kingdom of Christ will come to ruin. Calvin writes:

> From this let us learn that however numerous those enemies may be
> who conspire against the Son of God and attempt the subversion of
> his kingdom, all will be unavailing, for they shall never prevail against
> God's immutable purpose but, on the contrary, they shall . . . be laid
> prostrate at Christ's feet.[64]

In this same way, he understands Ps 110:5 ("he will shatter kings") as David's prophecy of Christ's triumph over the enemies of the messianic kingdom.[65] And when Calvin specifically names these enemies of Christ and the church, more often than not they are the Roman Catholics. In the end, he argues that the Roman Catholics are the real enemies of Christ and the church when they stand against the Protestant efforts to reestablish God's true kingdom and the practices of true worship and piety.

Calvin does retain a number of the negative images of the Jews and rhetoric against the Jewish interpretations of certain passages in these Psalms,[66] but he very rarely identifies the Jews explicitly as the enemies of Christ in these Psalms, contrary to Luther's constant and Bucer's occasional tendencies to do so. More significantly, he does not use a single one of the passages commonly deployed by Christian exegetes against the Jews in this way. Thus, Calvin does not identify the "enemy and avenger" in Ps 8:2 with the Jews but, rather, with the "despisers of God." Further, he does not read Ps 45:10, "O daughter . . . forget your people and your father's house," as concerning the Jews at all; rather, he aligns the church with "daughter" to exhort her to self-denial and the fleeing from impiety and corruption. Neither the "bees" in Ps 118:12 ("they surrounded me like bees") nor even the "builders" in Ps 118:22 ("the stone that the builders rejected") evoke an equation of these with the Jews for Calvin.[67] Instead, one finds several places where he promotes biblical Jews as positive examples for Christian imitation, the foremost of which is David himself.[68]

Calvin not only does not identify the Jews as the enemies of Christ and the church or use the passages against the Jews that Christian tradition has typically used against the Jews but also at several points lifts up the Jews as exemplars of faith, prayer, and perseverance worthy of imitation. For instance, he applies Ps 22:4, "in you our fathers trusted," as an example of Israel's faith to give the church a teaching of comfort:

> Here the Psalmist assigns the reason why God sits amidst the praises of the tribes of Israel. The reason is because his hand had been always stretched forth to preserve his faithful people. David . . . gathers together the examples of all past ages in order thereby to encourage, strengthen, and effectually persuade himself that as God had never cast off any of his chosen people, he also would be one of the number of those for whom deliverance is securely laid up in the hand of God.[69]

Rather than applying Ps 45:10 ("forget your people and your father's house") negatively against the Jews, Calvin appeals to the example of the Jews teaching their foreign wives to flee previous superstitions and cling to the true worship of God—an example that demonstrates how the church needs to renounce its superstitions and cleave to true piety.[70] On Ps 118:25–26, he promotes the Jews as exemplars of prayer, faith, and perseverance:

> And as the Jews never ceased to put up this prayer during that sad desolation and those hideous devastations [i.e., during the Babylonian exile], their perseverance ought to inspire us with new vigor in these days. At that time they had not the honor of a kingdom, no royal throne, no name but with God; and yet amid this deplorable and ruinous state of things, they adhered to the form of prayer formerly prescribed to them by the Holy Spirit. Instructed by their example, let us not fail to pray ardently for the restoration of the church, which, in our day, is involved in sad desolation.[71]

Calvin, then, sets forth the faithful example of Jews in times of adversity for the Protestant churches to imitate during times of trial under the "captivity" of the Roman church.

Although he does often lift up the Jews of the Old Testament as examples for the church to imitate, there are several passages where he gives strong critique of rabbinic exegesis. Particularly in interpreting those passages that are in dispute between Jews and Christians, Calvin expresses disdain for how the rabbis corrupt the text, obscure the true sense of the passage, and are ignorant of the true meaning of Scripture.[72] Notably, he does argue for the christological meanings of these verses over and against rabbinic interpretations, lest my arguments thus far be misunderstood to say that Calvin is willing to concede everything to the Jews in his limitations on christological exegesis. However, just as notable are the reasons he gives for the places in which he finds the rabbinic readings to be "frivolous," "feeble," "obscure," and "without foundation": namely, Calvin does not think that the rabbis maintain the simple and natural sense of the passage as a whole. For example, on Ps 22:16, he contends that the rabbinic translation of "like a lion" does not suit the meaning of the passage and requires the addition of a verb ("they surround") to complete the phrase and make it sensible. Though Calvin agrees that the Hebrew is problematic, he affirms the Christian translation as more in keeping with the simple sense of the text. In this same way, on Ps 45:6, he argues that even the rabbis have to admit that the simple sense of the phrase "your throne is forever" is not fully completed in Solomon or David, as their throne was not eternal, and thus must point to the Messiah.[73] These are examples of Calvin's critical engagement with rabbinic exegesis; however, in the final section of this chapter, I propose that Calvin is dealing much more positively with rabbinic exegesis than first meets the eye.

Calvin and Jewish Exegesis: The Case Study of Psalms 8 and 16

As the previous chapters have shown, reading these Psalms as literal prophecies of Christ is a commonplace in the antecedent Christian exegetical tradition. This is most certainly true of those Psalms that are quoted in the New Testament either in reference to Christ or from Christ's own mouth. Psalms 8 and 16 are two interesting cases in that the New Testament authors use them in reference to Christ and yet Calvin only very grudgingly interprets them concerning Christ.[74] Moreover, Calvin pointedly argues against the New Testament authors' christological use of them. Indeed, this chapter has shown that the overriding weight of his interpretations is to use David as a supreme teacher and exemplar for the church's imitation, rather than the christological readings of these Psalms. Furthermore, Psalms 8 and 16 become interesting cases because they figure prominently in the Lutheran Aegidius Hunnius's later accusations of judaizing against Calvin and in David Pareus's responding defense.

A comparison and contrast of the exegeses of Luther, Bucer, and Calvin on Psalms 8 and 16 reveal both striking parallels and distinctions among these three interpreters. Luther and the antecedent tradition read these two Psalms as prophecies of Christ's incarnation, death, resurrection, and ascension, and they find in them solid teachings concerning the two natures of Christ and Trinity. Whereas Bucer retains many of these teachings concerning Trinity and the two natures of Christ, neither Bucer nor Calvin reads the whole of Psalms 8 and 16 as prophecies of the saving events of Christ's life. Instead, they read Psalm 8 as concerning God's fatherly beneficence toward humankind and humanity's excellence, and they read Psalm 16 as instruction to believers to trust God, flee from impurity, and cleave to the society of saints. Indeed, these emphases of Bucer and Calvin are precisely the emphases of Jewish exegetes on Psalms 8 and 16.

One seemingly obvious difference between Bucer's and Calvin's exegeses of these two Psalms pertains to Bucer's overt use of Jewish exegesis. I contend, however, that when one walks step-by-step through Bucer's uses of Jewish exegesis in his comments on these Psalms, one can see real evidence of Calvin's own subtle uses of Jewish exegesis. In Psalm 8, Bucer applies Jewish exegesis to his interpretation of "how majestic is your name" (Ps 8:1). He points out that according to the rabbis—and he specifically cites David Kimhi—this is the same as saying "how majestic are *you*," for according to the rabbis, the divine name is equivalent to God.[75] Calvin addresses this very issue in his comments on Ps 8:1 by writing, "I do not approve of the subtle speculations of those who think the name of God means nothing else but God himself. It ought rather to be referred to the works and properties by which God is known, than to God's essence."[76]

The second reference to Jewish exegesis in Bucer's comments on Psalm 8 concerns in the second verse the translation of the Hebrew word יָסַד —a verb that can mean "you have made a beginning" or "you have established." Bucer cites Kimhi and Abraham Ibn Ezra's preference for the translation "you have made a beginning," for they emphasize that this refers to the suckling age as the time when humans begin to recognize the loving-kindness of the Creator. Bucer, however, prefers the second translation of "you have established" to make it a stronger reading for how this confounds "the enemy and avenger."[77] Calvin also addresses the question of how to translate this Hebrew verb and comes to the same preference as Bucer. He writes, "Some take the word *founded* as meaning that in the very birth or generation of man, God lays foundations for manifesting his own glory. But this sense is too restricted.

I have no doubt that the word put forth is *to establish*, as if the prophet had said, 'God needs not strong military forces to destroy the ungodly; instead of these, the mouths of children are sufficient for God's purposes.'"[78]

On this same verse in Psalm 8, Bucer provides great detail concerning Abraham Ibn Ezra's interpretation of "out of the mouths of babes and sucklings" as indicating the time when a human begins to speak. For speech, says Ibn Ezra, separates humans from the rest of creation and shows their rationality, superiority, and excellence.[79] Again, Calvin directly addresses this interpretation and rejects it: "In my judgment, those reason very foolishly who think that this is done when children begin to articulate, because then also the intellectual faculty of the soul shows itself."[80] Calvin instead proclaims that one should keep to the "clear and suitable" reading of this passage, which is that the verse speaks of God's providence. "Babes and sucklings" reveal God's providence by the fact that nourishment is ready for them as soon as they are born and by the fact that they are born with the skill to suck; in other words, all they need has already been provided by the Great Artisan. Incidentally, this is *precisely* the point made by David Kimhi in his comments on this text.[81] Indeed, Kimhi's emphases in his interpretation of the whole of Psalm 8 are that this Psalm portrays the providence of God that may be seen in the order of all creation and that demands humanity's recognition and praise. These are also Calvin's emphases: that David sets forth the example of praise of God's providence and calls all humanity to "apply their whole hearts" and efforts to the exercise of this praise. Yet, while Kimhi emphasizes that babes and sucklings have the power to recognize their Creator and should respond with praise, Calvin seems to especially emphasize that these babes and sucklings, *particularly*, are active and loud proclaimers of God's providence.[82]

Now it may just be a striking coincidence that Calvin reads Psalm 8 in very much the same light as does David Kimhi, for a reading in terms of divine providence is certainly a strong interest of Calvin's. One other element, however, makes one wonder whether Calvin is reading Kimhi in some way (probably through another Protestant commentary). Calvin makes a point to translate the Hebrew verb תִּנָה in the infinitive mood rather than the past tense. The reason he gives for this translation is that it retains the meaning of the verse better in indicating that the earth is too small to contain the glory of God. This is also precisely the point that Kimhi makes. Kimhi prefers the infinitive and supports this reading by saying the meaning of the verse is that the higher elements (the heavens) controls the lower elements (earth), for the earth is too small to contain those higher things.[83]

On Ps 16:4, Bucer uses Jewish exegesis to unravel the difficulties of the translation of two Hebrew words: מָהֲרוּ, which may mean "they hasten" or "they endow or offer" (i.e., they give gifts), depending on the tense of the verb, and עַצְּבוֹתָם, which may mean "idols" or "troubles or sorrows." He cites the translation of מָהָרוּ as "they endow" by Kimhi and Abraham Ibn Ezra, but he prefers Rashi's reading of "they hasten." Likewise, he cites the translation of עַצְּבוֹתָם as "troubles or sorrows," but he prefers to read this as referring to idols. Thus, Bucer concludes that he agrees more with the interpretation of Rashi, who translates this verse as referring to those who long to serve foreign gods (i.e., those who hasten after idols).[84] Calvin, on the other hand, prefers the translation of מָהָרוּ as "they offer" and עַצְּבוֹתָם as "sorrows" or "troubles," so that the verse means that the ungodly offer gifts to someone other than God and in doing so multiply their sorrows. Calvin's attention to grammar determines his reading of these Hebrew words: because עַצְּבוֹתָם is in the feminine, it properly denotes "sorrows"; likewise, because מָהָרוּ is a Kal conjugation, it properly means "they offer." Again, this is precisely the reading and the reasons for the reading given by David Kimhi.[85]

Bucer's other references to Jewish exegesis in his comments on Psalm 16 are less detailed and often in the form of one-liners. Most of these cite a comment by Kimhi. Thus, on Ps 16:2, he mentions the translation by Kimhi of this as "the good I do is not unto you" (rather than "I have no good apart from you"), so that the meaning is that we do no good for God because God has no need of any good from us, but we do this good for "the holy ones in the land." This reading, indeed, appears to be one of the things that supports Bucer's and later Calvin's emphases in this Psalm that David sets his affections upon the saints, teaches believers to connect themselves to the society of the righteous, and does good to the saints. Both Bucer and Calvin connect the second verse with the "holy ones in the land" of the next verse, just as Kimhi does.[86] In addition to his emphasis on David's affection and good deeds for the saints, Kimhi's reading of Psalm 16 also stresses David as an exemplar of obedience (Ps 16:3), trust in God (Ps 16:5), and the recognition of God alone as one's inheritance (Ps 16:5–6). Furthermore, Kimhi emphasizes that David himself was confident in God's delivery of him from all harm, even after death (Ps 16:9–11). These are all emphases found in Calvin's interpretation of Psalm 16.[87]

By walking through Bucer's uses of Jewish exegesis in these two Psalms and exploring Calvin's responses to them, we find that in many cases Calvin does refer to the ideas of Jewish exegesis cited by Bucer and rejects them, though in doing so, he does not explicitly name any as Jewish exegesis. There are also several ways, however, in which Calvin *positively* uses the ideas of Jewish exegesis, though again he does not openly credit Jewish exegesis. Indeed, even though Bucer overtly uses Jewish exegesis and Calvin does not, Calvin's particular emphases on divine providence and David as supreme exemplar in his interpretations of these Psalms fall even more closely to the heart of Jewish exegesis than do Bucer's. These emphases, as has been shown, are very much in line with those of David Kimhi. Hence, there is strong indication that Calvin's commentary on Psalms 8 and 16 contain clear echoes of parts of Bucer's accounts of Jewish exegesis when it suits his own theological purposes and that Calvin has knowledge of Jewish exegesis not cited by Bucer.[88]

These reasons alone would not be enough, though, to say that Calvin's interpretations fall closer to the heart of Jewish exegesis than do Bucer's. Two other important factors lead to this assertion. First, Bucer does give a christological reading of those particular verses cited by the New Testament in reference to Christ *without qualification*, whereas Calvin expresses real reservation and criticism of the New Testament authors' use of these Psalms and, thus, gives a *qualified* christological reading. In other words, Bucer does not disparage the New Testament authors' application of these Psalms; rather, he harmonizes their reading with his own emphases. Calvin, on the other hand, explicitly says the New Testament authors' applications present difficulties, do not actually explain the meaning of the text, and instead accommodate it to a different sense. Indeed, he is not at all willing to accept the reading of Ps 8:5 ("you have made him a little lower than angels") in reference to the humiliation of Christ, even though it is read this way by the author of Hebrews.[89]

Another reason that Calvin can be seen as more closely taking up the emphases of Jewish exegesis is that he—far more than Bucer on these two Psalms—wants to give a reading of these Psalms in reference to the person and history of David. Calvin stands apart from Bucer in his profound emphasis on the example of David.[90] Rather than giving a reading in reference to David, Bucer could be understood as giving a different kind of christological reading than Luther's, but a christological reading nonetheless. Although Bucer does not emphasize a reading of these Psalms as literal prophecies of Christ's death, resurrection, and ascension (though he still concedes these readings), he does give a powerful and emphatic reading of these Psalms in reference to Christ as the head of his members.[91] Though Calvin echoes Bucer's head-member reading to show how certain verses are properly interpreted in reference to Christ, Calvin's overwhelming emphasis is on David as exemplar of Protestant piety. In effect, it can appear to some that Calvin elevates the example of David where he should be promoting Christ. This is precisely one of Aegidius Hunnius's accusations against him. In point of fact, all of the reasons Calvin could be seen as promoting Jewish exegetical emphases that are highlighted here—emphases on David rather than Christ, on the excellence of humanity, and on divine providence and the lack of anti-Jewish rhetoric due to not interpreting these Psalms as literal prophecies of Christ—are exactly the reasons Hunnius raises in his 1593 treatise to support his accusations of judaizing against Calvin.[92]

Finally, Calvin reaches different conclusions than Bucer in his concern to render a reading of these two Psalms that is defensible against Jewish scrutiny. Whereas Bucer maintains the traditional christological readings of these two Psalms and harmonizes them with his weightier readings in reference to the church as the body of Christ, Calvin practically drops the christological readings altogether and finds a reading of these Psalms in reference to the life of David thoroughly sufficient to give meaning for the Christian church. For example, he clearly indicates his concern for the defensibility of his interpretations before the Jews as one of the reasons for his interpretation of Ps 16:10 as more appropriate to David than Christ:

> Both the Greek and Latin fathers, I confess, have strained these words to a meaning wholly different, referring them to the bringing back of the soul of Christ from hell. But it is better to adhere to the natural simplicity of the interpretation that I have given, that we may not make ourselves objects of ridicule to the Jews; and further, that one subtlety, by engendering many others, may not involve us in a labyrinth.[93]

Bucer many times expresses this same concern for rendering Christian readings that are defensible before the Jews, but it does not lead him to the same conclusions as it does Calvin, for Bucer states clearly that he wants to *strengthen* traditional christological readings by grounding them in the *historia*, not diminish them.[94] Of course, Calvin would not see himself as diminishing christological readings of the Psalms but, rather, strengthening them all the more by consistently applying certain exegetical principles. In this way, Calvin is more willing to break with the antecedent Christian tradition when it does not follow those principles he has set forth that call for such christological readings. Hence, we find between Bucer and Calvin important distinctions in their views of the authority of the previous Christian exegetical tradition or, at least, in how blatantly they are willing to counter it.[95]

Conclusions

In the context of prior Christian readings of these eight Psalms, Calvin makes a number of surprising exegetical shifts. Although he does interpret portions of most of these Psalms in reference to Christ, he gives much more limited and less frequent christological readings. In some key places, such as the interpretations of Psalms 8 and 16, he actually explicitly rejects the christological reading of the Psalm. Furthermore, he not only breaks with the prominence given to these Psalms in Christian exegesis as literal prophecies of Christ's incarnation, crucifixion, resurrection, and ascension but also does not use these Psalms to teach the doctrines of Trinity and the two natures of Christ.

Instead, Calvin applies his own specific exegetical principles to disclose what he considers to be the simple and natural sense of the text. By finding powerful doctrinal and pastoral messages for the church in the simple and natural sense of the Psalm—namely, in the historical life of David—Calvin believes he has fully discharged his duty as a biblical exegete. More often than not, such readings lead him to elevate the prominent messages of comfort and call to true Protestant piety as that which the Spirit speaks—through the mouthpiece of David—to downtrodden Protestant churches. Hence, Calvin's primary interpretations of these Psalms are readings through the person of David that bring comfort and teach true Protestant piety (over and against Roman Catholic piety) and expound upon the doctrines of the goodness of God, election, and divine providence.[96]

Moreover, this study of Calvin's interpretation of these eight Psalms reveals that the Jews play a very different role in his exegesis than in the interpretations of Luther or even Bucer. Calvin does not equate Jews with the "enemies" found in these Psalms, nor does he apply passages of these Psalms against the Jews that Christian interpreters had historically deployed against them. Indeed, at several points, he elevates the Jews as positive examples for the church's imitation. His concern to render a Christian reading that is defensible before the Jews is a crucial rationale for giving more limited christological interpretations of these Psalms and for dropping the Trinitarian applications of these Psalms altogether.

Like Luther and Bucer, Calvin views David as a prophet who foresees Christ; however, the content of these prophecies differs from the content that Luther, Bucer, and the late medieval Christian interpreters emphasize. Whereas Luther, Bucer, and the antecedent Christian tradition view David primarily as a prophet who foresees and foretells the incarnation, passion, resurrection, and ascension of Christ, when Calvin speaks of David as a prophet, he specifically means a prophet who foresees the messianic *kingdom*. The description of the kingdom of Christ given by David is the full content of David's prophecies, according to Calvin. Indeed, such differing perspectives on David's office as prophet have consequences for the treatment of Jews in these Psalms. The readings of these Psalms as prophesying Christ's passion and resurrection have tended to render the Jews as the enemies of Christ and the church, and Calvin's lack of doing so curbs these tendencies.

All three of these reformers—Luther, Bucer, and Calvin—use these Psalms to give a message of comfort to struggling Protestant churches. Luther gives a message of comfort to the churches that just as God did not forget Christ in his suffering, so God will not forget the church. Bucer, though in a very different way, also gives a message of comfort through Christ: Christ has brought the restoration of God's kingdom to the church so that all the good gifts of a beneficent God are restored to it. Calvin, on the other hand, brings a message of comfort through the example of *David*. David arises as the supreme exemplar of persevering faith, proper humility, devout prayer, true praise of God, and authentic Christian worship and piety.

The contrasting elements contained in the exegeses of these Psalms by Luther, Bucer, and Calvin also reveal the use of these Psalms to teach particular confessional emphases concerning tools of biblical interpretation and doctrinal content. Luther reads these Psalms as literal prophecies of Christ's passion and resurrection and uses them to teach about the doctrines of Trinity and the two natures of Christ. The Reformed theologians, Calvin and Bucer, on the other hand, share significant exegetical themes and tools. They both see in these Psalms prime teachings concerning the beneficence of God, election, the nature of faith, and the marks of true Christian piety. They also both exhibit the prominence given to historical exegesis and typological exegesis as proper and powerful tools for Christian interpretation of Scripture. And I have argued that both Bucer and Calvin are using Jewish exegesis to some extent to accomplish these purposes—though Bucer does this overtly and Calvin much more covertly.

Yet, there are also significant distinctions between our two Reformed exegetes. Different from Bucer, the primary doctrinal teaching Calvin finds in these Psalms concerns the providence of God—a teaching he then relates to the themes he shares with Bucer concerning the beneficence of God, election, and the cultivation of true piety. Furthermore, Calvin, even more profoundly than Bucer, offers a reading of these Psalms in reference to the person of David, whereas Bucer's primary readings remain christological (albeit with content that is often slightly different from that of Luther's). I have argued that both of these distinctions of Calvin—the emphasis on providence and the primacy of David—place him closer to the heart of the rabbinic readings of these Psalms than even Bucer and particularly close to the readings of David Kimhi. When one combines these factors with Calvin's tendency to eclipse the christological and Trinitarian readings and his general lack of anti-Jewish rhetoric in his interpretations of these Psalms, you basically have all the ammunition Aegidius Hunnius uses to accuse Calvin of judaizing. It is to these accusations and David Pareus's responding defense that we now turn.

5

The Judaizing Calvin

The Debate of Hunnius and Pareus

Calvin's emphasis on a Psalm's primary meaning concerning David
(and only secondarily concerning Christ) and his assertion of his
own interpretation of a Psalm as more in keeping with its plain
sense than that of the apostles themselves are two of the key issues
that are at the heart of the Lutheran Aegidius Hunnius's charges
of judaizing against him. Hunnius time and again accuses Calvin of
tearing the meaning of a Psalm away from the apostolic exegesis
of it and arrogantly asserting his own reading. Thus Hunnius
maintains that Calvin claims his own personal authority not only
over the patristic biblical interpretive tradition, but also above and
beyond the authority of the apostles themselves.[1]

Likewise, Hunnius also disparages Calvin's absence of employing
these eight Psalms to teach the doctrines of Trinity and the two
natures of Christ. He writes that Calvin's exegesis of these Psalms
entangles the doctrines of Trinity and the two natures of Christ in
"his thorn bush of tricks."[2] Thus, by not rendering the christological
reading as the primary sense and by denying the teachings of Trinity
and the two natures of Christ found in these Psalms, Hunnius
believes Calvin covers these most clear prophecies with "Jewish
perversions." He contends that the end result of Calvin's exegesis is
to shatter and undermine the exegetical foundations of Christian
teachings of Trinity and the two natures of Christ and, more generally,
the church's christological readings of the Old Testament. In these
ways, says Hunnius, Calvin opens up Scripture to Jewish and Arian

heresies.[3] Thus, I begin with some historical background to the debate between Aegidius Hunnius and Calvin's defender David Pareus. Next, I explore Hunnius's accusations against Calvin, especially as they appear in his critique of Calvin's interpretation of these eight Psalms. Lastly, I turn to David Pareus's defense of Calvin's exegesis of the messianic Psalms.[4]

Introduction to the Debate of Hunnius and Pareus

John Calvin has certainly had his share of Lutheran critics. During his lifetime, most of his Lutheran detractors attacked his Eucharistic theology, including most significantly the criticisms of Joachim Westphal and Tilemann Hesshus.[5] The accusations of Aegidius Hunnius (1550–1603) against Calvin's exegesis of Scripture appear after Calvin's death; thus, the Reformed theologian David Pareus (1548–1622) provides the formal rebuttal. Hunnius received his education from Württemberg and Tübingen. He began his career as a professor at the University of Marburg, but in 1592, he was called to Wittenberg. The central aim of his career was the restoration of Lutheran orthodoxy, which for him also crucially involved the fight against the growing presence of Calvinism in the electorate of Saxony, where he lived. Hence, Hunnius's treatises against Calvin were part of his larger program of reestablishing Lutheran orthodoxy and purifying Germany from what he saw as Calvinist contamination. David Pareus, on the other hand, was a student of Zacharias Ursinus in Heidelberg. Pareus spent most of his life as a pastor of various Reformed congregations in southern Germany and eventually finished the last two decades of his career as a teacher and the professor at the Collegium Sapientia in Heidelberg. Though he formally took the responsibility to confront Hunnius's accusations against Calvin, Pareus was by nature an irenicist who spent much of his career trying to find ways to unite Lutherans and the Reformed on such issues as the Lord's Supper.

The debate between Hunnius and Pareus begins with a 1589 treatise by Hunnius, in which he charges Calvin with undermining the exegetical foundations of the doctrine of the Trinity.[6] Although Hunnius recognizes that Calvin does believe in the doctrines of the Trinity and the deity of Christ (and therefore he is not actually an Arian), he contends that Calvin has rejected the patristic exegesis that has supported these dogmas and has, thus, "opened a window of opportunity for the corrupt theology of the Anti-Trinitarians," let alone that of Arians and judaizers.[7] David Pareus defends Calvin against these accusations of Arianism and judaizing by pointing to his work against contemporary Anti-Trinitarians, such as Servetus, Alciati, and Blandrata.[8]

Hunnius continues his attack on Calvin with a more thorough criticism of his exegesis in his 1593 treatise *Calvinus Iudaizans*, "The Judaizing Calvin," upon which this chapter focuses. In the *Calvinus Iudaizans*, Hunnius goes through Old and New Testament passages traditionally used to support the doctrines of the Trinity and the divinity of Christ.[9] In each case, he cites direct quotations from Calvin's exegesis of these passages to take issue with what he sees as the ways Calvin undermines the Trinitarian and christological teachings contained in these scriptures. Thus, Hunnius aims to give solid proofs from Calvin's own exegesis for his contention that he weakens the exegetical foundations of the key Christian doctrines of Trinity and the divinity of Christ.

David Pareus responds two years later to Hunnius's treatise on the judaizing Calvin. Pareus takes issue with Hunnius's selective quotations of Calvin's exegesis of the biblical passages cited, arguing that he has deliberately left out other aspects of Calvin's exegesis—namely, the christological readings Calvin does give to these biblical verses. Furthermore, Pareus adds more examples of Calvin's exegesis to prove that in many cases, Calvin does maintain the traditional patristic reading of Scripture and upholds the doctrines of Trinity and the divinity of Christ.[10]

Hunnius's Criticisms of Calvin's Exegesis

Hunnius begins his treatise on the judaizing Calvin by clarifying to Pareus that he has not accused and does not accuse Calvin of Arianism per se but, rather, of "offering an opportunity" and "opening a window" to lay a foundation for Arian impiety. In the preface, he sets forth the purpose of his treatise to "pierce through the impious glosses of Calvin," by which Calvin "darkens with Jewish darkness" many biblical passages that reveal and confirm Christ's divinity. Thus, he contends that Calvin distorts Scripture and drags it away from its genuine sense. Furthermore, decries Hunnius, Calvin not only "arrogantly looks down upon and mocks" the interpretations of the ancient and recent church fathers but also "in nothing does he inform himself of the sacred interpretations of the evangelists and apostles, badly mocking these and having no respect [for them]."[11] Hunnius proceeds first by pointing to biblical passages that the church fathers and the apostles interpret concerning the Trinity and that Calvin does not. Then he turns to biblical passages traditionally read concerning Christ's deity that Calvin does not apply in this way. Finally, he turns to biblical texts traditionally read as prophecies of Christ's passion, resurrection, and ascension that Calvin does not employ in these ways.

The Eclipse of Literal Prophecies of Christ and Apostolic Authority

Hunnius gives a lengthy exposition on Ps 2:7, "He said to me, 'You are my Son; today I have begotten you,'" to demonstrate that this verse must be read for the Trinitarian teachings it contains. His initial problem with Calvin's treatment of this verse is that Calvin first applies it literally to David and only secondarily to Christ—and this only via the type, by way of analogy and not by way of the literal sense. By applying this passage literally to David, argues Hunnius, Calvin renders unintelligible the apostles' interpretation in Acts 13:33 and Heb 1:5 of its plain sense as a literal prophecy of Christ. Hunnius points out that these New Testament passages reveal that the apostles understand the whole of Psalm 2 as David's prophecy of Christ's passion. Thus, he declares that Calvin departs from not only the authoritative and authentic apostolic exegesis of Ps 2:7 but also the mind of David himself and the whole apostolic church in general. Yet, even more deplorable in Hunnius's eyes is the fact that Calvin rejects the application of Ps 2:7 to the Trinitarian reading of Christ's eternal generation by the Father. He berates Calvin for his "singular audacity" in applying this passage to David as a son of God, rather than to Christ as the only begotten Son of God. "Therefore," asserts Hunnius, Calvin "is truly a Jew," for he "plucks" and "tears this Scripture from the apostles."[12]

Next, Hunnius turns to examine a set of biblical passages that the church fathers and apostles have traditionally interpreted concerning the deity of Christ, which include the interpretations of Ps 2:7, Ps 45:6–7, and Ps 68:18. The author of Hebrews uses both Ps 2:7 and Ps 45:6–7 to demonstrate the divinity of Christ. Thus, Heb 1:5, 6–9 reads (NRSV):

> For to which of the angels did God ever say, "You are my Son; today
> I have begotten you"? [Ps 2:7] . . . Of the angels he says, "He makes his
> angels winds, and his servants flames of fire" [Ps 104:4]. But of the Son
> he says, "Your throne, O God, is forever and ever, and the righteous
> scepter is the scepter of your kingdom. You have loved righteousness
> and hated wickedness; therefore God, your God, has anointed you with
> the oil of gladness beyond your companions" [Ps 45:6–7].

The apostle states that in these passages the Spirit undoubtedly speaks concerning the Son, but Calvin writes that the simple and natural sense of Ps 45:6–7 concerns Solomon and that it concerns Christ only via the type and not under the literal sense. Consequently, Hunnius accuses Calvin of judaizing: "For the Jews clamor in this same sense as Calvin when he says this to be the simple and natural sense!"[13]

Likewise, according to Hunnius, Calvin undermines the teachings of Christ's deity present in Ps 68:18. The Apostle Paul relates this verse to Christ in Eph 4:8, by which he declares Christ to be the same as the Lord in this Psalm, demonstrating the deity of Christ. Yet Calvin applies the verse to David's earthly kingdom rather than to Christ. Hunnius bemoans that Calvin "crucifies the brilliant predictions of the Prophets." Moreover, he accuses Calvin of arrogantly being his own teacher of Scripture by removing himself from the authority of apostolic exegesis. Even more to the point, Calvin has the audacity, says Hunnius, to criticize and correct the interpretation of the Apostle Paul when Calvin writes that "Paul *subtly bends* [deflectit]" Ps 68:18 toward Christ in Eph 4:8, implying that such a reading requires a "bending" of the passage away from its more natural sense. Again, he sees Calvin acquiescing to Jewish exegesis of this verse and undermining the scriptural foundations for Christ's deity.[14]

Hunnius next turns to Ps 8:4–6, which he sees as a literal prophecy of Christ's passion in accordance with the apostolic readings given of this text in Heb 2:6–8, 1 Cor 15:27, and Eph 1:22. Yet, instead of applying Ps 8:4–6 to Christ, Calvin "dares to twist" this passage and apply it to the excellence of humanity and to the dominion given to humanity over creation. Indeed, Calvin goes so far as to say that the excellence of humanity is such that it is "not far inferior to divine and heavenly glory." This, says Hunnius, is not only contrary to the apostles' reading concerning Christ's *humiliation* but also contrary to the message of the Old Testament prophets themselves, who point not to the proximity of humanity's condition to the Divine, but to their distance from it.[15] In so doing, Calvin "gnaws away as with dog's teeth the teaching of the Apostle Paul." And yet again Calvin asserts himself as a teacher of Scripture above the authority of Paul when he accuses the apostle of "dragging" [trahit] the meaning of Ps 8:4 to apply it to Christ's passion.[16] Thus, contends Hunnius, Calvin "plunders the plain sense" of these verses in the Psalms when he insists that the literal sense applies to the excellence of humanity and not to Christ:

> Will the judgment of Calvin stand better than that of the apostles? If so, then when other articles of the Christian faith wish to be founded upon the Prophets, will the Prophets be seen not to explain them . . . but, rather, to *bend* [deflectit] them toward the sense, of which others in the Prophets have said is the true sense? If concerning the Prophets their [the apostles'] words are considered to be embellished through *amplification* . . . if, furthermore, they [the apostles] are seen not so much as interpreting the Prophets' words but as accommodating them to some other thing through pious *deflection*

[deflexione]. . . . Well, even the Jews would not suffer the opening of so
many thousands of cracks![17]

In this way, Hunnius charges Calvin with separating the apostles' meaning
from that of the prophets' meaning and, thus, threatening the very unity of the
Testaments that Calvin claims to uphold.

After arguing for the literal sense of Ps 8:4–6 as a literal prophecy of
Christ's passion, Hunnius turns to Calvin's interpretation of Psalm 22, which
Christian tradition, the apostles, and the Gospels have undisputedly read in
reference to the crucifixion of Christ. He demonstrates the multiple parallels
between the Gospels' descriptions of Christ's suffering during the crucifixion
and Psalm 22. Thus, that Calvin should explain this Psalm first in reference to
David is an atrocity in Hunnius's eyes. He views Calvin as a Jew opposing
Christ when he shatters these most basic prophecies and weakens the Christian interpretation of Psalm 22 before the Jews. Hunnius quotes Calvin's
statement that David speaks of himself through the use of metaphors to bewail
his condition and exclaims in the margins beside this quote, "Away with your
metaphors!" Again, he disparages Calvin's "human invention" and blatant
disregard for the interpretations of the evangelists and the apostles. Indeed,
for him, Calvin is no better than a Jewish rabbi who devises ways to crucify
Christ all over again. Finally, Hunnius quotes Calvin's exegesis of the John 19
account of Christ's crucifixion, in which Calvin writes that the evangelists
inappropriately drag [trahit] Ps 22:18 to apply it to Christ, and thus they "neglect
the figure and depart from the natural sense." At this, Hunnius can hardly
contain his fury when he exclaims that Calvin not only exalts himself again
over the authority of the evangelists and the apostles but also acts as their
censor. In effect, fumes Hunnius, Calvin has accused the *evangelists*, rather
than the Jews, of bending [deflexione] the meaning of this Psalm to an
unnatural sense.[18]

Next Hunnius turns to Psalm 16 as a literal prophecy of Christ's resurrection, according to both the Apostle Peter (Acts 2:25–31) and the Apostle Paul
(Acts 13:34–37). Indeed, both apostles explicitly write that Ps 16:10 cannot be
applied to David, in that David died and experienced corruption, and must be a
prophecy of Christ's resurrection. Yet, Calvin proceeds to apply this passage to
David nonetheless.[19] In response, Hunnius, using the terms Calvin employs in
his criticisms of apostolic exegesis, sarcastically pronounces:

If Calvin was a servant of God, as his disciples proclaim of him, in no
way could he have led others away from this one simple sense that the
apostles set forth. . . . You see with what tortuous *bending* [reflexu] and
serpentine circles this spirit of darkness *twists* [torqueat] itself so that

this psalm is forced to be drawn away from the praise of Christ for which it is written. Therefore, he prefers to *drag* [trahere] the meaning to David in contradiction to Peter and Paul [who show] that David treated nothing of himself but entirely concerning Christ and his resurrection.[20]

Thus, Calvin weakens all the strong prophecies of David and departs from apostolic authority. Indeed, Hunnius points out that Calvin even notes the apostles' readings of Ps 16:8–11 concerning Christ alone and exclaims, "If this is so, why does he apply it to the person of David?" Thus, if one follows Calvin, bellows Hunnius, the testimony of Psalm 16 can no longer be a refuge of Christian teaching; instead, it is filled with "Jewish treachery, wantonness, and tricks."[21]

Finally, Hunnius turns to Ps 68:18 and Ps 8:6 as literal prophecies of Christ's ascension, according to apostolic usage. He appeals to the Apostle Paul's use of Ps 68:18 in Eph 4:7–10 concerning Christ's ascension and condemns Calvin's application of it to David.[22] Having already pointed out Calvin's accusation that Paul *bends* the meaning of Ps 68:18 to apply it to Christ, he moves on to discuss Ps 8:6. The literal sense of this verse, in accordance with 1 Cor 16:25–27, Eph 1:20–22, and Heb 2:7–8, speaks of the exaltation of Christ to the right hand of God and his dominion over all creatures, which occurs at Christ's ascension. Hunnius admits that Calvin does indeed "sprinkle some mentioning of Christ" into his exegesis of Ps 8:6, but far "too sparingly." More to the point, Calvin does not view this verse as prophecy. Hunnius is dissatisfied with the fact that Calvin will apply only minor parts of Psalm 8 to Christ and instead narrates the whole of the Psalm as concerning the excellence of humanity. Thus, he concludes, "Attend to this, whoever you are, how much the most putrid glosses of Calvin depart from the minds of the holy apostles, who without doubt understand this Psalm more rightly and profoundly than a hundred Calvins and just as many Bezas or even more than all the foggy fumings of Pareus and all of these put together!"[23]

Hunnius not only is horrified at Calvin's departure from apostolic exegesis and traditional Christian readings of these texts but also accuses Calvin of wicked and clever subterfuge. He views Calvin as "sprinkling" his interpretations with references to Christ, as if to avoid accusation, and then going on to explain these passages much more fully concerning David. Hunnius labels these as "pure tricks," "deception," and a "game of cheating the church." Indeed, as a final proof of Calvin's artifices, he turns to Calvin's exegesis of Ps 110:1. Although Calvin does clearly state that Ps 110:4 ("You are a priest after the order of Melchizedek") does apply to none other than Christ, Hunnius contends that he sprinkles Ps 110:1 "with the soot of Jewish corruptions," for Calvin nonetheless applies this verse to David. The problem is that while the prior Christian exegetical tradition applies the whole of Psalm 110 to Christ, Calvin applies only a small portion of it. Thus, Hunnius believes that Calvin acts as a trickster when he claims to apply a Psalm to Christ, when in actuality he is picking and choosing what applies to Christ and what does not.[24]

Hunnius brings his charges against Calvin up another whole notch, though, when he points out that Ps 110:1 is *Jesus'* answer to the Pharisees' question about who is the Messiah and whose son he is. Hunnius scornfully writes that if Calvin had been standing beside the Pharisees, he would have answered that this verse could be understood concerning David, and indeed, in this way Calvin puts forth the Pharisees' inanities. But more to the point, *Jesus himself* sets the proper interpretation of this verse as concerning himself, as seen in Matt 22:41–46, Mk 12:35–37, and Lk 20:41–44. In applying Ps 110:1 to David, Calvin dares even to go against Christ, the true Interpreter![25]

Hunnius's Charges against Calvin

In sum, Aegidius Hunnius's indictment against Calvin's exegesis of these Psalms amounts to four main charges. The first point of contention is the identification of the literal sense of these Psalms. Hunnius rightly points out that there is a long Christian exegetical tradition, guided by the New Testament usage of these Psalms, to identify their literal sense with the literal prophecies of Christ's deity, passion, resurrection, and ascension that they express. Calvin has time and again identified the literal sense of these Psalms with the meaning that pertains to David rather than with these prophecies of Christ. Though Calvin often does retain the christological reading of these Psalms in some way, he does so as a secondary figural or typological reading, in which he clearly states that these figural or typological readings are not the Psalm's "plain and simple" sense. Thus, Hunnius warns that Calvin's exegesis destabilizes clear testimonies of Christ's deity, passion, resurrection, and ascension.[26]

Second, Hunnius repeatedly accuses Calvin of arrogant disregard for apostolic authority in exegesis. He argues that Calvin removes the understandings of these Psalms from the interpretations given to them by the evangelists and apostles. Indeed, Calvin even claims the authority to censor the readings of the apostles and the evangelists when he alleges that they "drag" [trahit] or "bend" [deflectit] the sense to its application to Christ. On the contrary, says Hunnius, it is *Calvin* who bends [deflectit] the prophet's words for his own purposes and drags [trahit] the meaning away from the natural sense to his own interpretation. In a related move, then, Hunnius charges Calvin with "confusing and burying" the consensus of the church fathers on these passages—church fathers who rightly acknowledge apostolic authority and maintain the New Testament usage of these Psalms.[27]

As has been shown, Hunnius also implicates Calvin in practices of trickery and subterfuge. He paints Calvin as a crafty, devious, and deceitful exegete who is not completely honest or straightforward about the consequences of his exegesis. Hunnius intends to demonstrate for his audience the dangerous ramifications of Calvin's exegesis, namely, that it shatters the exegetical foundation of Christian teachings of Trinity and the deity of Christ, as well as christological prophecy in the Old Testament.[28] Hence, he judges Calvin to be "an angel of darkness, who comes forth from the abysmal pit to twist Scripture and destroy the grounds of defense of the Christian religion against Jewish and Arian adversaries."[29]

Finally, all of these charges culminate in Hunnius's charge of judaizing against Calvin. By denying the literal sense of these Psalms as prophecies of Christ, Calvin "bends the most sacred words from Christ to the gambling games of Jewish glosses."[30] When Calvin identifies the literal sense of these Psalms with their reading concerning the life of David, Calvin, says Hunnius, is reading like a Jew. When Calvin undermines the authority and power of apostolic readings of these Old Testament texts as prophecies of Christ and gives them a secondary or even a questionable status, then he—Hunnius contends—is promoting Jewish objectives. The deceitfulness and craftiness that Hunnius sees in Calvin's exegesis is, most unfortunately, very much in line with a long-standing medieval Christian depiction of Jews. Thus, Calvin's exegesis has not just opened Christianity to the heresy of Arianism but exposed it to the greatest danger of all, according to Hunnius—namely, to a way of reading the Old Testament in which Christ is no longer the primary or central content.

Pareus's Defense of Calvin

David Pareus writes a lengthy response to Hunnius's charges against Calvin—a response in two books published two years later in 1595. In the first and shorter book, he defends the orthodoxy of Calvin's doctrines of the Trinity and the eternal divinity of Christ as they are found mostly in biblical passages not covered by Hunnius. First, he demonstrates Calvin's orthodox expression of these doctrines in his *Institutes*. Next, he expounds on nine Old Testament passages to show that Calvin specifically applies them in reference to Christ's deity over and against Jews and heretics such as Servetus.[31] Moreover, he garners evidence of Calvin's orthodox doctrines of the divinity of Christ and Trinity in his commentaries on the synoptic Gospels, the Gospel of John, the Book of Acts, and the apostles' epistles.[32]

The heart and bulk of Pareus's defense of Calvin, however, appears in the second book of his treatise, where he takes to task the exegetical passages that Hunnius has used to argue his case against Calvin. Pareus divides these passages into six classes that he uses to refute Hunnius's accusations against Calvin. The first class includes passages that others have interpreted concerning Trinity and that Calvin interprets in another way.[33] The second class includes biblical texts that others interpret concerning the essential unity of the Persons and that Calvin does not.[34] The third class is biblical passages that others read concerning Christ and that Calvin interprets concerning God or according to the literal-historical sense.[35] The fourth class is texts others interpret in reference to Christ alone that Calvin accepts as principally concerning Christ but also applies to the type.[36] The fifth class concerns those passages that others interpret of Christ alone and that Calvin reads principally of Christ as head and secondarily of the church as members of the body of Christ.[37] The sixth and final class contains those biblical texts that Calvin interprets in reference to Christ alone that Hunnius has falsely accused Calvin of not doing so.[38] Two things are most notable in Pareus's defense of Calvin. First is his contention that Hunnius uses selective quotations of Calvin that render an inaccurate picture of his exegesis. Second, Pareus, unlike Hunnius, provides detailed references to the exegesis of the church fathers to demonstrate that Calvin has not departed as much from the antecedent Christian tradition as Hunnius has contended.

Defense against the Accusations of Arianism and Judaizing

Pareus begins the second book by quoting Hunnius's accusations that Calvin comes close to Arianism, while conceding that Calvin is not actually an Arian. He protests that if Hunnius must rightly concede Calvin's ultimate orthodoxy, why, then, does he continue to accuse? Pareus seethes, "If you confess that Calvin is orthodox, why do you accuse falsely? If you do not confess Calvin's orthodoxy, how do you not accuse him of Arianism? For it is necessary that either he is orthodox or he is an Arian!" Thus, he contends that Hunnius accuses falsely, cunningly, and vainly, and in doing so, he "snatches away" Calvin's Christianity. He avows that his own study of Calvin's exegesis will most "solidly dismantle" this accusation that Calvin lays a foundation for Arian impiety.[39]

Likewise, Pareus is even more displeased with Hunnius's accusation against Calvin of judaizing, as seen in the notably greater space he gives to this in his reply. First, Pareus defines a "judaizer" in New Testament terms and asserts that to be a "judaizer" one must be so in both practice and belief. To judaize, says Pareus, is to believe and teach and live against all the central Christian doctrines of the Trinity, the divinity of Christ, the virgin birth, the incarnation of Christ, and the fulfillment of messianic prophecies in Christ. These things cannot be said of Calvin, insists Pareus, neither in his life nor in his teaching. Indeed, he argues that it is insane to accuse Calvin of judaizing, when, as he will show in his treatise, Calvin consciously and deliberately takes a stand against Judaism.[40]

Pareus proceeds with a history of Calvin's exegetical works. He argues that Lutherans in Calvin's own day, such as Martin Luther and Philip Melanchthon, saw and read these very commentaries and did not find Calvin guilty of either Arianism or judaizing. Indeed, he exclaims, this cannot even be said of Calvin's harshest critics, such as Castellio, Westphal, Flacius, or Hesshus. Moreover, some Lutherans even cultivated a friendly relation with Calvin, as seen in the correspondences of Johannes Brentz and Jacob Andreas with Calvin. Thus, Pareus chastises Hunnius for seeing Arianism and judaizing in Calvin's works that significant Lutheran leaders in Calvin's own day did not see.[41]

Defense of Calvin's Relationship to the Exegetical Tradition

Concerning the charge that Calvin departs from previous exegetical consensus on these passages, Pareus sees little serious problem here. First of all, he contends that all agree that everyone should preserve and uphold those teachings fundamental to salvation. In this, Pareus is confident that Calvin has always maintained the consensus of the church. However, just as the rule of Augustine prescribes, in other matters it is possible—even useful—to depart from previous interpretations. Basing his arguments also upon the diverse gifts of the Spirit given to the church, Pareus argues for the necessity of multiple meanings of Scripture and the guiding goal of the edification of the church.[42]

Yet, Hunnius accuses Calvin of departing from previous tradition out of pride, for the sake of his own wisdom, and not out of necessity or edification for the church. By quoting from the preface of Calvin's commentary on Romans, Pareus lets Calvin answer this accusation in his own words. Calvin specifically states that he should be excused for differing from the previous tradition because he does not act out of presumption or lack of caution but, rather, with great care and concern for the edification of the church. He admits that one cannot find lasting agreement in this earthly life on the proper interpretation of biblical passages, a statement that warrants instruction on how to proceed: "When, therefore, we depart from the views of our predecessors, we are not to be stimulated by any passion for innovation, impelled by any desire to slander others, aroused by any hatred, or prompted by any ambition. Necessity alone is to compel us, and we are to have no other object than that of doing good."[43] In addition, points out Pareus, Calvin commends the "godliness, learning and sanctity" of the ancient commentators in this same preface.[44]

More important, Pareus provides multiple examples of the lack of exegetical consensus among the church fathers on the interpretation of such texts as Gen 1:1, Jn 8:25, Jn 16:28, and 1 Cor 7:2. If such is true of Augustine, Hilary, Ambrose, and Cyrillus, why, asks Pareus, can it not be equally granted to Luther, Calvin, and other recent interpreters? Finally, after pointing to some examples of extreme allegorizing among the ancient fathers, Pareus concludes that Calvin rightfully teaches caution against such allegories. In this way, it is true that Calvin sometimes prefers to retain the literal sense as the simple sense of the text in the context of its human author over and against the previous tradition's tendency to make the figural reading the literal sense. His purpose in doing so, insists Pareus, is precisely so that the exegetical foundations of Christian doctrine may remain secure.[45]

Defense of Calvin's Typology

After responding briefly to the first three classes of passages, Pareus focuses the details of his defense of Calvin's exegesis on the fourth class of these "difficult passages" by affirming Calvin's use of typology.[46] He insists that one must distinguish between kinds of types—some types are absolute and simple, whereas others are composite and complex. Simple types set forth things concerning Christ alone so that they speak absolutely about Christ and may not be transferred to another. Concerning these kinds of types, Pareus has no disagreements with Hunnius. However, the other kind of type—the composite type—can apply both to the type and to Christ. Indeed, the composite type can be further divided into four kinds: (1) those fulfilled literally both in Christ and in the type, (2) those fulfilled figuratively both in Christ and in the type, (3) those fulfilled literally in Christ and figuratively in the type, and (4) those fulfilled figuratively in Christ and literally in the type. Hence, one can speak of "composite prophecies" where there are twin fulfillments of the prophecies—one in Christ and the other in the type.[47]

Furthermore, parts of a biblical text might refer literally to the type, while other parts refer literally to Christ. In this way, there might be various manifestations of the composite type in, say, a single Psalm. Thus, for example, the verse concerning the kidneys that rebuke and wrestle with carnal desires (Ps 16:7) refers to David alone, the preservation from corruption (Ps 16:10) refers to Christ alone, and the rest of the Psalm applies to both David and Christ. Likewise, the eternal throne described in Ps 45:6 applies to Christ alone, and the rest of the Psalm applies to Solomon and his spouse. Similarly, the first three verses of Psalm 72 rightly and literally apply to Solomon, and the rest of the Psalm rightly speaks of the kingdom of Christ.[48] Furthermore, St. Augustine affirms this principle of exegesis concerning composite types, as seen in a passage from the *City of God*, where he says there is a "threefold meaning of the prophets, referring sometimes to the earthly Jerusalem, sometimes to the Heavenly City, sometimes to both at once."[49] To top it off, Pareus points to the fact that recent interpreters also utilize this principle of composite types in their exegesis of the Psalms in particular, and they interpret some Psalms to refer both to David and to Christ.[50]

Finally, Pareus takes up a defense against what he sees as Hunnius's basic objections to the reading of these passages as composite types and twin prophecies. First, Hunnius implies that only simple, absolute prophecies exist—that is, those that are clear promises and predictions that concern Christ alone—which Pareus believes he has already sufficiently shown to be false. Second, Hunnius appeals to the apostles' and evangelists' applications of these passages to Christ alone and argues that because they did not apply these passages to the type, neither should anyone else. But Pareus points out that this is analogous to saying that these passages suit Christ *by no reason of the type*. Yet, they cannot be fitting except by reason of the type, argues Pareus. Hence, the apostles and the evangelists cannot mean by their application to Christ that they deny the sacred history within the type, which is the very thing that gives the content that is then applied to Christ.[51]

Pareus sees Hunnius's third objection to composite types as his contention that the exegetical tradition has interpreted these passages concerning Christ alone. Pareus denies the truth of this assertion, for he has already shown the diverse readings of the fathers and will continue to demonstrate this in his treatment of the specific "difficult passages." At last, he raises Hunnius's objection that the application of the biblical text both to the type and to Christ weakens Christian arguments and exegetical proofs. Pareus argues that this can be true of only simple, absolute types and not of composite types. Because he believes the passages under debate are composite types, it is only right that they are applied both to Christ and to the type. One needs the historical referent to fully understand the content of the type; hence this dual application does not weaken the exegesis but, rather, strengthens it, for, avows Pareus, "truth does not weaken truth."[52]

Defense of Calvin's Readings of the Messianic Psalms

After having set up his case for composite types, Pareus turns to defend Calvin's typological exegesis of certain biblical texts. Beginning with Ps 2:7 ("You are my son; today I have begotten you"), he reiterates what he sees to be Hunnius's accusations against Calvin's interpretation of this verse: (1) Calvin impiously refers this verse to David *first* rather than to Christ, (2) Calvin refers this to David when it should be applied to Christ *alone*, (3) Calvin's exegesis is contrary to apostolic exegesis, and (4) Calvin judaizes because he rejects the Trinitarian reading that this verse speaks of Christ's coeternity with the Father. He deals with the first two accusations by arguing that to deny the application of this verse to David is to "deny the sacred history itself" upon which the type is based. Furthermore, not only does Calvin clearly state that this verse is *more fully* fulfilled by Christ but also Hunnius has deliberately left out this statement by Calvin and, thus, misrepresents him. As to the accusation that Calvin goes against apostolic exegesis, Pareus just does not see this to be the case. The apostles apply this Psalm to Christ, and so does Calvin. That the apostles do not explicitly apply it also to David does not mean, argues Pareus, that the application to David is contrary to apostolic exegesis, for in their application of the Psalm to Christ, "the type is not excluded."[53]

The fourth accusation, however, Pareus takes as much more serious. Hunnius argues that Calvin judaizes when he does not read Ps 2:7 as concerning Christ's eternal begetting by the Father. In defense, Pareus reiterates Calvin's position that this verse is about Christ's humanity, not his divinity. Thus, this verse refers to Christ being made manifest in the world, so that it declares beforehand Christ's heavenly glory displayed in the resurrection. Indeed, argues Pareus, this is exactly how the apostles read this passage as well. The larger context of the apostles' application of Ps 2:7 to Christ concerns not his eternal begetting by the Father but the manifestation of his glory through the resurrection. Thus, Pareus contends that Calvin's reading is even more in keeping with apostolic exegesis. Moreover, he demonstrates that Calvin is most definitely not alone in this interpretation, for many church fathers also interpret Ps 2:7 as concerning Christ's manifestation in the world in the incarnation and resurrection. He appeals to Chrysostom, Basil, Justin Martyr, Hilary, and Fulgentius's readings of Ps 2:7 as concerning not Christ's eternal begetting by the Father but the mysteries of his nativity and resurrection.[54]

Just in case the ancient church fathers are not proof enough, Pareus calls forth a number of recent interpreters who also interpret Ps 2:7 in reference to Christ's resurrection rather than to his coeternity with the Father. He focuses on the interpretation of Bugenhagen, a Lutheran known as "the most celebrated doctor of Wittenberg," who at length argues that Ps 2:7 concerns the humanity of Christ and refers to Christ's resurrection. Furthermore, Bugenhagen explicitly states that Ps 2:7 should not be interpreted concerning Christ's divinity, for apostolic use of this verse reveals that it is properly understood to concern the glorification of Christ's humanity in the resurrection. Why, then, asks Pareus, does Hunnius accuse Calvin of judaizing and not point to others, even others within his own confessional group?[55]

Pareus concludes his defense of Calvin's exegesis of Ps 2:7 by arguing that just because Calvin does not apply this verse to Christ's coeternity with the Father does not mean that he denies this doctrine; indeed, he assumes it. Pareus contends that not only does Calvin not judaize but also his application of this verse works even more strongly to cut short Jewish arguments. If one were to deny the application of Ps 2:7 to David, the Jews could easily outright dismiss the Christian reading. The affirmation that the verse does apply to David but more fully applies to the Messiah, however, is a statement with which the Jews agree. Thus, Pareus asserts, this leaves the Jews on the defensive concerning how this is not more fully fulfilled in Christ. He concludes, "Let the church judge whether or not [Calvin's] interpretation should be called impious or truly Judaic or whether these are impudent accusations, when nevertheless the Christian faith is upheld and the Jews are effectively refuted."[56]

On Ps 16:8–10, Hunnius has accused Calvin of wrongly applying to David what can only be said of Christ (i.e., the escape from the grave and decay). Hunnius has also pointed out that Calvin says the apostle *bends* the meaning to Christ in his use of Ps 16:8–10 in Acts 2:25–28. Pareus begins his defense of Calvin by first arguing that because Psalm 16 is a composite type, some things in it apply only to David, others only to Christ, and still other parts to both. He maintains that apostolic exegesis does not compel one to apply the whole Psalm to Christ. Indeed, some things in Psalm 16 apply properly to David *only*, such as Ps 16:7 in which the "kidneys rebuke," for many Christian expositors have interpreted kidneys as carnal pleasures.[57]

The core of Pareus's defense of Calvin's interpretation of Ps 16:8–10 is the contention that Hunnius resorts to tricks and omissions. To fully and properly understand Calvin's reading, Pareus asserts, one must consult not only his Psalms commentary but also his commentary on the Acts of the Apostles. He points out that Hunnius omits this interpretation of Calvin and only utilizes the interpretation as it appears in his Psalms commentary. In the Acts commentary, Calvin clearly states that this prophecy of escape from the corruption of the grave more solidly refers to Christ and that it applies to David only insofar as David is joined to Christ as a type and insofar as David receives this promise of resurrection as a member of the church. Pareus proposes that the Acts commentary is a more accurate representation of Calvin's thought.[58]

On Psalm 22, Hunnius argues against Calvin's application of it to David when it should be interpreted concerning Christ first and foremost, if not solely. Thus, he contends that in applying the Psalm to David just as much as to Christ, Calvin has weakened the Christian interpretation of the Psalm before the Jews. In Calvin's defense, Pareus begins with a series of quotations to emphasize that Calvin very much so interprets Psalm 22 concerning Christ first and foremost. He reiterates that one should not empty the type of its historical referent. Furthermore, he asserts that Calvin clearly states that these things are *foreshadowed* in David but more fully fulfilled in Christ, and he appeals to similar readings by Christophorus Cornerus (a Lutheran) and Wolfgang Musculus. Next, he argues that part of Psalm 22 is simple (i.e., refers to Christ alone) and part is composite. Verses twenty-seven to the end refer to Christ alone; however, all the rest of the Psalm is rightly understood as foreshadowed in David and more clearly fulfilled in Christ. He appeals to the exegesis of John Chrysostom, who plainly says that the first half of the Psalm can be understood as complaints of David. Thus that Calvin keeps Christ closely joined to the type does not go against apostolic exegesis nor undermine the Christian reading of this Psalm, argues Pareus; rather, it strengthens its defensibility before the Jews all the more.[59]

Finally, Pareus contends that Hunnius is guilty of calumny and sophistry in his inaccurate representation of Calvin's interpretation of Ps 22:18 ("they divide my clothes") in his commentary on Jn 19:23–24, where he has criticized Calvin's metaphorical application of these garments to David. What Hunnius failed to show, argues Pareus, is that in the whole context of Calvin's interpretation of John 19, he is "in the business of refuting the Jews." Thus, it is a calumny that Hunnius should accuse Calvin of judaizing. Furthermore, he contends that Hunnius uses sophistry by omitting the very response to his objections that can be found in the context of Calvin's comments on John 19, where Calvin writes that Ps 22:18 "ought not be restricted to David" but must be explained concerning Christ.[60]

Hunnius's main contention against Calvin's interpretation of Ps 45:6–7 is his statement that the "simple and natural sense" concerns Solomon.[61] In response, Pareus insists that Solomon as a type in Psalm 45 is partly composite and partly simple. Because the use of Solomon and his kingdom as types of Christ and his kingdom is founded on the principle that the history of Solomon foreshadows Christ, it cannot be wrong to say that the "simple and natural sense"—namely, the historical sense—pertains to Solomon. Indeed, Pareus contends that Calvin's reading is much more solid than the "allegorical" reading of Luther, for by grounding the Psalm within the history and the type, Calvin actually strengthens the Christian reading.[62]

Pareus's defense of Calvin's reading of Ps 8:4–6 involves a turn to his fifth class of passages—those passages that others interpret concerning Christ alone and Calvin interprets first concerning Christ and second concerning the members of Christ's body, the church. Very similar to his defense of Calvin's interpretation of Psalm 16, he appeals to Calvin's New Testament exegesis in his Hebrews commentary (i.e., Heb 2:6–8 cites Ps 8:4–6) as the more authoritative description of Calvin's views, rather than his Psalms commentary. In the Hebrews commentary, Calvin remarks, as he does in his Psalms commentary, that the Psalm "seems to be unsuitably applied to Christ." Yet, unlike his Psalms commentary, he proceeds to explain how these words apply properly to Christ by arguing that the passage refers both to Christ and to the humanity restored by Christ. In this way, the apostle's christological application of Ps 8:4–6 is true because all humanity has lost its excellence because of the Fall, but in Christ alone humankind is restored to its original excellence and enabled to participate in the dominion of Christ as members of his body.[63]

Next, Pareus brings forth the interpretations of four ancient expositors and three recent interpreters to demonstrate that Calvin is not alone in his application of Ps 8:4–6 to the excellence of humanity. He cites Basil's reading that Ps 8:4–6 concerns providence and the initial dignity of humanity and points out that both Chrysostom and Jerome assert that this passage speaks of humanity in general. As for recent interpreters, he indicates that Pellican applies the Psalm both to Christ and to all who participate in Christ and that Musculus emphasizes the contrast between the greatness of God and the insignificance of humanity and, yet, God exalts humanity. Most significant, Pareus appeals to the interpretation of Cornerus, a Lutheran, who argues that Ps 8:4–6 may be read literally concerning humanity and allegorically concerning Christ and his kingdom. How then, says Pareus, can Hunnius not blush when he casts these blasphemies upon Calvin?[64]

Next, Pareus addresses Hunnius's specific criticisms that Calvin interprets *Elohim* as "gods" rather than "angels," twists the scope of the passage to apply it to humanity in general, undermines apostolic exegesis, and hardly mentions Christ at all in his exegesis of Psalm 8. Concerning the first criticism, he points out that many other interpreters translate "*Elohim*" as "gods," including Luther's own affirmation that it can be understood as either "gods" or "angels." As for the second criticism, he simply refers the reader again to the proof of other exegetes on this matter. With regard to undermining apostolic exegesis, he concedes that in his Psalms commentary, Calvin applies this passage to the excellence of humanity; yet, he quickly points out that in his Hebrews commentary, Calvin follows the apostles' application of this passage to Christ's humiliation. How, asks Pareus, can the Holy Spirit speak in two such seemingly contradictory ways? The answer is that both concern the restoration brought by Christ. It is precisely the humiliation of Christ that brings about the restoration of humanity to its intended excellence.[65]

Furthermore, Pareus argues that Hunnius uses a logical fallacy in his contention that Ps 8:4–6 rightly applies to Christ *alone* and not more broadly to humanity because the apostle only applies this text to Christ. If one adheres to this principle of narrowly following the apostle's Old Testament applications, then one would have to reread such passages as Deut 30:14 and Ps 69:26. In Rom 10:8, Paul interprets Deut 30:14 concerning the gospel alone, but in Deuteronomy the whole of Moses' teaching—both law and gospel—is clearly meant. Thus, asks Pareus, does this mean that one should always understand the teaching of Moses as concerning gospel alone? Likewise, does the apostle's use of Ps 69:26 in Acts 1:20 to refer to Judas the traitor mean that this passage can be read *only* of Judas and not any others?[66] Finally, Pareus endorses Calvin's high regard for apostolic exegesis with a quotation from his comments on Matt 2:6:

> It ought always to be observed that whenever any proof from Scripture
> is quoted by the apostles, though they do not translate it word for word
> and sometimes depart widely from the language, yet it is applied
> correctly and appropriately to their subject. Let the reader always
> consider the purpose for which passages of Scripture are brought
> forward by the evangelists, so as not to stick too closely to the
> particular words, but to be satisfied with this that the evangelists never
> torture Scripture into a different meaning but apply it correctly in its
> native meaning.[67]

Pareus defends Calvin against Hunnius's attacks on his reading of Ps 110:1 in his last class of verses about passages that Calvin interprets concerning Christ alone but that Hunnius has falsely accused him of not doing. Pareus avows that Hunnius resorts to "attacking Calvin with specters," for he provides a long quotation in which Calvin clearly states that this Psalm concerns Christ alone. He buttresses his point by appealing also to Calvin's interpretation of the text concerning Christ alone in his commentary on Matthew (Matt 22:41–46). He chastises Hunnius for "fraudulently truncating" Calvin's interpretation and misrepresenting him through his evil sophistry. Moreover, Pareus asserts that Hunnius's accusation of judaizing against Calvin concerning Ps 110:1 does not stand, for when one reads Calvin's statement in its full context, one can see that his whole purpose is to contend against the Jews. Calvin repeatedly asserts that this Psalm speaks of Christ, and he does this, Pareus insists, specifically against the Jews.[68]

In sum, David Pareus uses several key tactics in his defense of Calvin's exegesis of these eight Psalms. First, he appeals to the understanding of simple and composite types to argue that most types are composite and require a careful preservation of the original historical referent. In this way, not only is it *not* wrong to read the simple and natural sense of these Psalms in relation to David or Solomon but also these very readings solidify their christological application. Second, Pareus repeatedly insists that Hunnius has misrepresented Calvin, particularly by the things he omits from Calvin's exegesis. Third, Pareus often appeals to Calvin's New Testament exegesis of the passages where these Psalms are quoted to show both Calvin's adherence to apostolic exegesis and the christological readings he gives. Fourth, Pareus garners many anti-Jewish statements in Calvin's exegesis of these texts to establish that far from judaizing intentions, Calvin endeavors to overthrow Jewish readings and make the foundations of Christian readings of these texts all the more secure.

Conclusions: The Judaizing Calvin?

No Christian wanted to be called a judaizer in the sixteenth century. As Jerome Friedman has pointed out, there was an immense growth in Christian Hebraica during the rise of Protestantism that led to conflicts among Christians concerning the usefulness of Jewish exegesis. Christian Hebraists were often attacked with the charge of judaizing, and a common method of defense against such allegations was to point to their own anti-Jewish statements and arguments against the Jews.[69] Amid Pareus's attempts to defend Calvin of the charge of judaizing is precisely his identification of several of Calvin's anti-Jewish statements and readings of portions of these Psalms over and against Jewish readings.

John Calvin is not usually identified as a Christian Hebraist, though he does make great use of the grammatical and lexical tools of Hebrew for his Old Testament exegesis. Most Christian Hebraists are identified by their explicit, positive use of Jewish exegesis—something that Calvin does not do, at least overtly. Still, Aegidius Hunnius is not to be fooled. Though Calvin does not openly use Jewish exegesis, this study has found that he is very much doing so and that his own exegetical principles lead him to interpret these Psalms with limited christological applications. The eclipsing of these christological readings and the lack of teachings concerning the Trinity and the two natures of Christ in Calvin's exegesis have not at all escaped Hunnius's notice. These warrant for him the charge of judaizing against Calvin.

The debate studied here is not unlike most academic debates, where the two parties talk at and across each other, with their own agendas, and often retranslate their opponent's views in a manner that serves their own cause. One can just imagine Hunnius's response to Pareus's defense, for Pareus completely redefines Hunnius's views by using his own trope of simple and composite types. Furthermore, Pareus has often failed to address the equally serious accusations that Calvin's exegesis does not teach the traditional doctrines of the two natures of Christ or the Trinity. In those two critical cases where Calvin so explicitly writes against apostolic exegesis (Ps 8:4 and Ps 16:10), Pareus does not actually defend Calvin's reading of the Psalms in his Psalms commentary but utilizes Calvin's New Testament commentaries (where these passages are quoted) as the more authoritative and accurate expression of his views.

This leads us to a valuable revelation. Pareus's defense of Calvin by appealing to the interpretation of these Psalms within his *New Testament* commentaries discloses a distinction that can be found between Calvin's Old Testament and New Testament exegesis. This study of Calvin's exegetical principles has already noted his concern for authorial intention as one of the criteria molding his more limited christological readings of the Psalms. Yet these christological readings emerge more prominently in his interpretation of these Psalms as they appear in the New Testament. Indeed, this is consistent with Calvin's concern for authorial intention. When Calvin reads these Psalms in their original literary context of the Old Testament, he reads them according to the *Psalmist's* intention, first and foremost. For him, with his emphasis on David as the exemplar of Protestant piety, this renders a reading that need not be explicitly christological in content. However, when he interprets the use of these Psalms by the New Testament authors in his New Testament commentaries, his concern is then more for the authorial intention of that New Testament author. Thus, Calvin renders a more robust christological application in keeping with apostolic intention.

This chapter has divulged the central place of Calvin's interpretation of this particular set of Psalms for Hunnius's charges against him. It also makes initial inroads in delineating the beginnings of a divide between Lutheran and Reformed principles of biblical interpretation and their relation to the prior exegetical tradition. Hunnius maintains the need for a stricter adherence to the antecedent exegetical tradition, though it should also be said that he appears to view this tradition as more monolithic than does Pareus. Luther affirms the efficacy of knowledge of the Hebrew language for exegesis but soundly rejects the merit of Christian employment of Jewish exegesis. Luther and Hunnius both insist that these Psalms should be read as literal prophecies of Christ's incarnation, passion, resurrection, ascension, and exaltation. Furthermore, they maintain that these Psalms contain clear teachings of the doctrines of Trinity and the two natures of Christ. Indeed, the study of Luther's and Hunnius's views on these Psalms reveals that a possible consequence of Lutheran tendencies to read these Psalms as literal prophecies of Christ's passion, crucifixion, resurrection, and ascension is the blatant and sometimes violent identification of Jews as the prototypical enemies of Christ and the church.[70]

Pareus, on the other hand, illustrates a Reformed fondness for the tool of typology and a commitment to the principle of simple and composite types. Much like Calvin, he emphasizes a more deeply critical stance toward the previous tradition's christological exegesis and sets forth principles to be followed to interpret rightly and more soundly an Old Testament passage concerning Christ.[71] Rather than reading these Psalms as literal prophecies of Christ, Calvin and Pareus both assert the need to affirm the simple and natural sense of these Psalms in relation to their original historical referent. Only then can one give a christological reading of the Psalm—a reading that is secondary because it must be first grounded in this very historical referent that is the Psalm's literal sense. Likewise, Pareus contends that Calvin upholds the traditional Christian doctrines of Trinity and the two natures of Christ, but just as christological exegesis needs a solid foundation (in the literal-historical sense of these Psalms), so do these doctrines need to be grounded upon irrefutable principles of exegesis.

Finally, this analysis underscores the use of the accusation of judaizing to undermine another confession or, at least, a confession's exegetical practices. Hunnius has deployed the accusation of judaizing against Calvin to reveal the dangers of his Reformed methods of interpretation and doctrinal teachings. Apparently, the accusation of judaizing is a very effective, debilitating tool in the sixteenth century, for above all, Pareus focuses his defense of Calvin against this charge of judaizing to show the soundness of Calvin's exegesis and of Reformed exegetical principles more broadly. Indeed, the very heart of Pareus's defense is that Calvin's exegetical practices are precisely aimed at providing more defensible Christian readings of the Old Testament—particularly against the Jews.

Is Hunnius right? Is Calvin a judaizer? Given Calvin's historical context, he certainly would have been dismayed at such a charge and would not have understood himself to be judaizing. Yet, Calvin really has done something fundamentally different with these traditionally messianic Psalms, even vitally different from the interpretations of an outright Christian Hebraist such as Martin Bucer. Though Bucer explicitly uses Jewish exegesis to undergird his historical readings of these Psalms, he also sustains the central place of their christological meaning and their doctrinal readings concerning Trinity and the two natures of Christ. Calvin may not be a judaizer, but it is certainly understandable that Hunnius sees in his exegesis significant departures from the antecedent Christian tradition and a challenge to the assumptions and principles of that tradition.

Conclusion

I conclude this study of these eight Psalms first with a suggestion for
further research and then, more centrally, with an attempt to place
Calvin and the significance of his exegesis within the history of Christian
biblical interpretation. I believe this study of these Psalms points
to an initial emergence of differing theological content and principles
of exegesis that in time begins to translate into defining aspects of
confessional identities. In other words, this analysis hints at the
significance of biblical exegesis in the formation of Protestant
confessional identities, though admittedly, it just makes tantalizing
suggestions to this effect and cannot prove this point within the scope
of the project. With this clearly said, I do want to explore just what
I think this study can begin to unearth concerning the role of biblical
exegesis in the formation of, specifically, the emerging distinctive
aspects of Lutheran and Reformed identities. Finally, I conclude with
an exploration of the significance of Calvin and his commentaries
within the larger history of Christian biblical exegesis that such as
study as this highlights.

Psalms Reading and Emerging Protestant Confessional Identities

This study of these eight Psalms raises some titillating suggestions
concerning the significance of biblical exegesis for the emergence

and formation of Protestant confessional identities. Scholarship on confessional formation and confessionalization has tended to neglect the centrality of the religious aspects and instead focus on the role of the state. John O'Malley shrewdly notes in his book *Trent and All That* the inadequacies of the confessionalization thesis in its overemphasis on the function of the state and its neglect of the role of religion. Likewise, other scholars of confessionalization, such as Bodo Nischan, also submit the need to return to religion as a centerpiece of these studies.[1] Thomas Brady points scholars of this history back to the works of Ernst Walter Zeeden, who was one of the initial founders of the concept of confessional formation. Brady argues that this field of study would benefit from a return to Zeeden's central attention to the religious life and practices of German Protestantism—both its enduring Catholic elements and departures.[2] I submit that a crucial task in returning to the importance of the religious aspects of confessional formation is the examination of the role of biblical exegesis in the development of Protestant confessional identities.[3] Indeed, the promotion of the authority of Scripture above that of the church—its leaders and tradition—is central to the larger Protestant confessional formation program. The biblical commentary was a key tool for the promotion of the authority of Scripture and, specifically, for the advancement of key Protestant teachings—first over and against the Roman Catholics and then over and against varying Protestant confessions.[4]

Protestant commentaries on the Psalms seemed to me to be a fruitful place to begin such an examination of the role of biblical exegesis in Protestant identity formation, given the vital use of Psalms not only for doctrinal instruction but also for practices of worship and the larger program of the cultivation of piety. In addition, I suspected that a study of Protestant readings of the Psalms would reveal significant disparities of exegetical method among different Protestant confessions—namely, when and where christological exegesis appears, definitions of the literal sense of the texts, use of typology, and employment of Jewish exegesis (or not). I was not disappointed in my search.[5] This study has shown that the vast majority of Christian medieval and late-medieval interpreters read this set of eight Psalms as literal prophecies of Christ's incarnation, crucifixion, resurrection, ascension, and kingdom. They also find within them key doctrinal teachings, particularly concerning the two natures of Christ and the Trinity. Secondarily, these expositors read these Psalms as prophecies of the church, in which Christ is the head and the church is the mystical body of Christ. Furthermore, these interpreters consistently identify the Jews as the enemies of Christ and the church. Finally, I have argued that one can note the trends of an increasing insistence upon christological readings of these Psalms as the only proper reading, as well as an increasingly emphatic assertion of these christological readings over and against Jewish historical readings.

Martin Luther and Martin Bucer both maintain key elements of this previous tradition, though Luther even more so than Bucer. They both maintain the primacy of the christological readings of these Psalms and the key doctrinal teachings of Trinity and the dual nature of Christ. Luther specifically stresses these Psalms as literal prophecies of Christ and offers the new, characteristically Lutheran emphases upon justification by faith alone, the distinction between law and gospel, and the use of his Jews-as-enemy reading strategy to depose Roman Catholic authority, teachings, and practices in favor of Protestant ones. Bucer's exegesis of these Psalms, on the other hand, reveals the emerging Reformed doctrinal emphases on the beneficence of God and election, the use of the Psalms to promote a program for the cultivation of true piety, and the exegetical tool of typology. Although Luther's later Psalm commentaries demonstrate that he, too, turns to greater use of the Psalms to give messages of comfort or give instruction in piety, this focus becomes the centerpiece of Bucer's exegesis. Thus, while Bucer retains these Psalms as literal prophecies of Christ, he equally, if not more so, places the experience of the church in these Psalms (which is also very much present in the antecedent tradition) and emphasizes their teachings concerning the restoration Christ brings to the church.

John Calvin appears to follow the lead of Martin Bucer, for he maintains Bucer's emphases upon the doctrines of God's beneficence and election, the use of these Psalms to cultivate true piety, and typological exegesis. Calvin, however, takes the course of Bucer's exegetical moves in a logical but different direction. He departs from reading these Psalms as literal prophecies of Christ and instead gives primacy to the experience of the church that he finds therein—an experience particularly located in the experience of David (rather than Christ). Calvin maintains a reading of these Psalms as prophecies of Christ mostly, if not only, when it is warranted by the royal elements of a Psalm (i.e., prophecies of Christ's kingdom).[6] In eclipsing the tradition of reading these Psalms as prophecies of Christ's incarnation, crucifixion, resurrection, and ascension, he also discards the use of these Psalms to teach Trinity and the two natures of Christ and the identification of the Jews as the enemies of Christ and the church. Instead, Calvin primarily employs these Psalms to promote his program for the cultivation of Protestant piety through the example of David and to teach, especially, the doctrine of God's providence. This is to say, Calvin advances a particularly Reformed reading that begins to help buttress an emerging Reformed confessional identity.

The debate between Aegidius Hunnius and David Pareus reveals the potential of ongoing and lasting effects from the use of biblical exegesis to maintain and promote certain confessional identities. Hunnius argues for an adherence to the primacy of the literal sense of these Psalms as literal prophecies of Christ and their uses to teach Trinity and the two natures of Christ. He maintains that he has the unquestioning support of Luther and the Christian exegetical tradition behind him. David Pareus, on the other hand, offers an extended defense of Reformed exegetical principles and readings—particularly the use of typology and the need to give christological readings that are defensible and based on clear exegetical principles (and not "allegory," with which he identifies Luther's interpretations).[7] Thus, the proper interpretation of these eight Psalms and Old Testament prophecy in general becomes an illuminating piece to begin to understand the potential role of biblical exegesis in confessional identity formation.

The Charge of Judaizing and Confessional Identity Formation

I have also argued that the accusation of judaizing was one of the polemical tools employed for purposes that include confessional identity formation in the sixteenth century.[8] In the case of Hunnius and Pareus, it was a device especially utilized by Lutherans to disparage and make suspect Reformed exegetical principles and readings of Scripture. Likewise, differing views on the usefulness of Jewish exegesis for Christian readings of the Psalms may very well be involved in the charge of judaizing. Martin Bucer overtly used Jewish exegesis to support his historical, typological readings of the Psalms and to buttress his doctrines of election and God's beneficence. To be clear, Luther was concerned about this use of Jewish exegesis by Bucer. Such concern may be seen in Luther's 1531 *Defense of the Translation of the Psalms*, where he wants his readers to understand that while he is aware of Jewish translations and interpretations, he does not at all feel compelled to follow them, nor does he find them helpful.[9] However, I agree with the argument set forth by Stephen G. Burnett that Luther's rejection of the usefulness of Jewish exegesis is not necessarily the key element that sets him apart from his Reformed counterparts.[10] Instead, Burnett points to Luther's conviction of the threat Jews and Jewish exegesis, in particular, pose to Christianity. As Burnett indicates, in his *Against the Sabbatarians*, Luther had already connected the upsurge of judaizing exegesis among Christians with efforts of actual Jews current in his day.[11] Thus, for Luther, the Jews continued to remain the archenemies of the church, now the Protestant church. Luther was not simply concerned about the use of Jewish exegesis among Christian expositors, but more clearly the use of it for what he deemed as judaizing purposes, purposes that he believed completely undermined the causes of the Reformation and Protestant (later, Lutheran) confessional identity.

Hence, although Luther is not exactly pleased with Bucer's use of Jewish exegesis, in the end he will have recognized that Bucer maintains the basic Christian readings of these Psalms in reference to prophecies of the salvation history through Christ, Trinity, and the two natures of Christ. Moreover, Bucer has done this while arguing against Jewish anti-Christian polemic, particularly polemic against christological readings and the doctrine of Trinity. The same, however, cannot be said of Calvin. From Lutheran eyes, Calvin's exegesis is more deeply and, indeed, more craftily a kind of judaizing exegesis, for it overturns the primacy of the christological readings and yet still claims to be giving a Christian reading for the church—a reading that suspiciously sounds very Jewish.

The debate of Hunnius and Pareus fruitfully demonstrates the use of the allegation of judaizing in the hands of a Lutheran against a Reformed church leader in order to promote confessional interests. I believe that part of Hunnius's charges of trickery and subterfuge against Calvin involves Calvin's veiled use of Jewish exegesis or, at least, his tendency to promote the very theological themes emphasized by particular Jewish exegetes, such as David Kimhi. And indeed, Pareus is at pains to prove that such Reformed techniques as typology and clear principles of christological exegesis are not giving credence to Jewish readings of these texts but actually strengthen Christian exegesis in the face of Jewish criticisms.

Two Protestant Schools of Exegesis?

This study confirms much of what has been written concerning the importance of Bucer for Calvin's theological and, I would add, exegetical development.[12] Scholars have pointed to their shared emphases on election, predestination, church discipline and structure, and the centrality of the Spirit for the foundation of the church.[13] Willem Van't Spijker particularly highlights the continuities of their thought concerning the church as the body of Christ and the manifestation of God's kingdom on earth. This includes their emphases on the cultivation of piety and the goal of shaping a Christian society.[14] My own study finds that Calvin very much shares many of Bucer's theological emphases and exegetical strategies. They both emphasize the doctrines of the beneficence of God and election found in these Psalms—to which Calvin specifically adds teachings of God's providence. They both strongly endorse the importance of historical readings of these Psalms through the method of typology. They both appeal to David as an example for Christians, and they both state a vital concern for keeping the plain sense of the text.

On the other hand, there are a couple of significant divergences between our two Reformed exegetes. Bucer uses Jewish exegesis explicitly to anchor the christological readings in the text's *historia*, whereas Calvin uses Jewish exegesis more subtly to give instruction to the Christian church through the example of David. Calvin and Bucer demonstrate very different uses of Jewish exegesis for significantly different purposes, at least when it comes to possible christological readings.[15] Although they agree on the use of typology to read these Psalms, even here there are important distinctions. Whereas Bucer's typological readings render both prophecies of Christ's earthly life (incarnation, crucifixion, resurrection, etc.), Christ's kingdom, and the church, Calvin's typological readings are mostly in reference to David as a type of the pious member of God's church. And almost all other typological readings pertain to Christ's kingdom alone, where David's kingdom foreshadows Christ's kingdom.

Furthermore, despite sharp distinctions between Luther and Bucer and between Luther and Calvin, there are also some significant correspondences between Luther and Bucer. Even as they differ radically about the value of Jewish exegesis, they both have similar goals in their interpretations of these Psalms. They both ultimately aim to set forth the christological readings of these Psalms as their true and proper interpretation, over and against Jewish readings that undermine these. Indeed, one can very well argue that despite Bucer's positive use of Jewish exegesis, his main intent is to use it to support these precise christological readings. Luther may not agree with Bucer's method, but his exegesis concurs with Bucer's intention to promote these christological readings. Furthermore, both Luther and Bucer maintain the usefulness of these Psalms to teach the doctrines of Trinity and the two natures of Christ and to encourage the downtrodden Protestant churches of their day.

Advocates of the existence of two Protestant schools of exegesis, usually regionally named as the Wittenberg School and the Basel-Strasbourg-Zurich School (or Rhenish School), argue that these two schools can be distinguished first and foremost by their views of Jewish exegesis and the different exegetical strategies they employ (literal-prophetic versus historical typology).[16] I propose through this work that perhaps a better way to understand these exegetical differences is not the existence of two actual schools of exegesis but, rather, the ties of exegetical practices to their corresponding confessions and, more specifically, the emerging use of exegetical practices to help define and distinguish confessional identities. This would help to explain the actual and significant differences between the various forms of Reformed confessions (Bucer versus Calvin versus Zwingli) rather than constraining them to fit within one school. Hence, this work adds voice to the cautions of such studies as those of Stephen G. Burnett and Barbara Pitkin when they warn that while common exegetical strategies can be regionally named, there remains exegetical variety between these regions—such as those represented by Bucer and Calvin—that cannot be ignored.[17]

Calvin in the History of Biblical Exegesis

I conclude with the three cumulating arguments of this book concerning Calvin's exegesis of these eight Psalms and his contributions to the history of Christian biblical exegesis. The first pertains to my depiction of the basically positive contribution Calvin's Old Testament exegesis can make to the history of Christian-Jewish relations. The second implicit argument in this book concerns Calvin's role in redefining the literal sense of Old Testament Scripture. Finally, I explore the question of the relationships of Calvin to precritical and modern exegesis. Though I place Calvin squarely within the precritical tradition, I argue that there is good reason to see in him the distant seeds of the principles of modern exegesis.

Calvin and the Role of Exegesis in Christian-Jewish Relations

Any astute reader will see that I have painted a picture of Calvin's exegesis that positions it in a more positive space concerning its implications for Christian-Jewish relations than the exegeses of the Christian antecedent tradition, Luther, and even Bucer. This is indeed my estimation, but it must also be stated with some clear provisos. First, I am not claiming that Calvin is not anti-Jewish.[18] It is clear that Calvin falls prey to many of the anti-Jewish views common among his Protestant and Roman Catholic contemporaries. Second, I am not alleging that it was Calvin's deliberate exegetical intention to set forth an exegesis of the Old Testament that may be viewed as kinder to Jews and Judaism; indeed, I do not believe this was one of his exegetical objectives. Finally, I am also not claiming that there are no problematic implications of Calvin's exegesis for Christian-Jewish relations. Calvin certainly holds to the principle of the fulfillment of the Old Testament by the New, which is viewed by many as a form of insurmountable supercessionism. Though I may not perceive it as "insurmountable," the problem is most certainly palpably present.

With these provisions clearly stated, I do believe that Calvin's exegesis offers a glimmer of hope within a rather bleak interpretative history when it comes to the matter of the treatment of Jews and Judaism in premodern Christian biblical exegesis. I certainly am not the first to see this. C. A. Pater argues that Calvin's theology is the least anti-Jewish "of the major classical theological systems."[19] Though Salo Baron notes Calvin's negative views of Jews and attacks on Jewish exegesis, he also discusses the ways that Calvin advanced positive views of the law, Jewish interpretations of the Ten Commandments, and principles of the separation of church and state that Baron deems as working to the eventual benefit of the Jews. Thus, Baron concludes that although Calvin may have set out to curse the Jews, "in the end [he] turned out to have blessed them."[20] Hans-Joachim Kraus goes as far as to claim that "one cannot accuse Calvin of being guilty of that ecclesiastical arrogance and pride toward Judaism [that] has everywhere been characteristic of the history of the church."[21]

My concern is not necessarily to argue one way or another about how anti-Jewish or not Calvin and his exegesis are in actuality. I am much more in agreement with the evenhanded views of Mary Potter Engel, who argues for the fundamental ambiguity of Calvin when it comes to the consequences of his exegesis for and views of Jews and Judaism. Engel demonstrates that Calvin has made both very positive statements and very negative statements concerning Jews and Judaism.[22] I am interested in proffering Calvin as one model of how to read the Old Testament (and not necessarily the New Testament)[23] that escapes most of the anti-Jewish tendencies of premodern Christian exegesis while simultaneously preserving a very Christian reading that maintains the premodern Christian convictions of the christological center and import of the Old Testament and the insistence that good exegesis aims to edify the church. At the end of this chapter I argue in detail about how Calvin's exegesis of the Old Testament may still be viewed as christological even as it eclipses prior traditional christological readings.

Calvin and the Literal Sense of Scripture

The heart of the debate between Hunnius and Pareus over Calvin's exegesis of the Old Testament, and specifically this set of eight Psalms, is over the identity of the literal sense of the text. Particularly for these Psalms that are cited by the New Testament in reference to Christ, there has been a long-standing Christian tradition of identifying their literal sense with their christological reading. This tradition has consistently viewed them as literal prophecies of Christ's incarnation, passion, resurrection, ascension, kingship, and kingdom. In other words, the plain, simple sense of each of these eight Psalms is the history and teachings about Christ that it conveys and prophesies. Thus, the literal sense of these prophecies is their fulfillment in Christ. Although many exegetes in the Christian tradition before and up until the time of Calvin have identified the literal sense of other Psalms not necessarily with their christological reading, this particular set of Psalms carries a remarkable agreement as literal prophecies of Christ even among such medieval proponents of historical exegesis as Nicholas of Lyra or the Victorine school.

In the history of Christian biblical exegesis, scholars have noted significant shifts in understandings of the "literal sense" of Scripture. These shifts include the move from the medieval fourfold sense to a more literal interpretation of Scripture in the work of Albert the Great and Thomas Aquinas, the redefining of the literal sense by Aquinas as that which the divine Author intends, the "double literal sense" introduced by Nicholas of Lyra, and the singular, completely spiritual literal sense espoused by Jacques Lefèvre d'Étaples.[24] Brevard Childs, echoing Hans Frei, identifies Luther and Calvin's contributions to this history as proffering an understanding of the literal sense that united the theological and grammatical senses of Scripture. Though he notes that there are differences between the ways in which Luther and Calvin accomplish this, Childs tends to gloss over just how great this difference is when he aligns Luther's uniting of the grammatical and the theological with Calvin's fusing of the historical and the theological.[25] Indeed, this study has demonstrated that it is precisely the question of history that is at issue here—more specifically, *which* history identifies the literal sense of the text. Is it the history of Christ that fulfills the prophecies of these texts? Or is it the history of the human author? Or is it some kind of combination of both?

I want to suggest that we see in Calvin's exegesis of these eight Psalms another significant shift in the understanding of the literal sense of Old Testament texts, particularly among Old Testament texts that have been traditionally viewed by Christian exegetes as literal prophecies of Christ. Naturally, this also has larger implications for Christian practices of christological exegesis of the Old Testament. Calvin very often identifies the literal sense of these Psalms with the historical life and experience of David or Solomon. Calvin is much more concerned with the human author's intention in these Psalms and identifies this intention less with David's (or Solomon's) prophetic experience and more with David's life experiences within his own historical context. Thus, frequently in these Psalms, Calvin hardly sees a prophecy of Christ at all—at least not prophecies of Christ's incarnation, passion, resurrection, and ascension.

Calvin's identification of the literal sense of Old Testament texts, such as these Psalms, with the human author's intention and original historical context has often been mistakenly applied to name him as a forerunner of the principles of modern historical criticism. The most obvious examples appear in the work of Philip Schaff and Frederic Farrar.[26] Schaff claims Calvin as the founder of modern exegesis, and Farrar points to Calvin's interpretation of messianic prophecy as particularly pioneering and applauds in Calvin's exegesis of traditional messianic prophecies the very things Hunnius despised:

> The most characteristic and original feature of his Commentaries is his anticipation of modern criticism in his views about Messianic prophecies. He saw that the words of psalmists and prophets, while they not only admit but demand "germinant and springing developments," were yet primarily applicable to the events and circumstances of their own days. The use of them by Evangelists and Apostles he regarded as ἐπεξεργάσιαι; as illustrative references; as skilful [sic] adaptations; as admissible transferences; as metaphoric allusions; as fair accommodations; as pious deflections.[27]

Similarly, Gerhard Ebeling has identified Protestantism's decision to follow the historical critical method as maintaining the concerns and decisions of the sixteenth-century Protestant reformers when he writes, "Wherever they [Protestants] made way for the critical historical method and, however grievous their errors, took it seriously as their task, there, if certainly often in a paradoxical way, they were really asserting the fundamental principle of the Reformers in the intellectual situation of the modern age."[28]

Calvin's Relationships to Precritical and Modern Exegesis

I entirely agree with those who refuse to allow the Protestant reformers—and Calvin in particular—to be co-opted by historical criticism or aligned with modern principles of exegesis.[29] Placing Calvin in the modern historical critical camp is mistaken on many fronts. It fails to take into strong enough consideration Calvin's assertion of the divine inspiration and self-authenticating quality of Scripture, his conviction of human depravity, his principle that meaning resides in the text itself (and not outside, under, behind, or beyond it), his practice of reading canonically, and his insistence that all biblical interpretation is focused on the goal of the edification of the church—namely, that the Christian biblical reader is always asked to move beyond the grammatical sense to theology, ethics, and a vision for the life of the church.[30]

Furthermore, it cannot be forgotten that there are clear places where Calvin does see prophecies of Christ in these Psalms, so that he does actually give several christological readings of them. These readings especially appear on passages prophesying Christ's kingdom. In such cases, there is an unmistakable principle of typology, where David acts as a type of Christ and where prophecies of the kingdom's expanse, eternity, and glory clearly are not fulfilled in the life and experience of David but only in Christ. Yet, even when Calvin appears to be much more concerned with the human author's intention in these Psalms and identifies this intention more with the life of David than its meaning explicitly concerning Christ, he does so specifically by unfolding David's function as a great Christian teacher and example for the church. The point is that Christ is not absent from even this reading. Calvin's reading concerning David as teacher and example for the church is founded upon his understanding of David both as a type of Christ and as a type of the church.[31] The former's christological focus is self-explanatory, but the second—David as a type of the church—is equally christological in content and focus because Calvin envisions the church as precisely the body of Christ.

Yet, it also cannot be denied that these very elements that modern exegetes have applauded in Calvin's exegesis are noted by someone like Hunnius as troubling because they do represent some kind of departure and change from what has come before. The change, as I have argued in this work, is not only a change in the identification of the literal sense of these Psalms but also a narrowing and sharpening of the principles and practices of christological interpretation of the Old Testament. Calvin ties the simple and natural reading of the text much closer to not only the grammatical reading of the text (i.e., what the words actually say) and its literary context (i.e., what comes before and after it in the broader context of Scripture) but also, even more important, to the historical context of the text—and by this Calvin does mean the human author's historical context and what the author intended in the text for the particular historical context in which the author writes. Calvin works with the conviction that the history or historical context of the human author is central to the text's meaning; thus his readings of these Psalms are grounded first and foremost in the history of David (or, in a few cases, Solomon).

In other words, Calvin wants a clearer and stronger role for the history of the human author in the definition of "literal sense." And this expresses itself in three basic ways. First, Hans Frei is right to argue that Calvin assumes a "natural coherence between literal and figural reading, and of the need of each for supplementation by the other."[32] Calvin may not see the literal sense of much of these Psalms as literal prophecies of the saving events of Christ's life, but he certainly gives *figural* readings of these Psalms in clear reference to Christ, and these figural readings are intimately related to their plain, simple sense that is understood in reference to the historical life and experience of David. David's life and experiences are used to point to the life of the church, the body of Christ, and also to some aspects of the life of Christ, particularly Christ as king. These figural readings, which are Calvin's expression of the christological readings of these Psalms, are deeply rooted in the history of the human author. Hence, Pareus is right to argue that these Psalms must apply to Christ only by reason of the sacred history within the type and not apart from it.[33]

But the central role of history in Calvin's readings of Scripture is not only because of his emphasis on the natural coherence and deep intimate tie between literal and figural readings but also because of his emphasis on authorial intention, by which Calvin does not simply mean the authorial intention of the Divine but also very much includes in this the *human* author's intention. The appeal to the human author's intention already appears in several places in Calvin's exegesis of these Psalms, and it famously appears in the dedicatory letter of his commentary on Romans to his friend Simon Gryneus. In this letter, he sets forth authorial intention as a crucial exegetical principle when he writes, "Since it is almost [the interpreter's] only task to unfold the mind of the writer whom he has undertaken to expound, he misses his mark, or at least strays outside his limits, by the extent to which he leads his readers away from the meaning of his author."[34] Hence, the import of this statement is that Calvin sees the rule of attending to authorial intention as an effective tool in setting a clear parameter for good exegesis.

It needs to be clarified that Calvin's emphasis on the human author's intention does not yield the same results as those of historical criticism. This is because Calvin never means exclusively the human author; it is always, for him, a consideration of the Divine intention expressed through the particularities, circumstances, and experiences of the human author. In other words, his principle of taking into account the human author's intention must be seen within his larger principle of accommodation and his overarching vision of divine providence.[35] Calvin's description of his doctrine of Scripture in the *Institutes* demonstrates that one of the crucial starting points is the understanding that *God* speaks in Scripture through the human authors.[36]

Yet, while it is God who ultimately speaks in Scripture, Calvin also describes Scripture as God's Word and revelation accommodated to human capacity. In God's essence, God is far beyond all human comprehension or perception; thus, God must accommodate God's Self to human capacity through revelation—one of the central acts of revelation being Scripture.[37] In the *Institutes*, Calvin explicates this principle of accommodation perhaps most clearly at the end of his section on the differences between the Old and New Testaments, where he explains why God would permit such differences:

> God ought not to be considered changeable merely because he
> accommodates diverse forms to different ages, as he knew would be
> expedient for each.... Thus, God's constancy shines forth in the fact
> that he taught the same doctrine in all ages, and has continued to

require the same worship of his name that he enjoined from the beginning. In the fact that he has changed the outward form and manner, he does not show himself subject to change. Rather, he has accommodated himself to men's capacity, which is varied and changeable.[38]

I imagine Calvin has much the same explanation concerning God's working through the human writers of Scripture and the apparent differing emphases or pictures of God they portray. God's constancy likewise shines through all of the various human authors in the biblical canon so that they always ultimately accomplish the purpose God intends.

Furthermore, the very particularities, circumstances, and experiences of the human author play an important role in their being vessels and instruments of God's Word. Calvin's vision of divine providence envisions a sovereign God whose perfect good will works sometimes "through an intermediary, sometimes without an intermediary, sometimes contrary to every intermediary."[39] The human authors of Scripture can be understood as intermediaries of God's revelation, Word, and intention. Calvin's arguments that God uses even the circumstances, personalities, and attributes of the ungodly to carry out God's purposes surely also applies to God using these very things in the godly![40] Thus, for Calvin, the distinct history and historical context of the human author are vital to the expression of God's accommodation and the accomplishment of God's intention through that particular author.

Finally, Calvin's insistence upon the human author's history as central to the literal sense of the text needs to be understood within the larger context of his understanding of the unity of the Old and New Testaments. Calvin's emphases in his conception of this unity are different from Luther's in important ways, which leads to some significant nuances between their thought. At the risk of a slight caricature of each, often it appears that for Luther the unity of the Old and New Testaments warrants the christological reading of Old Testament texts as their literal sense. On the other hand, it is precisely the unity of the Old and New Testaments for Calvin that leads him to find in the Old Testament author's particular history, experience, and context a message, teaching, or example for the church.[41] Both Luther and Calvin ultimately hold that both testaments narrate a single integral history—a history of how God acts in the world and brings salvation. Both would argue that Christ is the central figure of that history, and thus, both also claim that Christ is the content of all Scripture. Yet, again I want to argue that the nuances of their vision of this very history—salvation history—is exactly what is at stake. For Luther, salvation history is made up of the saving events of Christ's life: Christ's incarnation, passion, resurrection, and ascension. It is precisely these things, then, that Luther finds in certain Old Testament passages, particularly Old Testament prophecy. Of course, these events are also part of Calvin's understanding of salvation history, but even more principally, Calvin's vision of salvation history is framed first and foremost by a vision of divine providence—the unfolding of the great beneficent will of the sovereign absolutely good God in sacred history. Hence, when Calvin gives readings of these Psalms as teaching divine providence, the goodness of God, God's providential care of the elect and the church, and the great blessings God has bestowed upon humanity in general and the church in particular, he understands himself as maintaining the centrality of Christ, for Christ is central to divine providence and the very means by which God restores all good things to the church and, specifically, to the elect.

Thus, Calvin uses the centrality of the history of the human author to understand both the literal sense of Old Testament texts and the viable christological readings within them. Namely, the christological reading must have a clear and intimate tie with the basic plain, historical reading of the text, hence rendering typological or figural readings deeply tied to the literal sense. This is one of the clearest ways that Calvin has effectively limited the christological possibilities in the text. And this is rightfully understood within Calvin's larger program to restrict allegorical readings of Scripture.[42] The surprise, at least for me, in the study of this particular set of Psalms is how often and effectively Calvin has curtailed christological readings of *even these Psalms*, which are cited by the New Testament in reference to Christ and, as such, embody one of Calvin's rules for proper christological exegesis of the Old Testament.[43] If ever there is a warrant to give primacy to the christological reading of an Old Testament text, this would be it! Yet, in the end, Calvin's other principles of christological exegesis—namely authorial intention and retaining the simple and natural sense of the text—appear to be more determinate for him. Furthermore, his vision of salvation history as framed by divine providence enables his readings to be understood still as retaining the christological center of Scripture.

Ironically, Calvin's use of the literal sense as deeply tied to the history of the human author has been accused as judaizing by Hunnius, whereas Calvin precisely appeals to this use of history as providing a reading that is more defensible before Jews. Whenever I have read this explanation by Calvin, though (and I suspect Hunnius would agree), it seems to carry with it a kind of hollow echo that is not present when I read Martin Bucer making these same claims. I may be wrong, but I have come to suspect that Calvin uses the surrounding anti-Jewish climate of his day and concerns for defensible readings against Jews as a tool to further his actual program of liberating Christian exegesis from the practices of allegory. In other words, he argues for more stringent principles of interpretation, particularly in cases of christological or Trinitarian interpretations of the Old Testament, with the rationale of providing readings that are more defensible before Jews, when his real program is a more basic concern for what he deems are better Christian readings—readings that are in keeping with the grammatical reading of the text, the meaning of the verses that precede and follow it, and the larger narrative aim of Scripture. Yet, regardless of his actual intentions in delimiting christological readings of the Old Testament (which we can never be sure that we know rightly), Calvin emerges as a fascinating figure in the history of biblical exegesis precisely because, while he remains soundly within the precritical tradition, he foreshadows and embodies significant exegetical emphases— namely, focus on authorial intention, the importance of the human author's historical setting, and restrictions on christological exegesis of the Old Testament—that will later be taken up by different interpreters in different contexts with effectively different exegetical assumptions and outcomes.

Notes

INTRODUCTION

1. David Steinmetz, "The Superiority of Pre-Critical Exegesis," *Theology Today* 37 (1980): 27–38.

2. Here I name a few of the important books written by these authors concerning the significance of biblical exegesis in the Protestant Reformation. See John L. Thompson, *John Calvin and the Daughters of Sarah: Women in Regular and Exceptional Roles in the Exegesis of Calvin, His Predecessors, and His Contemporaries*, Travaux d'Humanisme et Renaissance 259 (Geneva: Librairie Droz, 1992); *Writing the Wrongs: Women of the Old Testament among Biblical Commentators*, Oxford Studies in Historical Theology (New York: Oxford University Press, 2001); and *Reading the Bible with the Dead: What You Can Learn from the History of Exegesis That You Can't Learn from Exegesis Alone* (Grand Rapids, MI: William B. Eerdmans, 2007). See also Susan Schreiner, *The Theater of His Glory: Nature and the Natural Order in the Thought of John Calvin* (Durham, NC: Labyrinth, 1991; repr., Grand Rapids, MI: Baker, 1995) and *Where Shall Wisdom Be Found? Calvin's Exegesis of Job from Medieval and Modern Perspectives* (Chicago: University of Chicago Press, 1994); Timothy J. Wengert, *Human Freedom, Christian Righteousness: Philip Melanchthon's Exegetical Dispute with Erasmus of Rotterdam*, Oxford Studies in Historical Theology (New York: Oxford University Press, 1998); Craig S. Farmer, *The Gospel of John in the Sixteenth Century: The Johannine Exegesis of Wolfgang Musculus*, Oxford Studies in Historical Theology (New York: Oxford University Press, 1997); Barbara Pitkin, *What Pure Eyes Could See: Calvin's Doctrine of Faith in Its Exegetical Context*, Oxford Studies in Historical Theology (New York: Oxford University Press, 1999); Irena Backus, *Reformation Readings of the Apocalypse: Geneva, Zurich and Wittenberg*, Oxford Studies in Historical Theology (New

York: Oxford University Press, 2000); Mickey Leland Mattox, *"Defender of the Most Holy Matriarchs": Martin Luther's Interpretation of the Women of Genesis in the* Enarrationes in Genesin, *1535–45* (Leiden: Brill, 2003); Beth Kreitzer, *Reforming Mary: Changing Images of the Virgin Mary in Lutheran Sermons of the Sixteenth Century,* Oxford Studies in Historical Theology (New York: Oxford University Press, 2004); and Raymond A. Blacketer, *The School of God: Pedagogy and Rhetoric in Calvin's Interpretation of Deuteronomy,* Studies in Early Modern Religious Reforms 3 (Dordrecht: Springer, 2006).

3. See, for examples, David C. Steinmetz, ed., *The Bible in the Sixteenth Century* (Durham, UK: Durham University Press, 1990); Richard A. Muller and John L. Thompson, eds., *Biblical Interpretation in the Era of the Reformation* (Grand Rapids, MI: William B. Eerdmans, 1996); Timothy J. Wengert and M. Patrick Graham, eds., *Philip Melanchthon (1497–1560) and the Commentary* (Sheffield: Sheffield Academic, 1997); Wim Janse and Barbara Pitkin, eds., *The Formation of Clerical and Confessional Identities in Early Modern Europe,* Dutch Review of Church History 85 (Leiden: Brill, 2005); and Kathy Ehrensperger and R. Ward Holder, eds., *Reformation Readings of Romans,* Romans through History and Cultures Series (New York: T&T Clark, 2008).

4. In addition to the volumes on Calvin's exegesis by Susan Schreiner, Barbara Pitkin, and Raymond Blacketer previously cited, see also T. H. L. Parker, *Calvin's New Testament Commentaries* (Louisville, KY: Westminster John Knox, 1993, 1st ed., 1971) and *Calvin's Old Testament Commentaries* (Edinburgh: T&T Clark, 1986; Louisville, KY: Westminster John Knox, 1993); Wulfert de Greef, *Calvijn en het Oude Testament* (Amsterdam: Ton Bolland, 1984); David L. Puckett, *John Calvin's Exegesis of the Old Testament,* Columbia Series in Reformed Theology (Louisville, KY: Westminster John Knox, 1995); Wilhelm H. Neuser, ed., *Calvinus Sacrae Scripturae Professor: Calvin as Confessor of Holy Scripture* (Grand Rapids, MI: William B. Eerdmans, 1994); and Donald K. McKim, ed., *Calvin and the Bible* (Cambridge: Cambridge University Press, 2006). These are only a select few in a very long list. Interestingly, Calvin has received the notice of scholars outside the field of sixteenth-century history. For example, Hans W. Frei paints Calvin as the quintessential biblical expositor in his classic text, *The Eclipse of Biblical Narrative: A Study in Eighteenth and Nineteenth Century Hermeneutics* (New Haven: Yale University Press, 1974), esp. 18–37. The biblical scholar Brevard S. Childs also lauds Calvin as a superior exegete. See his "The Sensus Literalis of Scripture: An Ancient and Modern Problem," in *Beitrage Zur Alttestamentlichen Theologie,* ed. Herbert Donner, Robert Hanhart, and Rudolf Smend (Göttingen: Vandenhoeck & Ruprecht, 1977), 80–87. Wesley A. Kort, as well, names Calvin's doctrine of Scripture as an excellent culmination of the scriptural reading practices preceding and contemporary to him, so that Kort uses Calvin to set forth both an understanding of the Bible as "Scripture" and a theory of reading. See *"Take, Read": Scripture, Textuality, and Cultural Practice* (University Park: Pennsylvania State University Press, 1996), esp. 14–36.

5. See Philip Schaff, "Calvin as a Commentator," *Presbyterian and Reformed Review* 3 (1892): 462–69; Frederic W. Farrar, *History of Interpretation* (Grand Rapids, MI: Baker Book House, 1961, reprint from 1886), 342–54; and Kember Fullerton, *Prophecy and Authority: A Study in the History of the Doctrine and Interpretation of Scripture* (New York: Macmillan, 1919), 133.

6. Richard A. Muller, "Biblical Interpretation in the Era of the Reformation: The View from the Middle Ages," in *Biblical Interpretation in the Era of the Reformation*, 3.

7. WA 10/1:99; CO 31: 15–20.

8. See R. Gerald Hobbs, "An Introduction to the Psalms Commentary of Martin Bucer" (PhD dissertation, University of Strasbourg, 1971), 77–100.

9. See, for examples, W. Stanford Reid, "The Battle Hymns of the Lord: Calvinist Psalmody of the Sixteenth Century," in *Sixteenth Century Essays and Studies*, ed. Carl S. Meyer (St. Louis: Foundation for Reformation Research, 1971), 2:36–54; and John D. Witvliet, "The Spirituality of the Psalter: Metrical Psalms in Liturgy and Life in Calvin's Geneva," in *Calvin and Spirituality/Calvin and His Contemporaries*, Calvin Studies Society Papers, 1995, 1997 (Grand Rapids, MI: CRC Product Services, 1998), 93–117. See also Édith Weber, "Le chant au service de la Réforme," in *Les deux réformes chrétiennes: Propagation et diffusion*, ed. Illana Zinguer and Myriam Yardeni, Studies in the History of Christian Traditions 114 (Leiden: Brill, 2004), 443–59; and Eckhard Grunewald, Henning P. Jürgens, and Jan R. Luth, eds., *Der Genfer Psalter und seine Rezeption in Deutschland, der Schweiz und den Niederlanden, 16–18. Jahrhundert*, Frühe Neuzeit 97 (Tübingen, 2004).

10. Acts 4:25–27 quotes Ps 2:1–2 in order to apply it to the persecution of Christ by Herod, Pilate, the Gentiles, and the Jews. Acts 13:32–33 quotes Ps 2:7 to argue for Jesus as the Son of God and the promised Messiah. Likewise, Heb 1:5 and Heb 5:5 quote Ps 2:7 for these same purposes. The author of the Gospel of Matthew also appears to be echoing Ps 2:1–6 in his account of King Herod's attempt to kill the Christ Child. See Matt 2:1–4. The author of the Gospel of Matthew explicitly quotes Ps 8:2 as Jesus' reply to the chief priests and scribes' rebuke of the children crying out concerning Jesus, "Hosanna to the Son of David." See Matt 21:15–16. Hebrews 2:6–10 quotes Ps 8:4–6 to apply it to the abasement and exaltation of Christ in his passion and resurrection and dominion. Acts 2:25–31 applies Ps 16:8–11 to Christ's resurrection. Likewise, Acts 13:34–39 quotes Ps 16:10 to argue that David prophesies Christ's resurrection for the forgiveness of sins. The parallels between the Gospel accounts of Christ's crucifixion and the descriptions in Psalm 22 are numerous, and I will not recount them here. Suffice it to say that two Gospel writers quote Ps 22:1 out of the mouth of Jesus as he hangs on the cross (Matt 27:46; Mk 15:34), and all of them describe the sufferings of Jesus in ways that clearly echo Psalm 22 (e.g., the mockery of Jesus, the dividing and bartering over Jesus' clothes). John 19:24–25 explicitly says that the soldiers' casting lots for Jesus' garments fulfills Ps 22:18. The author of Hebrews quotes Ps 22:22 concerning the incarnation of Christ (Heb 2:12). Hebrews 1:8–9 quotes Ps 45:6–7 concerning Christ's throne and kingdom. John 12:13 alludes to Ps 72:17–19 to apply it to Jesus' entry into Jerusalem and the inauguration of Jesus' reign. The Gospel of Matthew (21:9) also alludes to Ps 72:17–19 in its account of Jesus' entry into Jerusalem but more clearly cites Ps 118:25. The Gospel writers quote Ps 110:1 as Jesus' response to the Pharisees' question about whose son the Messiah is. See Matt 22:41–46, Mk 12:35–37, and Lk 20:41–44. Acts 2:34 and Heb 1:13 also quote Ps 110:1 to argue for the divinity of Christ and the identification of Christ as the promised Messiah. The author of Hebrews quotes Ps 110:4 multiples times to demonstrate the high priesthood of Christ and his divinity.

See Heb 5:6, 7:17, 7:21. Finally, the Gospel writers quote Ps 118:22 from the mouth of Jesus as a prophecy of the Jews' rejection of Jesus. See Matt 21:33–46, Mk 12:1–12, and Lk 20:9–19. The Apostle Peter also quotes Ps 118:22 as a prophecy of the Jews' rejection of Christ in Acts 4:11 and 1 Pet 2:7, and the Apostle Paul does the same in Rom 9:33.

11. These eight Psalms are most prominently applied in the New Testament as literal prophecies of Christ; however, they are not exhaustive. There are a few other Psalms that could have been included in this study. These include Ps 40:6 (quoted in Heb 10:5–6 to teach that Christ is the one, true, and final sacrifice), Ps 89:26 (alluded to in Heb 1:5 to teach Christ's relationship to God the Father), and Ps 68:18 (quoted in Eph 4:8 in reference to Christ's ascension).

12. For studies on the importance of Nicholas of Lyra for Martin Luther's biblical exegesis, see the conclusion of Skevington Wood's article, "Nicolas of Lyra," *Evangelical Quarterly* 33 (1961): 205. Wood argues that early on, Luther "had no liking for Lyra" but in later years came to appreciate Lyra's emphasis on the literal sense (205). On the other hand, in the introduction to his translation of Lyra's commentary on Song of Songs, James George Kiecker notes that in his lectures on Psalms, "Luther refers to Lyra several dozen times and by an overwhelming margin favorably" (*The Postilla of Nicholas of Lyra on the Song of Songs* [Milwaukee: Marquette University Press, 1998], 19). As to the importance of Lefèvre for Luther, see Guy Bedoulle's *Le Quincuplex Psalterium de Lefèvre d'Étaples: Un guide de lecture* (Genève: Droz, 1979), 226–40 and "Lefèvre d'Étaples et Luther: Une Recherche de Frontières (1517–1527)," *Revue de Théologie et de Philosophie* 63 (1983): 17–31. Heiko Oberman argues that Lefèvre was as much or more of an important source for Luther's *Dictata* than Lyra ("Biblical Exegesis: The Literal and the Spiritual Sense of Scripture," in *Forerunners of the Reformation: The Shape of Late Medieval Thought*, trans. Paul L. Nyhus [New York: Holt, Rinehart, & Winston, 1966], 291). Gerhard Ebeling also notes Luther's debt to both Lefèvre and Lyra and his criticisms of the latter ("Luthers Psalterdruck von Jahre 1513," *Zeitschrift für Theologie und Kirche* 50 [1953]: 43–99).

13. Beryl Smalley, *The Study of the Bible in the Middle Ages* (Notre Dame, IN: University of Notre Dame Press, 1964), 19.

14. Smalley, 19, 20, 18, 192–93.

15. Aegidius Hunnius, *Calvinus Iudiazans, hoc est: Iudaicae Glossae et Corruptelae, quibus Iohannes Calvinus illustrissima Scripturae sacrae Loca & Testamonia, de gloriosa Trinitate, Deitate Christi, & Spiritus Sancti, cum primis autem ascensione in caelos et sessione ad dextram Dei, detestandum in modum corrumpere no exhorruit. Addita est corruptelarum confutatio per Aegidium Hunnium* (Wittennberg, 1593). David Pareus, *Libri Duo: I. Calvinus Orthodoxus de Sacrosancta Trinitate: et de aeterna Christi Divinitate. II. Solida Expositio XXXIIX. Difficilimorum Scripturae Locorum et Oraculorum: et de recta ratione applicandi Oracula Prophetica ad Christum. Opposti Pseudocalvino Iudaizanti nuper a quodam emisso* (Neustadt: Matthaeus Harnisch, 1595). There are few detailed studies of this debate. Ken Schurb analyzes the debate on the single text of Gen 3:15. See "Sixteenth-Century Lutheran-Calvinist Conflict on the *Protevangelium*," *Concordia Theological Quarterly* 54 (1990): 25–47. David Steinmetz studies Hunnius's and Pareus's use of the Johannine passages in their debate in "The Judaizing Calvin," in *Die Patristik*

in der Bibelexegese des 16. Jahrhunderts, ed. David C. Steinmetz and Robert Kolb, Wolfenbütteler Forschungen, Band 85 (Wiesbaden: Harrassowitz, 1999), 135–45.

16. I realize and agree that the use of the term "judaizing" is offensive for our current context, especially when it is used as an insult. I sincerely apologize to any who are offended. I choose to retain the term because it is a word used in the history of Christian-Jewish relations that is difficult to substitute and because it is particularly used by Hunnius to accuse Calvin. When I use the word "judaizing," I employ it under the meaning that Hunnius gives it. Hunnius describes Calvin's exegesis as "judaizing" because he believes it eclipses—much like Jewish exegesis—the christological and Trinitarian teachings of Old Testament passages in favor of the plain, historical meaning of the human author. Of course, it is a Christian misrepresentation of Jewish exegesis to assume that it always reads these texts only in their historical sense or *peshat*.

17. The term *confessionalization* specifically focuses on the close cooperation of church and state in the process of confessional formation. *Confessional formation*—the term I use because of its broader connotations including but beyond church-state relations—refers to the process in which individual confessions became consolidated and integrated into particular societies. Key scholarship defining confessionalization and confessional formation in the sixteenth century include the following: Ernst Walter Zeeden, *Die Entstehung der Konfessionen: Grundlagen und Formen der Konfessionsbildung im Zeitalter der Glaubenskämpfe* (München: R. Oldenbourg, 1965); Wolfgang Reinhard and Heinz Schilling, eds., *Die Katholische Konfessionalisierung: Wissenschaftliches Symposion der Gesellschaft zur Herausgabe des Corpus Catholicorum und des Vereins für Reformationsgeschichte 1993* (Münster: Aschendorff, 1995); and Heinz Schilling, *Konfessionskonflikt und Staatsbildung: Eine Fallstudie über das Verhältnis von religiösem und sozialem Wandel in der Frühneuzeit am Beispiel der Grafschaft Lippe* (Gütersloh: Gütersloher Verlagshaus G. Mohn, 1981); "Die zweite Reformation," in his *Die reformierte Konfessionalisierung in Deutschland—Das Problem der "Zweiten Reformation"* (Gütersloh: Gütersloher Verlagshaus G. Mohn, 1986), 387–438; "Die Konfessionalisierung im Reich: Religiöser und gesellschaftlicher Wandel in Deutschland zwischen 1555 und 1620," *Historische Zeitschrift* 246 (1988): 1–45; and "Confessional Europe," in Thomas A. Brady Jr., Heiko A. Oberman, and James D. Tracy, eds., *Handbook of European History 1400–1600: Late Middle Ages, Renaissance and Reformation*, Vol 2: *Visions, Programs and Outcomes* (Leiden: Brill, 1996), 641–81.

18. See volume 85 in the Dutch Review of Church History series: *The Formation of Clerical and Confessional Identities in Early Modern Europe*. My deepest thanks to Barbara Pitkin and Wim Janse for inviting me to contribute to this volume and, thus, encouraging me to pursue an understanding of this project through the lens of confessional identity and confessional formation. This volume demonstrates the much-needed realization of the use of biblical interpretation and preaching as recently neglected tools for confessional formation and, more generally, the need to explore the social history of the Reformation and the history of theological thought as mixed and deeply related realities rather than separate ones.

19. For important case studies of Lutheran, Reformed, or Catholic confessional formation, see Lorna Jane Abray, *The People's Reformation: Magistrates, Clergy and*

Commons in Strasbourg, 1500–1598 (Oxford: Oxford University Press, 1985); Gerald Strauss, *Luther's House of Learning: Indoctrination of the Young in the German Reformation* (Baltimore: John Hopkins University Press, 1978); James D. Tracy, ed., *Luther and the Modern State in Germany* (Kirksville, MO: Sixteenth Century Journal Publishers, 1986); Hartmut Lehmann, *Pietismus und weltlich Ordnung in Württemberg vom 17. bis zum 20. Jahrhundert* (Stuttgart: Stuttgart W. Kohlhammer, 1969); Volker Press, *Calvinismus und Territorialstaat: Regierung und Zentralbehörden der Kurpfalz 1559–1619* (Stuttgart: E. Klett, 1970); and R. Po-Chia Hsia, *The World of Catholic Renewal, 1540–1770* (Cambridge: Cambridge University Press, 1998).

20. The literature on this subject is far too vast to recite here. Please see my selected bibliography at the end of the book for numerous key sources on this subject.

21. Pretty much any premodern Christian treatise concerning Jews and Judaism will be full of biblical citations and allusions. Just to name a few, see Justin Martyr's *Dialogue with Trypho*; John Chrysostom's "Homilies against the Jews," in *Patrologia Graeca* (Paris, Garnier, 1857–1866), 48:843–942; and Martin Luther's 1543 treatises *On the Jews and Their Lies* and *Von Schem Hamphorus und Vom Geschlecht Christi*.

22. One could claim a Christian reading of the Hebrew Bible and not necessarily have to denigrate others—in this case Jews and Judaism—by doing so.

23. To be clear, I am not arguing that Calvin is not anti-Jewish. I think that it is clear that he is and that he has not escaped the theological climate of his time. I do, however, think that much of his exegesis of the Old Testament offers some promising alternatives—especially where instead of depicting Jews as blind or faithless or as the crucifiers of Christ in these texts, he uses biblical Jews as positive examples for the church.

24. See also Mk 13:1–2.

25. See Parkes, *The Conflict of the Church and the Synagogue: A Study in the Origins of Antisemitism* (New York: Atheneum, 1969); Ruether, *Faith and Fratricide: The Theological Roots of Anti-Semitism* (New York: Seabury, 1979); and Siker, *Disinheriting the Jews: Abraham in Early Christian Controversy* (Louisville, KY: Westminster John Knox, 1991).

26. See Ex 32:9; 33:3, 5; 34:9.

27. In this passage in John 8, Jesus is cited as arguing that Jews—since they will not love and believe God's word given through him—are not the children of Abraham but, rather, of the devil, the father of lies.

28. The use of Jewish exegesis for the support of historical readings of the Psalms is not anything new, for it can be seen in the work of Andrew of St. Victor and Nicholas of Lyra. Yet, even these exegetes did not read these Psalms in reference to David's historical situation. This is discussed in more detail in chapter 1.

29. While there are many studies of Jewish and/or Protestant readings of the messianic Psalms, very few take the anti-Jewish polemic involved in Christian exegesis of the Psalms or the anti-Christian polemic involved in Jewish exegesis of the Psalms as a centerpiece of the study. One exception is U. F. Bauer, "Antijüdische Duetungen des ersten Psalms bei Luther und im neueren deutschen Protestantismus," *Communio Viatorum* 39 (1997): 101–19.

30. David Kimhi (1160–1235), also known as Radak, was a Jewish commentator and grammarian from Narbonne, Provence. He, along with Solomon ben Isaac (Rashi,

1040–1105) and Abraham ibn Ezra (1092/93–1167), tended to emphasize the importance of the historical context of the author and biblical text. For this reason, they were the three favorites to read among Christian Hebraists, as can be seen in the work of Nicholas of Lyra and among sixteenth-century Christian Hebraists.

1. MEDIEVAL AND LATE-MEDIEVAL INTERPRETERS: THE LEGACY OF LITERAL PROPHECIES OF CHRIST

1. See Aegidius Hunnius, *Calvinus Iudiazans, hoc est: Iudaicae Glossae et Corruptelae, quibus Iohannes Calvinus illustrissima Scripturae sacrae Loca & Testamonia, de gloriosa Trinitate, Deitate Christi, & Spiritus Sancti, cum primis autem ascensione in caelos et sessione ad dextram Dei, detestandum in modum corrumpere no exhorruit. Addita est corruptelarum confutatio per Aegidium Hunnium* (Wittennberg, 1593), 18, 30, 122, 128, 140, 145–46, 170, 175–76.

2. Hunnius, 6, 18, 22–23, 30, 32, 123–24, 131–34, 145–46, 150, 170–71, 180–89, 185.

3. Denis the Carthusian, *Commentarium in Psalmum*, in *Dionysii Opera Omnia* (Monstroli: Typis Cartusiae S. M. de Pratis, 1898), 5:415–16, 451–52, 488, 529; 6:1, 205, 499, 534.

4. Denis the Carthusian, 5:415.

5. Nicholas of Lyra, *In se continens glosam ordinarium cum expositione Lyre litterali et morali, necnon additionibus ac replici, super libros Job, Psalterium, Proverbiorum, Ecclesiasten, Cantica canticorum, Sapientie, Ecclesiasticum* (Basil: Froben & Petri, 1506), 88b, 96d, 105a–b, 113b, 149b, 186c, 251a, 260c. See, for example, Philip Krey's emphasis on Lyra as "famous for the literal and historical interpretation of the Bible" in "Many Readers but Few Followers: The Fate of Nicholas of Lyra's '*Apocalypse Commentary*' in the Hands of His Late-Medieval Admirers," *Church History* 64 (1995): 185. In fact, Lyra emphasizes the historical interpretation in reference to David for most Psalms; however, on this particular set of eight Psalms, he adamantly maintains their literal sense as literal prophecies of Christ. Theresa Gross-Diaz notes the particular challenge that the Book of Psalms poses for literal-historical exegesis in "What's a Good Soldier to Do? Scholarship and Revelation in the Postills on the Psalms," in *Nicholas of Lyra: The Senses of Scripture*, ed. Philip D. Krey and Lesley Smith (Leiden: Brill, 2000), 111–28, esp. 111. Gross-Diaz argues that Lyra resorts to the christological reading of a Psalm only when certain verses of that Psalm are cited by the New Testament in reference to Christ (127).

6. Lyra usually begins by briefly stating the Psalm's original historical setting and the historical readings of Jewish interpreters of a Psalm in reference to David, but he proceeds to argue that their primary reading is in reference to Christ. The exception is his comments on Psalm 118, where Lyra reads the first half in reference to David and the second half as literally concerning Christ. Nicholas of Lyra especially emphasizes the interpretation of Solomon ben Isaac, also known as Rashi. See the important study by Herman Hailperin on the use of Rashi by Christian interpreters and particularly his chapter on Nicholas of Lyra in *Rashi and the Christian Scholars* (Pittsburgh: University of Pittsburgh Press, 1963), 137–246. Although Hailperin notes that Lyra does not speak of Jewish corruption of many passages in the Psalms that Christian tradition typically finds (173), Jeremy Cohen in *The Friars and the Jews* (Ithaca, NY: Cornell University

Press, 1982) sees Lyra as the culmination of the anti-Judaic missionizing efforts of the school of Raymond Martini. See also the more recent work by Deeana Copeland Klepper, *The Insight of Unbelievers: Nicholas of Lyra and Christian Reading of Jewish Text in the Later Middle Ages* (Philadelphia: University of Pennsylvania Press, 2007).

7. See Jacques Lefèvre d'Étaples, *Quincuplex Psalterium*, 1513 edition (Genève: Librairie Droz, 1979), Aii, Aiii. Lefèvre argues this in the preface to his Psalms commentary. For an English translation of his preface, see Heiko A. Oberman, *Forerunners of the Reformation: The Shape of Late Medieval Thought* (New York: Holt, Rinehart, and Winston, 1966), 297–301. My placing of Lefèvre as a late-medieval interpreter involves a particular position on his relationship to Protestantism. Scholars have debated this topic. Some have hailed Lefèvre as the first French Protestant. See, for example, the very early work of Charles-Henri Graf, *Essai sur le Vie et les Écrits de Jacques Lefèvre d'Étaples* (Strasbourg: G. L. Schuler, Print, 1842). Others have emphasized him as a predecessor of Protestant reform, especially given his stress upon the centrality of Scripture and its availability in the vernacular. See, for example, the article by James Jordan, "Jacques Lefèvre d'Étaples: Principles and Practice of Reform at Meaux," in *Contemporary Reflections on the Medieval Christian Tradition: Essays in Honor of Ray C. Petry*, ed. George H. Shriver (Durham, NC: Duke University Press, 1974), 95–115. Guy Bedouelle argues that Lefèvre is a good precursor to Protestant reform, but not necessarily specifically Luther's or Zwingli's precursor. See "Lefèvre d'Étaples et ses disciples," *Bulletin de la Société de L'histoire du Protestantisme Français* 134 (1988): 669–72. Finally, some argue that Lefèvre is ultimately Catholic because he staunchly envisioned reform within the boundaries of the Catholic Church and saw schism as a greater evil than the evils within the church. See, for example, the article by M. Cecily Boulding, "Jacobus Faber Stapulensis, c 1460–1536—Forerunner of Vatican II," in *Opening the Scrolls: Essays in Catholic History in Honor of Godfrey Anstruther*, ed. Dominick Aidan Bellenger (Bath, UK: Downside Abbey, 1987), 27–49. My own view is that Lefèvre is an important predecessor to Protestant reform; however, he remains a Catholic who never embraced Protestantism. Furthermore, Lefèvre's views on Scripture are convincingly understood within the context of Renaissance humanism. This argument is nicely and concisely made in a review article critiquing Philip Hughes's alignment of Lefèvre with Protestantism. See Maxine B. Morel, "Jacques Lefèvre d'Étaples: A Review Article," *Iliff Review* 42 (1985): 43–48; and Philip Edcumbe Hughes, *Lefèvre: Pioneer of Ecclesiastical Renewal in France* (Grand Rapids, MI: Eerdmans, 1984). I place Lefèvre in this chapter, as well, because of his importance as a backdrop to Martin Luther.

8. *Biblia Latina cum Glossa Ordinaria*, facsimile reprint of the editio princeps, Adolph Rusch of Strassburg 1480–81 (Brepols: Turnhout, 1992), 2:459, 471, 478, 508, 509, 543, 598, 599. Denis the Carthusian, 5:415, 451, 485, 529; 6:2, 206, 499, 500, 501, 502, 534. Lefèvre, 3a, 10a, 20b, 33a, 69a, 104a, 163a, 170a.

9. *Glossa Ordinaria*, 459; Nicholas of Lyra, 88b–d, 89a; Denis the Carthusian, 5:415–16, 417–18; Lefèvre, 3a–3b.

10. *Glossa Ordinaria*, 465; Nicholas of Lyra, 96d, 97b, 97c; Denis the Carthusian, 5:451–52, 453–54; Lefèvre, 10a–10b.

11. *Glossa Ordinaria*, 471, 472; Nicholas of Lyra, 105b, 105d–106a; Denis the Carthusian, 5:485, 487–88; Lefèvre, 20b, 20b–21a.

12. Nicholas of Lyra, 105d; Denis the Carthusian, 5:487. However, the Gloss and Lefèvre prefer to interpret this as the temptations of the flesh. *Glossa Ordinaria*, 472; Lefèvre, 20b. Lyra also identifies the Jews with "those who hasten after another god" (Ps 16:4). See Nicholas of Lyra, 105b.

13. *Glossa Ordinaria*, 478; Denis the Carthusian, 5:529.

14. *Glossa Ordinaria*, 478, 479, 480; Nicholas of Lyra, 113b, 114a–d; Denis the Carthusian, 5:529–31, 532–33, 534–38; Lefèvre, 33a–33b.

15. *Glossa Ordinaria*, 509; Nicholas of Lyra, 149c–149d, 150a–150d, 151a; Denis the Carthusian, 6:1, 3–4, 7–10; Lefèvre, 69a–69b, 70a.

16. *Glossa Ordinaria*, 543–44; Nicholas of Lyra, 186c–d, 187a–d, 188a–c; Denis the Carthusian, 6:205, 207, 208–12; Lefèvre, 104a–105a.

17. *Glossa Ordinaria*, 598–99; Nicholas of Lyra, 251b, 251d, 252a, 252b, 251c; Denis the Carthusian, 6:499–505; Lefèvre, 163a.

18. *Glossa Ordinaria*, 606; Nicholas of Lyra, 261c–d; Denis the Carthusian, 6:538–40; Lefèvre, 170a–b. Lefèvre, however, does not interpret Ps 118:5–18 as concerning Christ's passion but as a promise to the church that Christ will help in its struggles against its enemies.

19. *Glossa Ordinaria*, 605, 606; Nicholas of Lyra, 260c, 261c–d, 261d, 262a–b; Denis the Carthusian, 6:534–40, 534, 536, 537, 539; Lefèvre, 170a–b.

20. Nicholas of Lyra, 88a–d, 89a.

21. Portions of Psalm 2 are quoted in Acts 4:25–26, Acts 13:33, Heb 1:5, and Heb 5:5. Hailperin makes these same observations concerning Lyra's interpretation of Psalm 2 in *Rashi and the Christian Scholars*, 176–79.

22. Nicholas of Lyra, 88b (emphasis added).

23. Nicholas of Lyra, 251b.

24. For example, Lyra writes on Psalm 22, "Noteworthy theologians have explained this psalm concerning David and his persecution by Saul . . . but it is the determination of the church that this psalm is explained *ad litteram* of Christ's passion and his divine liberation in the glory of the resurrection" (Nicholas of Lyra, 113b). Similarly, Lyra only discusses the original historical context of Psalm 72 in his treatment of the Psalm's title "of/for Solomon." He concludes, "Concerning the subject matter of this psalm, it seems to me that it is better understood not concerning the prosperity under the reign of Solomon but of the magis who brought gifts to Christ the king, which is seen in many places in this Psalm. These things are not accomplished concerning Solomon but only concerning Christ and his kingdom" (Nicholas of Lyra, 186c). See Hailperin's emphasis on Lyra's view of David as a prophet of the "highest grade" in *Rashi and the Christian Scholars*, 224, 228, 230–31.

25. Nicholas of Lyra, 105a, 186c, 186d, 187a–d, 188a–c, 149b–c.

26. Denis the Carthusian, 5:415.

27. Denis the Carthusian, 6:534. This is an assumption about Jewish exegesis that Denis and most of medieval Christian tradition make that is not necessarily always true.

28. Note that this is a circular argument. For readings of Denis in comparison with the exegesis of the Protestant reformers, see David C. Steinmetz: "Luther and the Drunkenness of Noah," "Luther and the Ascent of Jacob's Ladder," and "Luther and

Calvin on the Banks of the Jabbok," in *Luther in Context*, 2nd ed. (Grand Rapids, MI: Baker Academic, 2002); "Calvin and the Natural Knowledge of God," "Calvin and Tamar," and "Calvin and Isaiah" in *Calvin in Context* (New York: Oxford University Press, 1995), 23–39, 79–94, 95–109; "Calvin as Interpreter of Genesis," in *Calvinus Sincerious Religionis Vindex: Calvin as Protector of the Purer Religion*, ed. Wilhelm H. Neuser and Brian G. Armstrong, Sixteenth Century Essays and Studies 36 (Kirksville, MO: Sixteenth Century Journal, 1997), 53–66; and "John Calvin on Isaiah 6: A Problem in the History of Exegesis," *Interpretation* 36 (1982): 156–70.

29. The method of Jacques Lefèvre d'Étaples in his interpretation of the messianic Psalms is quite different from that of his predecessors. Lefèvre provides three parallel columns that give three Latin versions of each Psalm, portraying his concern for discovering the best translation. He then deals with the meaning of the title of each Psalm, provides a paraphrase of the Psalm along with his verse-by-verse interpretation, brings in the harmony of the Psalm's content and prophecies with the New Testament and other Old Testament prophecies, and concludes by addressing certain passages that are often debated among exegetes—to which Lefèvre gives his own preferred reading.

30. Lefèvre, 3b.

31. Lefèvre, 10a–10b. The other interpreters also draw this parallel: see *Glossa Ordinaria*, 465; Nicholas of Lyra, 97b; and Denis the Carthusian, 5:453. Bedouelle provides his own examination of Lefèvre's interpretation of Psalm 8 in his study of the *Quincuplex Psalterium* (*Le Quincuplex Psalterium de Lefèvre de'Étaples: Un guide de lecture*, 121–33) and points out the parallels Lefèvre makes between Psalm 8 and Phil 2:6–11 (127).

32. Lefèvre, 10b, 21a. Lefèvre also connects the prophecies of Ps 8:2–3 with Matt 21:15–16, Ps 33:6, and Is 40:12.

33. Lefèvre quotes Matt 27:46, 26:39, 27:39–40, 27:41–43, 26:59, and 27:35. The other Old Testament prophecies concerning Christ's suffering and crucifixion that he quotes include Ps 88:1, Ps 76:13, Ps 115:9, Ps 107:6, Is 41:14, Ps 108:25, Ps 72:6, Ps 142:4, Ps 54:3, Ps 109:2–3, Ps 40:12, Is 53:7, Zech 13:6, Ps 40:11, Ps 144:11, and Ps 35:17. See Lefèvre, 34a–34b. Concerning Psalm 110, Lefèvre cites Ps 45:6, Matt 7:28–29, and Acts 4:33 in support of the description of Christ's authority and power found in this Psalm, and he cites Is 9:6 and Is 7:14 in support of the virgin birth of Christ (Lefèvre, 163a–b).

34. Lefèvre, Aii; Oberman, *Forerunners*, 298.

35. Lefèvre in Oberman, *Forerunners*, 300.

36. Lefèvre in Oberman, *Forerunners*, 301.

37. Each of our interpreters, however, has differing methodologies and emphases. The Gloss mingles the christological and ecclesial readings, tends to have almost equal emphasis on the ecclesial readings of these Psalms as on their christological readings, and portrays a greater accent upon the messages of comfort found in these Psalms than the other commentators. Nicholas of Lyra and Denis the Carthusian provide two separate expositions of each Psalm—a literal exposition and a moral one. Lyra is less inclined than the Gloss to draw out messages of comfort for the church; Denis emphasizes the tropological reading of each Psalm, in which these Psalms may be read

concerning the individual, faithful Christian soul. Lefèvre aims for the one, literal, true sense intended by the Spirit, which is the christological reading; however, within this emphasis, he also finds prophecies concerning the church.

38. *Glossa Ordinaria*, 459; Nicholas of Lyra, 87d, 88d, 89a; Denis the Carthusian, 5:419; Lefèvre, 3b.

39. Nicholas of Lyra, 105b, 105d, 106a; Denis the Carthusian, 5:485, 488.

40. *Glossa Ordinaria*, 478–80; Nicholas of Lyra, 113d, 114b, 114d, 115b; Denis the Carthusian, 5:531; Lefèvre, 33a–b. The Gloss cites the statement of Augustine that Christ bears the weakness of the members of his body and "speaks for the sake of those who are members of his body and yet are afraid of death" (*Glossa Ordinaria*, 478–79, 479–80). Hence, the request that God "deliver my soul from the sword" (Ps 22:20) is Christ's request to save the church.

41. *Glossa Ordinaria*, 605, 606; Denis the Carthusian, 6:535–36, 542; Lefèvre, 170a–170b.

42. For example, on Psalm 8, see Nicholas of Lyra, 260d, 261b, 261d, 262b; Denis the Carthusian, 5:451, 455–56. Both Lyra and Denis write that the first half of Psalm 8 describes the church militant and the second half (from Ps 8:6, "you have given them dominion") describes the church triumphant (Nicholas of Lyra, 96d, 97b, 97c; Denis the Carthusian, 5:451, 453, 455–56). The Gloss also reads Psalm 8 as a description of the church; however, it describes the mixed nature of the church (*Glossa Ordinaria*, 465).

43. *Glossa Ordinaria*, 471, 472; Nicholas of Lyra, 106a; Denis the Carthusian, 5:489, 490.

44. Nicholas of Lyra, 251b, 251d, 252b; Denis the Carthusian, 6:501.

45. *Glossa Ordinaria*, 508, 509, 510; Nicholas of Lyra, 149b, 149d, 150b, 149c, 150b–c; Denis the Carthusian, 6:1, 7, 8; Lefèvre, 69a–b.

46. *Glossa Ordinaria*, 544, 543; Nicholas of Lyra, 186c, 186d, 187a; Denis the Carthusian, 6:212, 207; Lefèvre, 104a–105a. Furthermore, Lyra and Denis interpret Ps 72:15–16 as indicating the institution of the sacrament of Eucharist and other practices of the triumphant church (Nicholas of Lyra, 188b; Denis the Carthusian, 6:211). The Gloss reads Ps 72:15–16 concerning the authors of divine Scripture rather than concerning the Eucharist (*Glossa Ordinaria*, 544).

47. *Glossa Ordinaria*, 459, 480, 605. Thus, the Gloss concludes with a statement by Cassiodorus concerning the hope of salvation that Psalm 22 offers the church in its suffering: "This Psalm speaks of the Lord's passion and finds its end most of all in the hope of Christians so that they may know that they will be saved from suffering" (*Glossa Ordinaria*, 480).

48. Denis the Carthusian, 5:531, 536; there 531.

49. *Glossa Ordinaria*, 459, 472, 598, 605, 606. See Lyra, 149b, 149d, 150b, 188d, 187b, 188b.

50. The Gloss, Lyra, and Denis clearly maintain the tradition of seeing certain Psalms as providing particularly clear teachings of the two natures of Christ. For example, the Gloss often cites key statements by Cassiodorus, such as "this is the first Psalm to teach the two natures of Christ... this is the second Psalm to teach the two natures of Christ" and so on. Psalms 2, 8, 45, and 72 are precisely the first four Psalms

understood to contain the clearest teachings of the two natures of Christ. See *Glossa Ordinaria*, 459, 465, 508, 543. Psalms 16 and 22 are also seen as teaching the two natures; however, Cassiodorus names these even more so as particularly vivid prophecies of Christ's passion and resurrection. For example, see Denis the Carthusian, 5:417, 417–18.

51. *Glossa Ordinaria*, 465; Nicholas of Lyra, 97b, 97a; Denis the Carthusian, 5:452–54; Lefèvre, 10a, 10b, 11a. For these commentators, the "mouths of babes and sucklings" (Ps 8:2) also confess his divinity.

52. *Glossa Ordinaria*, 471, 472.

53. Nicholas of Lyra, 105d.

54. Denis the Carthusian, 5:485, 487.

55. Lefèvre, 20b.

56. *Glossa Ordinaria*, 478; Nicholas of Lyra, 113b–c; Denis the Carthusian, 5:529; Lefèvre, 34b.

57. However, while the Gloss and Denis focus upon the pictures of Christ's humanity contained in Psalm 22, both Lyra and Lefèvre maintain that clear depictions of Christ's divinity may also be found, especially in the latter half of the Psalm. See Nicholas of Lyra, 113d, 114c; Lefèvre, 33a, 34b.

58. Namely, this refers to God's promise of the Word made flesh. *Glossa Ordinaria*, 598–99.

59. Nicholas of Lyra, 251b–c, 252b.

60. Denis the Carthusian, 6:499, 500. Yet, Denis adds that this also can be understood of Christ's humanity in that Christ's body ascends to the right hand of God.

61. Lefèvre, 163a. See *Glossa Ordinaria*, 606; Nicholas of Lyra, 262b, 261d.

62. *Glossa Ordinaria*, 508. The Gloss is citing the teaching of Cassiodorus here. Lyra, Denis, and Lefèvre all maintain this tradition. See Nicholas of Lyra, 149c–d; Denis the Carthusian, 6:3; Lefèvre, 69a–b, 70a.

63. Nicholas of Lyra, 150a–b; Denis the Carthusian, 6:7–8.

64. *Glossa Ordinaria*, 543–44; Nicholas of Lyra, 186d, 187a, 188b; Denis the Carthusian, 6:207. For example, according to Denis, the request of Ps 72:1 ("Give the king your justice, O God") is a request made by Christ in his humanity.

65. *Glossa Ordinaria*, 543; Nicholas of Lyra, 187a–b; Denis the Carthusian, 6:207. However, Lyra is less clear that the "moon" indicates Christ's humanity. He also sees the "moon" as indicating Christ's divinity.

66. *Glossa Ordinaria*, 459; Nicholas of Lyra, 88d; Denis the Carthusian, 5:419; Lefèvre, 3a–3b. Denis the Carthusian, more than any of the other interpreters considered here, exhibits a profound emphasis on the doctrine of the Trinity. He very often depicts God as Trinity throughout a whole Psalm so that it is the "whole most blessed Trinity" that is ultimately the actor within it. For example, for Denis, the whole Trinity judges those who revolt against Christ (Ps 2:4–5). See Denis the Carthusian, 5:416–17.

67. *Glossa Ordinaria*, 465; Lefèvre, 10a, 11a; Denis the Carthusian, 5:452. Denis sees the whole Trinity working in this Psalm as well. For example, the whole Trinity gives dominion to Christ (Ps 8:6–8).

68. Denis the Carthusian, 5:487; Lefèvre, 10a, 11a, 20b, 21a. Here Lefèvre quotes from the Gospel of John that God has "given all things into his [Christ's] hands" (Jn 13:3) and "all that the Father has is mine" (Jn 16:15).

69. Nicholas of Lyra, 115a; Denis the Carthusian, 5:529, 531–32; Lefèvre, 33a. Nicholas of Lyra specifically points to Ps 22:26 as a word that Christ the Son directs to the Father. Denis, especially, wants the reader to understand that Christ's cry "why have you forsaken me" (Ps 22:1) cannot mean that God has departed from Christ, for "neither the personal union of the Word nor the blessed delight of the mind of God did he [Christ] lose" (Denis the Carthusian, 5:530).

70. *Glossa Ordinaria*, 508; Denis the Carthusian, 6:1–2; Lefèvre, 69a, 70a. The Gloss also sees a distinction of the persons of the Trinity in the expression "therefore God, your God" of Ps 45:7 that points to God the Father and God the Son (*Glossa Ordinaria*, 509). Again, Denis finds even more Trinitarian overtones in Psalm 45. According to Denis, "I speak my words to the king" (Ps 45:1) is God the Father speaking to Christ the king (Denis the Carthusian, 6:1–2, 2), and the beauty of Christ expressed in Ps 45:2 is not only a bodily beauty but also a divine, uncreated beauty grounded in Christ's coeternity with the Father (Denis the Carthusian, 6:3).

71. *Glossa Ordinaria*, 543, 544; Nicholas of Lyra, 186d, 187a, 187b; Denis the Carthusian, 6:206, 211; Lefèvre, 105b.

72. *Glossa Ordinaria*, 598, 599; Nicholas of Lyra, 251b–d; Denis the Carthusian, 6:499–500, 501–502; 163b; Lefèvre, 163a.

73. *Glossa Ordinaria*, 479, 599; Nicholas of Lyra, 113d, 251d; Denis the Carthusian, 5:533; Lefèvre, 33b, 163a–b. There are a few other isolated places where particular interpreters find allusions to the virgin birth. For example, Nicholas of Lyra also sees a reference to the Virgin Mary as the moon in Ps 72:5 ("May he live while the sun endures and as long as the moon") and a reference to Christ's humanity as one who is "born of a virgin" in Ps 8:4 ("son of man"). See Nicholas of Lyra, 187b, 97b. The application of Ps 72:5 to the Virgin Mary does not appear in the Gloss, nor does the specific mention on Ps 8:4 that Christ is born of a virgin; however, the Gloss sees the virgin birth in Ps 22:6 ("But I am a worm") and Ps 45:4 ("Come forth")—readings that do not appear in Lyra. Denis finds teachings concerning the virgin birth in other portions of these Psalms not found by our other interpreters. For example, he argues that the beauty of Christ expressed in Ps 45:2 includes an account of Christ's human beauty—a beauty based upon the fact that the body of Christ "was chosen from the most beautiful material, namely from the cleanest blood of the most dignified Virgin" (Denis the Carthusian, 6:3).

74. *Glossa Ordinaria*, 509; Denis the Carthusian, 6:5–6.

75. *Glossa Ordinaria*, 543; Nicholas of Lyra, 187b; Denis the Carthusian, 6:208; Lefèvre, 104b–105a.

76. *Glossa Ordinaria*, 543.

77. Denis the Carthusian, 5:533. Scholars have noted the importance of Mary for Denis; doctrines concerning Mary's perpetual virginity and status as coredemptrix reach their height during Denis's day.

78. Denis the Carthusian, 6:500 (emphasis added).

79. Denis the Carthusian, 6:1, 11, there 11. Denis goes on to apply the rest of Ps 45:9–15 to Mary. Lefèvre also reiterates the interpretation of the Psalm 45 concerning Christ and the Virgin. See Lefèvre, 69a.

80. *Glossa Ordinaria*, 480; Nicholas of Lyra, 115a, 115b; Denis the Carthusian, 5:537–38, 538, 543; Lefèvre, 33a–b.

81. *Glossa Ordinaria*, 599, 606; Nicholas of Lyra, 252a, 262a, 261c–d; Denis the Carthusian, 6:503, 593; Lefèvre, 163a, 170b.

82. Nicholas of Lyra, 188b; Denis the Carthusian, 6:211; Lefèvre, 105a. The Gloss, however, does not see the ties to the Eucharist in Ps 72:16.

83. Except, as already noted, he does read the first half of Psalm 118 in reference to David.

2. MARTIN LUTHER: LITERAL PROPHECIES REDEPLOYED

Many of Luther's commentaries on the Psalms are translated into English in the Concordia Publishing House's volumes of *Luther's Works*. Several of my quotations of Luther on the Psalms are based on the translations provided in these volumes and often slightly edited, based on my reference to the original Latin and in order to modernize the language. A number of Luther's commentaries on the Psalms are not translated in the volumes of *Luther's Works*, particularly his *Operationes in Psalmos* (except for Psalm 2, which can be found in *Luther's Works* 14:313–49) and also a handful of his commentaries or sermons on single Psalms. All translations from these sources are my own.

1. Though, in doing so, Luther recognized that this might at times undermine faithfulness to the Hebrew source. See WA 38:9–17.

2. Heinrich Bornkamm, *Luther and the Old Testament*, trans. Eric W. Gritsch and Ruth C. Gritsch (Mifflintown, PA: Sigler, 1997), 7–8. Martin Brecht also comments on the centrality of the Psalms for Luther's life and work. See *Martin Luther: Shaping and Defining the Reformation, 1521–1532*, trans. James L. Schaaf (Minneapolis: Fortress, 1990), 380.

3. WA 10/1: 99.

4. WA 40/2:195, 45:207, and 40/2:586.

5. WA 41:79.

6. WA 31/1:66. Luther comments only once, and briefly, on Psalm 72, so it plays almost no role in my analysis of Luther's interpretation of the messianic Psalms.

7. Interestingly enough, there are no comments recorded in the *Dictata* on Psalm 22. Of course, *Operationes in Psalmos* covers only Psalms 2, 8, 16, and 22 (and not Psalms 45, 72, 110, 118). There is, however, a commentary on Psalm 110 written in 1518. See WA 1:689–710 and 9:180–202. The 1530s sermons and commentaries include the following: a commentary on Psalm 2 in spring/early summer of 1532, a sermon on Psalm 8 in November of 1535, a commentary on Psalm 45 in 1532, a commentary based on eight sermons on Psalm 110 in May/June of 1535, and a commentary on Psalm 118 in the summer of 1530. This leaves Psalm 16 without comment in the 1530s.

8. I found only one instance where Luther used typology: in *Operationes in Psalmos* on Ps 2:3, Luther parallels David's experience with Saul with Christ's experience with the Jews (WA 5:52). There are two exceptions in his exegesis of the messianic Psalms, where Luther does make reference to David's historical context, both of which appear in his exegesis of Psalm 118. In Luther's comments on Ps 118:2, he writes that David is thanking God for his kingdom and recognizing that temporal government is a gift from God (WA 31/1:77–78). In his comments on Ps 118:10–13, Luther says that David is writing about himself and his own people (WA 31/1:115–16).

9. See WA 45:233, 237, 239 and 41:80–81. Contrary to prior studies of Luther's exegesis that argue that in Luther one finds a "new" hermeneutic that is far more different from the antecedent tradition than similar, this study of at least these Psalms finds much more agreement in Luther with the antecedent tradition than dissonance. Gerhard Ebeling wrote an article, "Die Anfänge von Luthers Hermeneutik" (*Die Zeitschrift für Theologie und Kirche* 48 [1951]: 172–230), that argues that Luther developed a "new" hermeneutic during the years of 1516–1519—a hermeneutic that had been in the process of formation during his first lectures on the Psalms (1513–1515). Ebeling defines this new hermeneutic as reading Scripture through the lens of existential struggle and with the tool of antithesis or dualism (e.g., letter versus spirit or law versus gospel). He goes on to argue that Luther's new exegesis is a "disruptive force" to the prior tradition. See the three-part series of the English translation of this essay: "The Beginnings of Luther's Hermeneutics," *Lutheran Quarterly* 7 (1993): 129–58, 315–38, 451–68, esp. 130, 133, 317, 452. In a later article, "The New Hermeneutics and the Early Luther" (*Theology Today* 21 [1964]: 34–46), he also emphasizes Luther's departure from prior tradition, by which he means primarily scholasticism. My question is the following: Is not this departure actually in many ways a return to an earlier Christian tradition rather than a "new" hermeutic? Not only does Ebeling emphasize the discontinuity of Luther's exegesis with the prior exegetical tradition but also he argues that for Luther the relationship of the Old and New Testaments is one of antithesis so that the Old Testament is always a shadow or figure of the New Testament ("The Beginnings of Luther's Hermeneutics," 329–31). James Preus agrees with Ebeling and develops this argument further ("Old Testament *Promissio* and Luther's New Hermeneutic," *Harvard Theological Review* 69 [1967]: 145–61). See also his book *From Shadow to Promise: Old Testament Interpretation from Augustine to the Young Luther* (Cambridge: Harvard University Press, 1969). Later in this chapter, I more explicitly challenge such readings of Luther—at least when it comes to this particular set of Psalms.

10. On Psalm 2: WA 3:32, 33–34; WA 5:47–51, 53–54, 56–57, 58–59, 60–61, 67, 72–73; WA 40/2:196–97, 237–38, 242–43, 260–62, 276–77, 285–86, 304–305. On Psalm 8: WA 3:81–82; WA 5:249, 253, 254, 271–72, 273–74, 277, 284; WA 45:206–207, 213–14, 216–17, 229–30, 237, 239–49. On Psalm 110: WA 4:229, 230, 232–35; WA 41:79–80, 82–84, 86–93, 107–108, 122–23, 131–32. On Ps 110:4: WA 4:234–35; WA 41:167–68, 174–75, 186–87, 187–89, 190–91. On Psalm 22: WA 5:598–672. On Psalm 16: WA 3:104, 105; WA 5:443, 445–46, 456, 461–63, 464, 466. On Psalm 45: WA 3:253; WA 40/2:479.

11. WA 3:467; WA 4:233.

12. WA 5:51, 61, 70. Luther writes, "Again you see that the rule of Christ is not one that he has arrogantly assumed, but that it was established by the command and authority of the Father" (WA 5:61).

13. WA 5:251–52, 275–76, 456, and 465. Luther interprets the "inheritance" in Ps 16:6 as Christ receiving everything from the Father.

14. WA 40/2:196. Likewise, Luther concludes with an affirmation of Psalm 2's teachings concerning the dual natures of Christ and Trinity: "Now, then, you have the chief articles of our faith set forth in this psalm, who and what sort of king Christ is, namely, begotten of the Father from eternity and set upon Mount Zion; then, what his kingdom is like, namely, that he is a teacher beyond the Law and Moses" (WA 40/2: 258).

15. Luther writes, "Thus the Holy Spirit through the prophet David instructs us in this Psalm by short, clear words about the following topics: the two natures of Christ so united in a single undivided person; Christ's dominion and kingdom . . . the glory and renewal of creation; Christ's humiliation, suffering, death; Christ's resurrection, exaltation, and glorification . . . . In a fine and happy way this Psalm proves these sublime doctrines with simple and short words" (WA 45:249).

16. WA 45:207–208, 230.

17. For examples, see WA 40/2:483–85, 515–17, 585–89; WA 41:79–80, 89; WA 31/1:179–80. He also praises Psalm 110, especially, as giving one of the clearest and most powerful descriptions of Christ's person in the Old Testament, providing teaching concerning the kingship and priesthood of Christ. See WA 41:79–80, 88–89, 194–195.

18. WA 4:234. See also WA 41:144, 159. Luther maintains some of the medieval readings of parts of these Psalms concerning the virgin birth of Christ. The typical passages that evoke comments on the virgin birth are Ps 22:9–10, Ps 45:4, Ps 72:6, and Ps 110:3. Luther does give a brief mention of the virgin birth in his interpretation of Ps 22:9–10 in his *Operationes* (WA 5:624); however, his focus is on the birth of the church (WA 5:624–26). Psalm 45:6 does not evoke for him a mention of the virgin birth; and he briefly mentions the readings of Lyra and Cassiodorus concerning the virgin birth in his comments on Ps 72:6 in the *Dictata* (WA 3:468). Although Luther interprets Ps 110:3 concerning both the virgin birth of Christ and the birth of the church in the *Dictata* (WA 4:234), he applies this to only the birth of the church in his later 1535 commentary on Psalm 110 (WA 41:158–67).

19. On Psalm 2: WA 3:33; WA 5:52, 55; WA 40/2:205, 217, 233, 270, 282, 300–301, 305, 309. On Psalm 8: WA 3:82; WA 5:280, 281; WA 45:213–14. On Psalm 16: WA 3:105–108; WA 5:445, 447, 449, 452–53. On Psalm 22: WA 5:620–21, 627, 628–29, 632. On Psalm 45: WA 3:257–58; WA 40/2:483, 563–74. On Psalm 110: WA 4:230, 231, 235; WA 41:112–13, 144–45, 161, 226. On Psalm 118: WA 4:279–80, 280; WA 31/1:103–104, 164, 168, 171, 172.

20. Luther, however, adds the emphasis of the Jews' wrong reliance upon the law and works-righteousness much more than the antecedent exegetical tradition of these Psalms. This added emphasis will be shown to be part of his larger concern to use these Psalms to teach the doctrine of justification by faith alone.

21. WA 3:34; 4:279, 279–80.

22. WA 5:50, 52–53, 74, 270–72, 274, 612–13, 660–61.

23. WA 40/2:196–97, 199, 201–202, 205–206, 227–29, 228, 266–67, 276, 312, 498–99, 506–507, 511–12; WA 41:144, 223–24, 227–30; WA 31/1:137–39, 145, 146–47, 149–50, 153–55, 154. Especially look at Luther's comments on Ps 2:1, 2, 5, 9, 11; Ps 45:3–5; Ps 110:3, 5–6; and Ps 118:15–18. Luther writes that one can find a rule that "whenever in the Psalter and Holy Scripture the saints deal with God concerning comfort and help in their need, eternal life and resurrection of the dead are involved" (WA 31/1:154). Furthermore, according to Luther, the "rule over consciences" is part of Christ's office as king (WA 40/2:242–43). Likewise, the oath the Lord swears in Ps 110:1 "serves to strengthen and comfort poor and disturbed consciences" (WA 41:473). Finally, not only is Christ's office as king one of comfort but also even more so is his office as priest (WA 41:192).

24. Eric Gritsch, "The Cultural Context of Luther's Interpretation," *Interpretation* 37 (1983): 266–67. See also Luther's own statement on this hermeneutical principle (WA 16:385). Luther writes, "You must keep your eye on the word that applies to you."

25. The other verses written on the walls were Ps 1:6 and Ps 74:21. See Martin Brecht, *Martin Luther: Shaping and Defining the Reformation*, 372, 376, 391–93. Luther writes concerning Psalm 118: "Although the entire Psalter and all of Holy Scripture are dear to me as my only comfort and source of life, I fell in love with this Psalm especially. Therefore I call it my own. When emperors and kings, the wise and the learned, and even saints could not aid me, this Psalm proved a friend and helped me out of many great troubles. As a result, it is dearer to me than all the wealth, honor, and power of the pope, the Turk, and the emperor. I would be most unwilling to trade this Psalm for all of it" (WA 31:66).

26. WA 40/2:196, 248, 259–60. Similarly, Luther writes that Ps 2:10 teaches that while the law is good, it does not extend to salvation (WA 40/2:278). We will see in the next chapter that Martin Bucer also uses Psalm 2 to teach about the true nature of faith.

27. WA 40/2:472, 481.

28. See WA 40/2:482–83, 488–93, 563–67. Luther consistently contrasts Christ's way of righteousness over and against Moses and the law, particularly in his explanation of Ps 45:2 ("You are the most handsome of men" and "grace is poured upon your lips") and Ps 45:10 ("forget your people and your father's house").

29. WA 31/1:114. Luther uses Ps 118:5 to give a definition of faith. See WA 31:96.

30. WABr 5:435–36. Luther quotes Ps 118:22 in his reply.

31. WA 3:82.

32. WA 3:254.

33. WA 3:82, 256, 258, 107–108. This view of the twofold sense of Scripture is based on a longer explanation of the "cup of pure wine" in Ps 74:8, where the dregs are the letter and the pure wine is the spirit.

34. WA 4:280. Herein, we may very well find an important clue to Luther's lack of the use of typology in his exegesis of the Psalms. "Why would one need the type, the figure or shadow, when the clear, spiritual reading is already manifest?" asks Luther. Indicating another important reason that Luther is not interested in David as a type of Christ, he writes that he will not expound on the prophet David himself or his life

because David is the very mouthpiece of Christ, so that *Christ's* words are actually spoken by David. See Luther's preface to the scholia (WA 3:15).

35. See Heiko Oberman, "Biblical Exegesis: The Literal and the Spiritual Sense of Scripture," in *Forerunners of the Reformation: The Shape of Late Medieval Thought*, trans. Paul L. Nyhus (New York: Holt, Rinehart, and Winston, 1966), 281–96, esp. 290–91. One can see a growing appreciation of the literal sense in Luther's exegesis in his increasing attention to the biblical text's historical setting. Even between the *Dictata* and the *Operationes*, he displays much more concern for the Psalms' historical setting in the *Operationes*. This turn to the importance of historical context continues in Luther's 1530s exegesis of the prophets and his last lectures on Genesis. Several of Luther's teachings of comfort in his 1530s expositions of the Psalms are grounded in a greater appreciation of the historical sense of each Psalm.

36. Though he does not drop letter versus spirit completely in all of his exegeses. He does, however, drop it completely from his interpretation of the messianic Psalms studied in this chapter.

37. WA 3:254, 255–56; WA 40/2:485–86, 490–91, 492–93.

38. WA 3:82, 106, 107–108, 255–56, 259, 263; WA 4:280.

39. WA 5:61, 68; WA 40/2:242, 265, 278, 285–86, 301–302, 483, 572–73; WA 41:152; WA 31/1:180–81.

40. WA 5:52, 280, 281, 447, 453, 463; WA 40/2:205–206, 270, 282, 309, 473, 563–66, 572–73, 586–87; WA 45:213–14, 236; WA 41:144–45, 161, 169–71, 174–75, 230–31; WA 31/1:164–65, 171–72.

41. WA 3:105, 258, 106, 107.

42. WA 5:69, 74, 447.

43. WA 40/2:273–74, 486–87; WA 45:217; WA 41:109–10.

44. WA 40/2:219–20, 222, 273–74; WA 41:96–98; WA 31/1:91.

45. WA 4:278–80; WA 5:53, 280, 281, 447; WA 45:219; WA 41:170; WA 31/1:103–104.

46. WA 3:107; WA 5:54, 445, 447, 452, 453; WA 40/2:270, 300–301, 305, 309, 563–65, 572–73, 575; WA 41:150–52, 161–63; WA 31/1:166–67, 168, 171.

47. WA 5:54, 447, 453; WA 40/2:273, 545–47, 576–77; WA 45:228; WA 41:112–13, 145, 225–26; WA 31/1:103–104.

48. WA 5:447, 450, 452–53.

49. WA 5:447, 450, 452–53; WA 40/2:205–206, 273–74, 301, 564–65, 572–75; WA 41:161–63; WA 31/1:166–67, 168–69, 174–75, 178.

50. WA 5:305–306; WA 41:151–52; WA 31/1:162–63.

51. WA 45:219, 224–26; WA 40/2:534–35, 546–47, 564–65, 570–72.

52. WA 40/2:309–10, 546–47; WA 45:226–29; WA 41:112–15. Other enemies make brief appearances in these commentaries, such as the Turks and the sectarians, especially in the 1532 commentary on Psalm 45.

53. WA 40/2:567, 583.

54. Much work has been done on the topic of Luther and the Jews. Early scholarship tends to follow one of two extremes: either an overly apologetic portrayal of Luther or the depiction of Luther as the father of modern anti-Semitism. Neelak Tjernagel

(*Martin Luther and the Jewish People*) and A. K. Holmio (*Martin Luther: Friend or Foe of the Jews*) follow the former tendency; William Shirer's *The Rise and Fall of the Third Reich* follows the latter tendency. More balanced views include those of Wilhelm Maurer ("Die Zeit der Reformation," in *Kirche und Synagoge: Handbuch zur Geschichte von Christen und Juden*, Vol. 1, ed. Karl Heinrich Rengstorf and Siegried V. Kortzfleisch [Stuttgart: Klett, 1968], 363–452), Heiko Oberman (*The Roots of Anti-Semitism: In the Age of the Renaissance and Reformation*, trans. James I. Porter [Philadelphia: Fortress, 1984]), Mark U. Edwards ("Against the Jews," in *Essential Papers on Judaism and Christianity in Conflict: From Late Antiquity to the Reformation*, ed. Jeremy Cohen [New York: New York University Press, 1991], 345–79), and Eric Gritsch ("The Jews in Reformation Theology," in *Jewish and Christian Encounters over the Centuries: Symbiosis, Prejudice, Holocaust, Dialogue*, ed. Marvin Perry and Frederick M. Schweitzer [New York: Peter Lang, 1994], 197–213). See also the recent essay by Thomas Kaufmann, "Luther and the Jews," in *Jews, Judaism, and the Reformation in Sixteenth-Century Germany*, ed. Dean P. Bell and Stephen G. Burnett (Leiden: Brill, 2006), 69–104.

55. Preus, "Old Testament *Promissio* and Luther's New Hermeneutic," 146, 148, 153–55, 160.

56. WA 40:195–96; WA 45:207, 239; WA 40/2:586; WA 41:79, 80, 81.

57. WA 10/1: 99, 100, 101.

58. As several scholars have pointed out, law and gospel are found in both the Old and New Testaments, so that the division between the Old Testament and the New is not one of law and gospel. See David Steinmetz, *Luther and Staupitz: An Essay in the Intellectual Origins of the Protestant Reformation* (Durham, NC: Duke University Press, 1980), 55. I suppose one would have to define what one means by affirming the Old Testament "on its own terms." If by this Preus means that Luther would have to affirm the Old Testament apart from its gospel content, this would be foreign to Luther. If he means that Luther affirms the New Testament vision of the Old Testament people as Old Testament people, then this Luther does do.

59. There is one other point of contention that I have with James Preus's thesis. He places a fair amount of weight on the appearance and use of the "faithful synagogue" in the second half of the *Dictata super psalterium*. Preus sees in Luther's references to the faithful synagogue a fundamental change in the meaning of "prophetic": while in earlier Psalms David's word is prophetic because he speaks the words of Christ, in the later Psalms the prophetic speaker is "the faithful synagogue awaiting Christ's first advent." Thus, Preus concludes, "The voice of the Old Testament people, speaking as themselves, is heard" ("Old Testament *Promissio* and Luther's New Hermeneutic," 154–55). What he fails to point out is that Luther identifies the faithful synagogue with the primitive church (WA 3:535) and with the early church (WA 4:394). See also Scott Hendrix's discussion of Preus's thesis in *Ecclesia in Via: Ecclesiological Developments in the Medieval Psalms Exegesis and the* Dictata super psalterium *(1513–1515) of Martin Luther* (Leiden: E. J. Brill, 1974), 271–78.

60. WA 3:15; WA 41:81.

61. WA 45:239.

62. WA 41:98.

63. WA 41:81–82. I suggest, in fact, that David is not only an exemplar of faith for Luther but also perhaps even more so a *teacher* of Christian doctrine, especially in Luther's 1530s writings on the messianic Psalms.

64. WA 41:187. The mention of Melchizedek (Ps 110:4), as well as Ps 22:25–26, 29; Ps 72:16; and Ps 118:19–20, 27, evoke Eucharistic connotations for the antecedent tradition. On Ps 22:25–26 in his *Operationes*, Luther very briefly refers to the Eucharist, but his emphasis is upon the gospel that is given as food for the poor (WA 5:664–65). He harmonizes all the various translations of the Hebrew in Ps 72:16 in his Eucharistic reading (WA 3:470–71). While in the *Dictata* Luther briefly uses Ps 110:4 to refer to the Eucharist (WA 4:234–35), he argues against such a reading in his later 1535 commentary on Psalm 110; the mention of Melchizedek, argues Luther, is not made to foreshadow the Eucharist but, rather, to demonstrate what kind of priesthood Christ would have—namely, an eternal priesthood that is apart from law (WA 41:180–83). Finally, Ps 118:19–20 and Ps 118:27 do not warrant an application to the Eucharist for Luther in either his *Dictata* or his 1530 exposition on this Psalm.

65. References to Hebrew in the *Dictata* occur mostly in Luther's discussion of a title of a Psalm. In addition, his references to the Hebrew in his coverage of the messianic Psalms deal with *other* scholars' translations, such as Reuchlin, Jerome, Lyra, and Burgensis, followed by Luther's attempts to harmonize these translations. See WA 3:33–34, 35, 104, 254. See Siegfried Raeder's works on Luther's use of Hebrew in the first and second lectures on the Psalms: *Das Hebräische bei Luther, untersucht bis zum Ende der ersten Psalmenvorlesung* (Tübingen: J. C. B. Mohr, 1961); *Die Benutzung des masoretischen Textes bei Luther in der Zeit zwischen der ersten und zweiten Psalmenvorlesung* (Tübingen: J. C. B. Mohr, 1967); and *Grammatica Theologica: Studien zu Luthers Operationes in Psalmos* (Tübingen: J. C. B. Mohr, 1977).

66. WA 5:250, 252–53.

67. WA 5:269–271, 271, 270.

68. WA 5:274. On the following verse (Ps 8:6), Luther pays lengthy attention to the Hebrew words כָּבוֹד and הָדָר. See WA 5:276.

69. WA 5: 449.

70. WA 5:462.

71. WA 40/2:474–76.

72. WA 40/2:474–75.

73. WA 40/2:231. Luther contends that even if knowledge of Hebrew was not useful, one should learn it out of gratitude to God, and he includes a warning: "Therefore, I earnestly admonish you not to neglect it. There is a danger that God may be offended by this ingratitude and deprive us not only of the knowledge of this sacred language, but of Greek, Latin, and all religion" (WA 40/2:474).

74. WA 40/2:481, 484–85; WA 45:207–208. He also uses the Hebrew to correct the Vulgate version of the biblical text of Ps 45:13–14. See WA 40/2: 599, 601.

75. See Martin Brecht's discussion of this in *Martin Luther: His Road to Reformation, 1483–1521*, trans. James L. Schaaf (Minneapolis: Fortress, 1993), 290–91.

76. These censures become particularly strong in his later works. See, for example, his lectures on Genesis. For a few examples, see WA 42:194–96, 198–99, 218, 223.

77. WA 3:13. Luther, of course, has Nicholas of Lyra in mind when he writes this.

78. WA 40/2:282, 473; WA 41:83, 169, 230.

79. For example, the first edition of Martin Bucer's commentary on the Psalms appeared in September 1529, and it was full of positive references to Jewish exegesis. A second edition of Bucer's commentary came out in 1532. Jerome Friedman argues that the first half of the sixteenth century witnessed the greatest growth in Christian Hebraica and the most significant internal conflicts among Christian Hebraists. See *The Most Ancient Testimony: Sixteenth-Century Christian Hebraica in the Age of Renaissance Nostalgia* (Athens: Ohio University Press, 1983), 5.

80. Johannes Forster, *Dictionarium Hebraicum Novum, non ex Rabinorum Commentis nec ex Nostratium Doctorum stulta imitatione descriptum, sed ex ipsis thesauris sacrorum Bibliorum et eorundem accurate locorum collatione depromptum, cum phrasibus scripturae Veteris et Novi Testamenti diligenter annotatis.* Translation from Frank Rosenthal, "The Rise of Christian Hebraism in the Sixteenth Century," *Historia Judaica* 7 (1945): 179. See also Friedman, 170–71.

81. WA 42:271–72.

82. Martin Luther, *Tischreden in der Matheischen Sammlung*, ed. E. Kroker (Leipzig, 1903), 588.

83. Martin Luther, *Von Schem Hamphorus und Vom Geschlecht Christi*, in Gerhard Falk, *The Jew in Christian Theology* (London: McFarland, 1992), 222–23, 222. For studies on sixteenth-century Christian Hebraists, see Frank Rosenthal, "The Rise of Christian Hebraism in the Sixteenth Century," *Historia Judaica* 7 (1945): 167–91; Jerome Friedman, *The Most Ancient Testimony*, and "Protestant, Jews, and Jewish Sources," in *Piety, Politics, and Ethics: Reformation Studies in Honor of George Wolfgang Forell*, ed. Carter Lindberg, Sixteenth Century Essays and Studies 3 (Kirksville, MO: Sixteenth Century Journal Publishers, 1984), 139–56; Bernard Roussel, "Strasbourg et l'école rhénane d'exégèse (1525–1540)," *Bulletin de la Société de l'Histoire du Protestantisme Français* 135 (1989): 36–41; Gerald Hobbs, "L'Hébreu, le Judaïsme et la Théologie," *Bulletin de la Société de l'Histoire du Protestantisme Français* 135 (1989): 42–53, and "Monitio Amica: Pellicon à Capiton sur le Danger des Lectures Rabbiniques," in *Horizons Européens de la Reforme en Alsace*, ed. Marijn de Kroon and Marc Lienhard, Société Savante D'Alsace et des Régions de L'est 17 (Strasbourg: Librairie Istra, 1980), 81–93; and Eric Zimmer, "Jewish and Christian Hebraist Collaboration in Sixteenth Century Germany," *Jewish Quarterly Review* 71 (1980): 69–88. Rosenthal, Roussel, Friedman, and Hobbs all espouse the predication of two schools of exegesis that are divided both regionally and concerning their views on the usefulness of Jewish exegesis. These two schools are identified as the Strasbourg-Basel-Zurich School (or Upper Rhineland School) and the Wittenberg School, where the former advocates the usefulness of Jewish exegesis for Christian exegesis and the latter does not. Stephen G. Burnett, however, questions whether the differences between these two "schools" are as clear as these authors contend. See "Reassessing the 'Basel-Wittenberg Conflict': Dimensions of the Reformation-Era Discussion of Hebrew Scholarship," in *Hebraica Veritas? Christian Hebraists and the Study of Judaism in Early Modern Europe*, ed. Allison P. Coudert and Jeffrey S. Shoulson (Philadelphia: University of Pennsylvania Press, 2004), 181–201.

3. MARTIN BUCER: CHRISTOLOGICAL READINGS THROUGH HISTORICAL EXEGESIS

1. R. Gerald Hobbs, "An Introduction to the Psalms Commentary of Martin Bucer" (PhD dissertation, University of Strasbourg, 1971), vi; and Hasting Eells, *Martin Bucer* (New Haven: Yale University Press, 1931), 65, 67. Hobbs provides an analysis of the various editions of Bucer's *Sacrorum Psalmorum Libri Quinque* (1529, 1532, 1547, and 1554) and the elements of the historical setting, the translations, and the Christian and Jewish sources of the commentary. He shows that the 1529 and 1554 editions of Bucer's Psalms commentary were the most popular and the most circulated (41).

2. Constantin Hopf, *Martin Bucer and the English Reformation* (Oxford: Basil Blackwell, 1946), 205, 206. See also 221–31. Hopf also argues for the likelihood that Coverdale knew both Bucer's commentary on the Psalms and its English translation when he wrote his English Bible (207, 223).

3. Erasmus's expositions and paraphrases of certain Psalms may be found in *Desiderii Erasmi Roterodami Opera Omnia* (Lugduni Batavorum, 1703–1706), 5:171–556. Jacques Lefèvre d'Étaples, *Quincuplex Psalterium*, reprint ed. (Geneva: Library Droz, 1979). Felix Pratensis, *Psalterium ex hebreo diligentissime ad verbum fere tralatum* (Venice, 1515; reprint ed., Hagenau, 1522). Martin Luther, *Operationes in Psalmos*, Weimar Ausgabe, Volume 5. Johannes Bugenhagen, *In librum Psalmorum Interpretatio* (Basel, 1524). Conrad Pellican, *Psalterium Davidis* (Strasbourg, 1527).

4. Hobbs makes this point in "How Firm a Foundation: Martin Bucer's Historical Exegesis of the Psalms," *Church History* 53 (1984): 480.

5. Hobbs, "An Introduction," 55, 56–58. Hobbs surmises that this translation of Bugenhagen's Psalms commentary stimulated Bucer to the task of writing his own commentary because of the inadequacies he found in Bugenhagen's work (59–60).

6. Hopf, 209. This was in contradiction to Bugenhagen's Lutheran views of the Eucharist.

7. Document 871 in the Zwingli Briefwechsel, CR 97:198. The quote is taken from Gerald Hobbs's translation of the letter in his article "Exegetical Projects and Problems: A New Look at an Undated Letter from Bucer to Zwingli," in *Prophet, Pastor, Protestant: The Work of Huldrych Zwingli after Five Hundred Years*, ed. E. J. Furcha and H. Wayne Pipkin, Pittsburgh Theological Monographs 11 (Allison Park, PA: Pickwick, 1984), 90–91.

8. For further details and explanations of Bucer's use of a pseudonym, see the discussions by Hopf, 208–10; Eells, 67–69; and Hobbs, "An Introduction," 77–100. Hobbs emphasizes Bucer's deliberate soft tone and aim to convince rather than convict (81, 79, 83–84, 99) and his refusal to advocate a *sola fideism* (to win over the Catholics; see 85) while also not condemning those church fathers who held this position (90). See also Hobbs's discussion of the pseudonym in "Exegetical Projects," 97–98.

9. Johannes Sturm, *Commonitio oder Erinnerungsschrift* (Newstatt, 1581), 16; Eells, 68. Hobbs gives a detailed discussion of the ongoing effectiveness of the pseudonym in France, England, and Italy. See Hobbs, "An Introduction," 125–28.

10. Erasmus, *Epistola contra pseudo-evangelicos*, in *Erasmi Opera* X: 1581, 1602. Martin Luther, WATr 4:4185. See also the discussion by Eells, 68; and Hobbs, "An Introduction," 111–15.

11. Bucer, *Epistola Apologetica*, f. F5v and cited in Eells, 68; P. Bayle, *Dictionnaire historique et critique* (Paris, 1820), 4:209; E. Middleton, *Evangelical Biography* (London, 1816), 2:282; and Hobbs, "An Introduction," 113–14.

12. CR 10:871. Hobbs, "An Introduction," 67, 78.

13. Typology, of course, is not a new tool. However, interestingly enough, even those interpreters who frequently used typology often did not use it for this particular set of Psalms. Beryl Smalley points out that the case of the messianic Psalms is a particularly special case (*The Study of the Bible in the Middle Ages* [Notre Dame, IN: University of Notre Dame Press, 1964], 18).

14. Martin Bucer, *Sacrorum Psalmorum libri quinque ad hebraicam veritatem versi et familiari explanatione eludicati* (Argentorati, George Ulrich Handlanus, 1529), 7a. Translation from Hobbs, "How Firm a Foundation," 480–81.

15. This is not a new concept; Augustine and Aquinas had already previously set the precept that the historical sense is the foundation of all doctrine. See Aquinas, *Summa Theologica*, 1a.1.10. Jerome also wrote, "The truth of the historical is the foundation of spiritual understanding" (*Lettres*, trans. Jerome Labourt, 8 vols. [Paris, 1949–63], Letter 129, 7:163–64).

16. Bucer, 8a. Thus, included also in Bucer's acclamation of the historical sense is a critique and warning against allegorical readings of Scripture.

17. Bucer, 19a, 21b, 58a, 93b, 90b, 91–92a, 123b, 124b–127a, 129a, 128b–129a, 341b, 343b, 355a, 266a, 268a. For examples: Bucer agrees with the use of Ps 22:22 in Heb 2:12 to describe Christ's communion with human nature (129a). He interprets "those who sleep in the earth" in Ps 22:29 in the light of Jesus' words concerning the resurrection of the dead in Jn 5:28 (131a). He also refers the "posterity," "future generation," and "people yet unborn" spoken of in Ps 22:30–31 to the perpetuity of the church (128b–129a). Likewise, Bucer supplements the description in Psalm 110 of Christ as seated at the right hand of God with all things under his feet with several New Testament references (Phil 2:10–11, Mk 16:19, Eph 1:20–23, and 1 Cor 15:25). See Bucer, 342a.

18. Bucer, 8a. The importance of this point will be seen more clearly when we look at Calvin's interpretation of these eight Psalms. Several times Calvin argues against the New Testament author's interpretation of a Psalm precisely because he does *not* think that it is in keeping with true historical exegesis.

19. The general format that Bucer follows in interpreting each Psalm is first to give the *argumentum* of the Psalm, his own paraphrastic translation, and the *explanatio*, which provides the original *historia* of the Psalm that is often supplemented with a combination of philological comments, Jewish exegesis, and variant Christian readings. He then turns to a typological reading of the Psalm, in which the *historia* is used to shed light on the meaning concerning Christ and the church.

20. Bucer, 22a–23b, 19b–21b, 22a, 20a, 23b, 27a–29b.

21. Bucer, 121a–127a, 127a–131b, 211a–215b and 265b–268b, 341a–344a, 353b–355b. Psalm 118 also exhibits through the type of David the defeat of the enemies and the true pious devotion of public gratitude to God that are, again, more truly accomplished by Christ. Psalms 8 and 16 represent different cases, which are discussed in a later section.

22. Bucer, 93b–94b, 123a–b. Bucer writes, "Certainly he [David] raises the eyes of his mind to the author of his hope…it is clear enough from the apostles that it appropriately and truly points to Christ, who alone conquered death and restored eternal life and who so gloriously in three days took himself back from death" (94b).

23. Bucer, 214b, 265b–266a, 268b, 342a, 343a.

24. Hasting Eells makes the point that Bucer's exegetical method is theological and homiletical, containing lengthy doctrinal forays. See Eells, 65.

25. Bucer, 23b, 22b–23a, 57b, 58a–b. On Ps 2:12, he also expounds on the two natures of Christ as the only begotten of the Father, true God and true human (27a). Likewise, Bucer argues that Psalm 22 teaches that in Christ taking on flesh, God renews and restores human nature through Christ (127b). His emphasis on the redemption and restoration of humanity accomplished through Christ's incarnation is also found in his comments on Ps 72:17–19 and Ps 110:4. See Bucer, 268b and 343b.

26. See Bucer, 23a–b, 24a–b, and 27a–b. In his comments on each of these verses in Psalm 2, Bucer extensively cites and refutes Kimhi's arguments against the Christian use of these verses to support the doctrine of the Trinity. This aspect is explored in more depth in a later section of this chapter.

27. Bucer, 21b, 22a–b, 20a, 20b, 21a, 21b, 22a, 23a–b, 24a–b, 26b, 27a, 27b, 127b, 129a. Bucer, however, does not give a Trinitarian reading of the second half of Ps 8:1 ("You have set your glory above the heavens"). Several scholars have noted the centrality of the Holy Spirit for Bucer's theology. See August Lang, *Der Evangelienkommentar Martin Butzers und die Grundzüge seiner Theologie* (Leipzig: Aalen, 1900), and W. P. Stephens, *The Holy Spirit in the Theology of Martin Bucer* (Cambridge: Cambridge University Press, 1970). For example, in the preface to his Psalms commentary, Bucer clearly states his belief that the Holy Spirit is the author of the Psalms (Bucer, 8b). Here he also contends that the very act of interpreting Scripture is first to discern the teaching that the Spirit intends (Bucer, 25b). His exegesis emphasizes that the Holy Spirit plays a crucial role in the election, justification, and sanctification of every Christian (Bucer 28b) and in the attainment of the church's calling as the kingdom of God (Bucer, 130b, 215a).

28. Bucer, 22a, 56a–58a, 123b, 215a. Bucer also writes on Ps 118:26 ("Blessed is the one who comes in the name of the Lord") that whenever the Hebrew word *baruch* ("blessed") appears in reference to God, it signifies God's favor and beneficence (355b).

29. Bucer, 89b–95a, 127b, 131a–b, 342a. See also 342b, 343a, 344a. He also comments on Ps 118:22 ("The stone that the builders rejected has become the chief cornerstone") that this is rightly called a foundation stone, since the elect rest upon it (355a).

30. Bucer 22a, 27b–28a. In defining faith, he refers to Cicero, Valla, and Budaeus to support his definition of faith as persuasion. But above all, he argues that this

definition is supported by Heb 11:1: "Faith is the *assurance* of things hoped for, the indication of things not seen." This assurance, says Bucer, is the same as undoubted persuasion (Bucer, 27b–28a).

31. Bucer, 28a, 28b, 29a–b, there 28b. Hobbs discusses this as a point of Bucer's moderation toward more Roman Catholic views of salvation and sanctification. See "An Introduction," 83–85. These depictions of faith as persuaded assurance and faith as intimately tied to a righteous life appear in Bucer's readings of Psalms 8, 16, 22, and 45, as well. See his comments on Ps 8:1, 16:2, 16:9, and 22:22–31 in Bucer, 55b–56b, 57b–58b, 90a, 93a–b, 127b, 128a–b, 129a, 130b, 131b. On the whole, Bucer does not maintain the medieval and late-medieval traditions of using these Psalms to teach about the virgin birth or Eucharist. The mention of the "mother's womb" in Ps 22:9–10 evokes from him praise of God's great care and goodness to humanity and to the elect in particular (Bucer, 123b). The image of the rains that water the earth in Ps 72:6 speak of the restorative work of Christ, rather than the virgin birth (see 266b). And "from the womb of the morning" (Ps 110:3) is about the birth of the church (and not Christ's virgin birth). See Bucer, 342b–343a. As to Eucharist, Bucer only maintains a brief mention of Eucharist on Ps 22:25–26 (130a) and 110:4 (343a–b).

32. We will see that these purposes are accomplished by Bucer's profound envisioning of the church as the body of Christ, so that what may be said of Christ, the head, is also said of the church, the members of Christ's body. Hence, Bucer's placement of the church as central to his readings of these Psalms is intimately tied to their christological import. This is important to note, because John Calvin will find the experience of the church in these Psalms primarily through the person of David (i.e., without a clear christological link).

33. Bucer, 21a, 26a, 26b, 55b, 56a, 57b, 59b, 94b–95a, 129a, 93a, 122b, 127a, 354a, 354b, 355b, 21a, 24b, 59a.

34. Bucer, 57a. He specifically identifies the "enemy and avenger" as atheists. Amy Nelson Burnett argues that Bucer's emphasis on moral reform and the cultivation of piety echoes the influence of Erasmus. See her article "Church Discipline and Moral Reformation in the Thought of Martin Bucer," *Sixteenth Century Studies Journal* 22 (1991): 454. Gottfried Hammann notes Bucer's preoccupation with holiness and piety in the context of his creation of the "Gemeinschaften" ("Ecclesiological Motifs behind the Creation of the 'Christlichen Gemeinschaften,'" in *Martin Bucer: Reforming Church and Community*, ed. D. F. Wright [Cambridge: Cambridge University Press, 1994], 141–42).

35. Bucer, 90a, 91a, 91b, 355b, 122b, 128a, 128a–b. Bucer contrasts Saul and David: "Saul's ruling of the people obscured the true religion of God. So David inaugurated it when he invited the people to bring the Ark of God back.... Therefore he [David] was encouraging them to know the wonderful and incomparable goodness of God so that they would come forth to all goodness, gather as one, and give praise and cleave to this religion alone and serve God's commands devotedly" (128a).

36. On the defeat of Christ's enemies, see Bucer, 20a–b, 21b, 24b–26a, 342a, 342b, 343b, 344a. On the splendor of Christ's kingdom, see Bucer, 24a, 131b, 212a, 215a, 266b, 267b–268a, 355a–b. On the establishment of righteousness and justice, see

Bucer, 130a, 131a, 131b, 212b, 215a, 266a, 343a. On the expansiveness, universality, and eternity of the kingdom, see Bucer, 121a, 122a–b, 131b, 215a, 215b, 268a, 341a, 343a. See T. F. Torrance, "Kingdom and Church in the Thought of Martin Butzer," *Journal of Ecclesiastical History* 6 (1955): 48–59, which argues that the doctrine of the two natures of Christ is the foundation of Bucer's concept of the relation between the heavenly and earthly kingdoms (58).

37. Bucer, 24b, 342b–343a, 90a, 92a, 127b. T. F. Torrance also points out Bucer's emphasis on seeing the church as the living body of Christ and eloquently describes the connection for him between election and incorporation into the body of Christ ("Kingdom and Church in the Thought of Martin Butzer," 51, 53–54).

38. See, for example, Bucer, 90b–91a. Moreover, he identifies the kingdom of Christ on earth as the "society of the saints." See, for example, Bucer, 92b. A fuller expression of Bucer's vision of Christ's kingdom on earth is given in his 1550 *De Regno Christi*, in which he sets forth a program for church reform in England. For a description of Bucer's concern to form a new Christian society, see Amy Nelson Burnett's article "Church Discipline and Moral Reformation in the Thought of Martin Bucer," 438–56, and her book, *The Yoke of Christ: Martin Bucer and Christian Discipline* (Kirksville, MO: Sixteenth Century Journal, 1994).

39. Bucer, 26a–b. For example, a good and pious prince never starts cruel wars, does not neglect piety and holiness, does not neglect the innocent, practices the virtue of study, and seeks to do justice. Most of all, such princes understand that they are stewards of God's kingdom (26b). Gerald Hobbs argues that Bucer uses the figure of David to exemplify the true pious prince. See Hobb's article "Bucer's Use of King David as Mirror of the Christian Prince," *Reformation and Renaissance Review* 5 (2003): 119.

40. Bucer, 213a, 266a–b, 129a–b, 131b, there 129a–b. Aspects exhibited by David that characterize a pious king include setting forth laws of peace, calling the people to faithfulness and praise of God, imploring the help of God in time of need, and caring for the poor and needy (129b–130a). Many scholars have noted the intimate tie Bucer places between civil and religious leaders in furthering the kingdom of Christ on earth. See Martin Greschat's article "The Relation between Church and Civil Community in Bucer's Reforming Work," in *Martin Bucer: Reforming Church and Community*, 17–31.

41. Bucer, 127b, 268b, 342a, 22a–b.

42. Bucer, 22b, 27b–28a, 131b, 21a, 59a, 92a, 128a–b, 129a, 90a, 92a, 127b, 342b–343a.

43. For examples: Bucer interprets Ps 16:10 concerning Christ having passed from death to life, but then he goes on to emphasize that the saints share in this victory so that through Christ the saints escape death, and the blessings of resurrection, eternal life, and eternal joy befall them (94a). Likewise, the weight of his interpretation of Psalm 22 is to show that Christ underwent these sufferings for the elect's salvation and restoration (127b).

44. Dates for these Jewish exegetes are the following: David Kimhi (1160–1235), Abraham Ibn Ezra (1092/93–1167), and Rabbi Solomon ben Isaac (1040–1105).

45. Gerald Hobbs provides an extensive analysis of the Christian sources (patristic and contemporary) that may have influenced Bucer. See Hobbs, "An Introduction," 185–226. In addition, Bucer also demonstrates influences of Renaissance humanism, as seen in his citations of Cicero and Laurentius Valla on Psalm 2 (27b) and his emphasis on human excellence in his exposition of Psalm 8 (57a, 58a, 58b, 59b). Likewise, on Ps 45:1–5, he underscores the king's eloquence and nobility, which he likens to that of the kings and heroes of the writings of Homer and Vergil (212a).

46. Bucer, 7a. Bucer does make a handful of explicit references to church fathers. For example, he cites Jerome's translation of Ps 2:12 as "worship purely," rather than "kiss the son" (27a), and he criticizes Origen's universalism in contrast to his interpretation of Psalm 110 as concerning the elect (342a). He also mentions several church fathers' views on faith—such as those of Augustine, Bernard of Clairvaux, and Chrysostom—in his excursus on the doctrine of faith at the end of his comments on Psalm 2 (28b–29b). For a more detailed analysis of Bucer's use of the church fathers, see Irena Backus, "Martin Bucer and the Patristic Tradition," in *Martin Bucer and Sixteenth-Century Europe: Actes du colloque de Strasbourg* (28–31 août 1991, Vol. 1), ed. Christian Krieger and Marc Lienhard (Leiden: Brill, 1993), 55–69.

47. This is his praise particularly of David Kimhi and Abraham Ibn Ezra. See Bucer, 8a.

48. Rashi, *Rashi's Commentary on Psalms 1–89*, with English translation by Mayer I. Gruber (Atlanta: Scholars, 1998), 1, 52. David Kimhi, *The First Book of Psalms According to the Text of the Cambridge MS Bible with the Longer Commentary of R. David Qimchi*, ed. S. M. Schiller-Szinessy (Cambridge: Deighton, Bell, 1883), 8 [Hebrew]. The English translations of Kimhi's comments on Psalms 2, 8, 16, and 22 can be found in *The Longer Commentary of R. David Kimhi on the First Book of Psalms*, trans. R. G. Finch (New York: Macmillan, 1919), here, 12. See Bucer, 19a.

49. Kimhi in Schiller-Szinessy, 9; Finch, 14. Bucer, 21a.

50. Kimhi in Schiller-Szinessy, 10; Finch, 15. Bucer, 22a–b. Kimhi also quotes 1 Sam 16:1, which is not explicitly quoted by Bucer, though Bucer refers to the context set by this verse (see 21b).

51. Kimhi in Schiller-Szinessy, 11; Finch 17–18. Bucer, 27a. Kimhi also quotes Jer 41:5, which Bucer leaves out.

52. Bucer, however, interprets Psalm 45 pertaining to Solomon, rather than David.

53. Though Rashi also adds, "However, according to its primary, literal meaning and for a refutation of the unrepentant infidels [i.e., Christians] is it correct to interpret it as a reference to David" (Rashi in Gruber, 1, 52).

54. David Kimhi in "The Commentary of Rabbi David Kimhi on Psalms 42–72" [Hebrew], ed. Sidney I. Esterson, *Hebrew Union College Annual* 10 (1935): 329–35, 436–43; and Abraham Ibn Ezra in R. Avrohom Chaim Feuer, *Tehillim: A New Translation with a Commentary Anthologized from Talmudic, Midrashic, and Rabbinic Sources* (Brooklyn, NY: Mesorah, 1985), 559–75, 893–906, 1401–1414. For Kimhi on Psalm 118, see the edition in *The Commentary of David Kimhi on the Fifth Book of the Psalms*, ed. Jacob Bosniak (New York: Bloch, 1954), 99–107 [Hebrew]. Rashi also makes note that other rabbis interpret Psalm 72 concerning the Messianic Age, though he interprets it

primarily within Solomon's historical context. See Rashi in Gruber, 35–36, 324–28. Likewise, he notes that parts of Psalm 118 are often read pertaining to the future war of Gog and Magog, particularly verse eleven (see Feuer, 1406). Rashi does not, however, interpret Psalm 45 in reference to the Messiah but instead as concerning the Torah scholar. See Rashi in Gruber, 22–23, 212–215.

55. See Kimhi in Esterson, 438, 441–42, and Feuer, 1402, 1412, 1413, 1414. On Psalm 22, however, the weight of the rabbis' exegesis falls on the meaning of the Psalm as a prophecy of Israel's exile, suffering, and redemption, rather than as a prophecy of the Messiah's suffering. See Rashi in Gruber, 12–13, 126–28; Kimhi in Schiller-Szinessy, 65–71; Finch, 97–109; Feuer, 269–85.

56. Kimhi in Schiller-Szinessy, 26, 27, there 27; Finch, 49–50, 53, there 53.

57. Bucer, 55b, 56b, 57b–58a.

58. Kimhi in Schiller-Szinessy, 42; Finch, 74. Bucer, 90a. David Kimhi cites his father's interpretation of Ps 16:2 as "the good I do is not done to You [God]," so that the meaning is that because God is the source of all good, God does not need our good deeds, but, rather, they are done "to the holy ones who are in the earth" (Ps 16:3).

59. Bucer, 56b. Kimhi translates the verb as "you have founded," and Ibn Ezra translates it as "you make a beginning." Bucer essentially harmonizes these two translations. Kimhi writes on Ps 8:2: "In the present psalm he says that the wonders of the Creator and His loving-kindness to man are to be recognized from the moment of his first coming into the air of the world and from his early infancy" (Kimhi in Schiller-Szinessy, 25–26; Finch, 49).

60. Bucer, 92b. See Kimhi in Schiller-Szinessy, 43; Finch, 76.

61. For example, all three Jewish commentators use the latter verses of Psalm 2 to teach about true worship of God—that the proper stance before God is holy fear, trembling, and complete trust in God. See Kimhi in Schiller-Szinessy, 11; Finch, 17, 18. Rashi in Gruber, 1–2, 53–54. Ibn Ezra in Feuer, 70–71. It is curious, though, that Bucer does not use the rabbis' comments on Ps 2:12 to support his emphasis on true piety and separation from impurity. Kimhi and Rashi both cite the possible translation of the Hebrew phrase נַשְּׁקוּ־בַר as "kiss purity" to point to the purity of heart of the righteous (see Kimhi in Schiller-Szinessy, 11; Finch, 17 and Rashi in Gruber, 1, 53). Instead, Bucer cites Jerome's interpretation of this phase as "worship purely" (see Bucer, 27a).

62. See Rashi in Gruber, 8, 99–100; Kimhi in Schiller-Szinessy, 42–44, and Finch, 75–78; Ibn Ezra in Feuer, 192, 193, 199.

63. Bucer, 127b–128b. For the citations of Kimhi and Ibn Ezra in Bucer, see 128b and 130a. See Kimhi in Schiller-Szinessy, 69; Finch, 106. On Psalm 118, see Bucer, 355b, and Feuer, 1402–1403. David is shown as the one who establishes true religion and worship of God over and against Saul's "rule in darkness" and "dull devotion" (Bucer, 128a). Bucer does then turn from the example of David to David as a type of Christ, for, argues Bucer, the institution of the true worship of God was more fully established by Christ. See Bucer, 128a–b, 130b.

64. Bucer, 91a, 127b–128b. See Rashi in Gruber, 8, 99.

65. Bucer, 90b and 91a.

66. Bucer, 90b and 92b. Kimhi comments on the phrase "you hold my lot" in Ps 16:5b that God provides help to those who choose God as their inheritance. See Kimhi in Schiller-Szinessy, 43, and Finch, 76.

67. See Bucer, 27a and Kimhi in Schiller-Szinessy, 11, and Finch, 17–18. Bucer then connects this reading to Christ, when Christ's wrath is kindled against those who are unwilling to worship him.

68. Bucer, 92b, 128b, and 130a.

69. See Kimhi in Schiller-Szinessy, 11–12, 70–71; Finch, 18–19, 108–109; Kimhi in Bosniak, 66–68. Bucer does not directly quote or address Kimhi's anti-Christian polemic in his comments on Psalms 72 and 110. Hobbs surmises that Bucer is most likely using the 1517 edition of David Kimhi's commentary on the Psalms, which may very well explain the absence of his response to Kimhi's attacks on Psalms 72 and 110, for they were censored in the 1517 edition. See Hobbs's discussion, "An Introduction," 269–71.

70. Kimhi in Schiller-Szinessy, 11–12; Finch, 18–19.

71. Kimhi in Schiller-Szinessy, 12; Finch, 19.

72. Bucer, 23a–b.

73. See Bucer, 20a, 21b, 22b, 23a, 23b, 27a.

74. The dispute is how to translate the Hebrew phrase: כָּאֲרִי יָדַי וְרַגְלָי. The medieval rabbis translate this phrase "as a lion, my hands and feet"; Christians read it as "they pierce my hands and feet."

75. Kimhi in Schiller-Szinessy, 70; Finch, 109. Kimhi also asks why Jesus is asking for help (Ps 22:1) when it is also said that he willingly faced death, why Jesus would speak of the *praises of Israel* (Ps 22:3) if it is Israel who is doing him harm, or how he can speak of all the nations bowing down to him (Ps 22:27–29) when the Jews and the Muslims do not believe in him.

76. Bucer, 124b.

77. Bucer cites Num 23:24, Judges 14:8, 1 Sam 17:34, 2 Sam 23:20, and Is 38:13. He argues that no one writes ארי with a *cof* and translates it as "like a lion." The only exception is Is 38:13, which is the only other place in Scripture (other than Ps 22:16) where a *cof* precedes the word.

78. Bucer, 125a. Yet, Bucer is still concerned about Jewish mockery of Christian interpretations, for in the very next line he states, "Nevertheless this is not without them exhibiting laughter at our expense. I urge them to follow me and not impede me on this passage concerning the word ארי."

79. See Bucer, 126b–127b. He also cites the parallels of the events recorded in the Psalm with those recorded concerning the life of Jesus in the Gospels. See Bucer, 122a, 123b, 126a, 126b–127a, 129a, 130b, 131a–b.

80. Constantin Hopf notes that Bucer applies this rule with all of his sources, whether church fathers or Jewish commentators. See Hopf, 212. Bucer's sentiments toward Jewish exegesis appear to echo those of Nicholas of Lyra, for both men find Jewish exegesis helpful in illuminating the literal sense and both limit the use of Jewish exegesis according to how well it maintains the simple sense of the text; however, Lyra preferred Rashi, and Bucer preferred Kimhi. Lyra writes in his Second Prologue to his

Postilla Litteralis super Totum Bibliam: "Likewise, my intention is to cite the statements not only of Catholic but also of Jewish teachers and especially Rabbi Solomon, who among all the Jewish exegetes has put forward the most reasonable arguments in order to illuminate the literal meaning of the text.... So one must not adhere to the teachings of the Jews except insofar as they are in accord with reason and the true literal meaning" (PL 113:30). This translation comes from A. J. Minnis, A. Brian Scott, and David Wallace, eds., *Medieval Literary Theory and Criticism, c. 1100–c. 1375: The Commentary Tradition* (Oxford: Clarendon, 1988), 270.

81. Bucer, 59a. See Kimhi in Schiller-Szinessy, 27; Finch, 52.

82. Bucer, 22a–b. See Kimhi in Schiller-Szinessy, 10; Finch, 15.

83. Bucer, 344a. There are other instances as well. For example, Bucer disagrees with Kimhi's interpretation of Ps 16:11 as a prayer, for he argues that the context of the previous verse proves that it is a praise that God has not deserted him and has saved him from the corruption of the grave (Bucer, 94b). See Kimhi in Schiller-Szinessy, 44; Finch, 78. On the title of Psalm 22, Bucer rejects Jewish interpretations of the Hebrew word אַיֶּלֶת, particularly Kimhi's application of this word as a metaphor for Israel. Through the quotation of various biblical passages, Bucer argues that the preferable meaning is that אַיֶּלֶת refers to Christ (122a–b).

84. Bucer, 91a–b. See Rashi in Gruber, 8, 99; Kimhi in Schiller-Szinessy, 42; Finch, 75.

85. Bucer, 213b. See Kimhi in Esterson, 331; Ibn Ezra in Feuer, 568–69.

86. Bucer, 267b. See Rashi in Gruber, 36, 326. Kimhi in Esterson, 440. Ibn Ezra in Feuer, 902.

87. My views on Bucer's anti-Jewish rhetoric are slightly different from those expressed by R. Gerald Hobbs in his "An Introduction," 272–75. Hobbs sees Bucer's remarks to be "significantly free of animus" and states that Bucer does not "indulge in an all-too-popular anti-semitic jargon." Though not so virulently or frequently as Martin Luther, Bucer does retain the two basic anti-Jewish sentiments of his day—Jews as enemies of Christ and the church and Jews as blind and ignorant interpreters of Scripture. I have not included in the body of this chapter a discussion of Bucer's dealings with contemporary Jews of his day, for my investigation is focused on his use of Jewish commentaries in his exegesis. The best known incident is, of course, the Cassel Advice, in which Bucer advocates several economic and religious restrictions on the Jews of Hesse to maintain the supremacy of Christianity and the church.

For studies on Bucer and the Jews of Hesse, see Hasting Eells, "Bucer's Plan for the Jews," *Church History* 6 (1937): 127–35; Robert Stupperich, ed., *Bucers Deutsche Schriften*, Vol. 7: *Schriften der Jahre 1538–1539* (Gütersloh: Gütersloher Verlagshaus Gerd Mohn, 1964), 336–37; Wilhelm Maurer, "Die Zeit der Reformation," in *Kirche und Synagoge: Handbuch zur Geschichte von Christen und Juden*, ed. Karl H. Rengsdorf and Siegfried von Kortzfleisch (Stuttgart: Ernst Klett, 1968), 1:363–448; W. Nijenhuis, "A Remarkable Historical Argumentation in Bucer's 'Judenratschlag'" and "Bucer and the Jews" in *Ecclesia Reformata: Studies on the Reformation* (Leiden: E. J. Brill, 1972), 23–72; Steven Rowan, "Luther, Bucer and Eck on the Jews," *Sixteenth Century Journal* 16 (1985): 79–90; John W. Kleiner, "The Attitudes of Martin Bucer and Landgrave

Philipp toward the Jews of Hesse," in *Faith and Freedom: A Tribute to Franklin H. Littel*, ed. Richard Libowitz (Oxford: Pergamon, 1987), 221–30; Martin Greschat, *Martin Bucer: A Reformer and His Times*, trans. Stephen E. Buckwalter (Louisville, KY: Westminster John Knox, 2004), 156–58, and "The Relation between Church and Civil Community in Bucer's Reforming Work," in *Martin Bucer: Reforming Church and Community*, ed. D. F. Wright (Cambridge: Cambridge University Press, 1994), 27–29; R. Gerald Hobbs, "Martin Bucer et les Juifs," in *Martin Bucer and Sixteenth-Century Europe: Actes du Colloque de Strasbourg* (28–31 août), ed. Christian Krieger and Marc Lienhard (Leiden: Brill, 1993), 2:681–89, and his more recent article, "Bucer, the Jews, and Judaism," in *Jews, Judaism, and the Reformation in Sixteenth-Century Germany*, ed. Dean P. Bell and Stephen G. Burnett (Leiden: Brill, 2006), 137–69.

88. Bucer, 20a.

89. See Bucer, 21b, 25a–b.

90. Bucer, 57a.

91. Bucer, 126a. However, it is notable that he does not carry out a continual reading of the Jews as the enemies and crucifiers of Christ in his interpretation of Psalm 22; indeed, this is the only explicit reference.

92. Bucer, 342a, 344a, 355a; there 344a.

93. Bucer, 94b, 130b, 213a; there 130b.

94. This is important to keep in mind once we consider John Calvin. Bucer maintains these Psalms as literal prophecies of Christ and anchors his placement of the church as the central player in these Psalms with the church's identity as the body of Christ; thus, the christological center is still maintained in various ways. Calvin, on the other hand, exhibits a significant shift to readings given through *David* (not Christ).

95. Bucer, 7a. Taken from Hobbs's translation in "How Firm a Foundation," 480–81.

96. This is not to say, however, that Bucer's readings are necessarily convincing to Jews.

97. This is a suggestion that should be made with caution, as this study looks at Luther, Bucer, and Calvin and, later, Hunnius and Pareus. I hope to indicate a trend, but it has yet to be seen whether such distinctions, especially concerning views of Jewish exegesis, can be maintained in later generations of Lutheran and Reformed thinkers.

4. JOHN CALVIN: THE SUFFICIENCY OF DAVID

The Calvin Translation Society provides an English translation of Calvin's commentaries on the Psalms. All of Calvin's commentaries on the Psalms are translated by James Anderson and may be found in five volumes: John Calvin, *Commentary on the Book of Psalms* (Edinburgh: Calvin Translation Society, 1845–49) and more recently republished with Baker Book House. All of my quotations of Calvin on the Psalms are based on these translations by James Anderson and often slightly edited because of my own references to the original Latin and in order to modernize the language.

1. See the discussions of Richard A. Hasler, "The Influence of David and the Psalms upon John Calvin's Life and Thought," *Hartford Quarterly* 5 (1964–65): 7–18;

James A. De Jong, "'An Anatomy of All Parts of the Soul': Insights into Calvin's Spirituality from His Psalms Commentary," in *Calvinus Sacrae Scripturae Professor: Calvin as Confessor of Holy Scripture*, ed. Wilhelm Neuser (Grand Rapids, MI: Eerdmans, 1994), 1–14; James Luther Mays, "Calvin's Commentary on the Psalms: The Preface as Introduction," in *John Calvin and the Church* (Louisville, KY: Westminster John Knox, 1990), 195–204; and Barbara Pitkin, "Imitation of David: David as Paradigm for Faith in Calvin's Exegesis of the Psalms," *Sixteenth Century Journal* 24 (1993): 843–63, and her book *What Pure Eyes Could See: Calvin's Doctrine of Faith in Its Exegetical Context* (New York: Oxford University Press, 1999), especially chapter 4. Pitkin, Hasler, and De Jong stress Calvin's use of David as an exemplar of Christian faith and prayer. A more recent work by Herman J. Selderhuis explores Calvin's doctrine of God in his Psalms commentary; see *Calvin's Theology of the Psalms*, Texts and Studies in Reformation and Post-Reformation Thought (Grand Rapids, MI: Baker Academic, 2007).

2. See, for examples, W. Stanford Reid, "The Battle Hymns of the Lord: Calvinist Psalmody of the Sixteenth Century," in *Sixteenth Century Essays and Studies*, ed. Carl S. Meyer (St. Louis: Foundation for Reformation Research, 1971), 2:36–54; and John D. Witvliet, "The Spirituality of the Psalter: Metrical Psalms in Liturgy and Life in Calvin's Geneva," in *Calvin and Spirituality/Calvin and His Contemporaries*, Calvin Studies Society Papers, 1995, 1997 (Grand Rapids, MI: CRC Product Services, 1998), 93–117.

3. CO 31:13–16. Calvin writes, "I began to perceive more distinctly that this was by no means a superfluous undertaking, and I have also felt from my own individual experience that to readers who are not so exercised I would furnish important assistance in understanding the Psalms."

4. James Luther Mays makes a similar argument in his article, "Calvin's Commentary on the Psalms: The Preface as Introduction," 95. Mays points out that Calvin names his intended audience and stresses parallels between the experiences of David and himself. I also find that the preface sets forth all of Calvin's key *theological* themes.

5. CO 31:15–20.

6. CO 31:19–22.

7. CO 31:21, 22, 27, 28. See also CO 31:13, 14, 35, 36.

8. Hans-Joachim Kraus notes, "Calvin always reveals himself as an unusually careful interpreter of the Old Testament when it comes to christological interpretations" ("Calvin's Exegetical Principles," *Interpretation* 31 [1977]: 9).

9. On the eternity of the kingdom, see CO 31:452–54, 663–65, 667, 671; CO 32:159–60, 202, 210. On the vastness of the kingdom, see CO 31:47, 458, 459, 669; CO 32:159–60, 162. On the invincibility of the kingdom, see CO 31:48, 459; CO 32:159–60, 165. On the priestly function, see CO 31:234–36, 666–67, 667; CO 32:159–60, 163–65. On peace and unity of the kingdom, see CO 31:234–35; CO 32:162–63.

10. See CO 31: 43, 45, 46, 47, 48, 233, 449, 451–53, 456, 664, 665, 667, 668, 669, 670, 671, 671–72, and CO 32:159–60, 161, 162, 163, 164, 165–66, 202, 203, 210–11. There are a few brief places in Psalm 22 where Calvin does refer to Christ's sufferings (see CO 31:222, 224, 227–28). Barbara Pitkin contends in her article "Imitation of

David: David as Paradigm for Faith in Calvin's Exegesis of the Psalms" that Calvin downplays David's prophetic status and concentrates on David's historical person (843). My study of these eight Psalms has found a need for this statement to be slightly revised. Although Calvin does very much emphasize David as a historical person, he also emphasizes a particular aspect of David's prophetic status, namely, his foresight of *Christ's kingdom* and less so his foresight of the earthly events of Christ's life. S. H. Russell studies the connection between Calvin's christological exegesis and the royal elements in the Psalms. See his article "Calvin and the Messianic Interpretation of the Psalms," *Scottish Journal of Theology* 21 (1968): 37–47. Yet, Russell's article does not address the lack of christological exegesis in Calvin's interpretation of passages that have been traditionally interpreted concerning Christ, nor does he note Calvin's larger emphasis on David as an exemplar for the church.

11. See Matt 22:41–46, Mk 12:35–37, and Lk 20:41–43.

12. See CO 31:220–22. Throughout his exposition of Psalm 22, Calvin lifts up David as an exemplar of persevering faith. When he turns to the application of this verse to Christ, his main concern is to address the apparent contradiction of how the Son of God (divine) can feel forsaken by God. On Psalm 110:1, see CO 32:160–62.

13. CO 32:208, 209, 210, there 209.

14. For an extended discussion of Calvin's notion of the dual authorship of Scripture, see David L. Puckett, *John Calvin's Exegesis of the Old Testament*, Columbia Series in Reformed Theology (Louisville, KY: Westminster John Knox, 1995), 26–37. See also Hans-Joachim Kraus, "Calvin's Exegetical Principles," 7–8; and Richard C. Gamble, "*Brevitas et Facilitas*: Toward an Understanding of Calvin's Hermeneutic," *Westminster Theological Journal* 47 (1985): 2.

15. CO 31:43 (emphasis added).

16. CO 31:230.

17. CO 31:156–57, 219, 230, 237, 669, 672; CO 32:161, 211.

18. CO 31:89.

19. See CO 31:90 (emphasis added).

20. See CO 31:91, 92–93, 93.

21. CO 31:219 (emphasis added).

22. CO 32:166.

23. CO 31:157 (emphasis added).

24. CO 31:92. Calvin writes, "The Septuagint renders אלהים, Elohim, by *angels*, of which I do not disapprove....But as the other translation [gods] seems more natural and as it is almost universally adopted by the Jewish interpreters, I have preferred following it."

25. CO 31:664 (emphasis added). The importance of not giving the Jews a reason to criticize Christian interpretations may also be seen in Calvin's comments on Psalms 45 and 110, where he uses the Jews' own application of the Psalms to the Messiah as support for a christological reading of the Psalm—something already seen in the exegeses of Lyra and Bucer. See CO 31:453; 32:159.

26. My reading of Calvin's christological interpretation differs from that of W. McKane, who emphasizes his extensive christological applications of the royal elements

in the Psalms. See "Calvin as an Old Testament Commentator," in *Calvin and Herme-neutics*, ed. Richard C. Gamble (New York: Garland, 1992), 256, 257–58. Insofar as Calvin sees David as a prophet who foresees Christ's kingdom, I agree that the Davidic element (i.e., the *royal* element) is a key guide for Calvin toward the application of a Psalm to Christ. However, my study of these eight Psalms reveals more of a deficit of his christological applications, for Calvin does not retain the tradition of reading these Psalms as literal prophecies of Christ's incarnation, passion, resurrection, or ascension.

27. CO 31:46–47.

28. Such a discussion of Ps 2:7 concerning the workings of the Trinity at Christ's baptism are prevalent in medieval readings and emphasized in the interpretations of Luther and Bucer. See WA 5:59–51; WA 40/2:250–60; and Bucer, 21b–23b.

29. CO 31:88, 90–91; CO 32:163, 205–206. Indeed, he appears to be very conscious of his rejection of the Trinitarian reading of Ps 110:3, for he states, "It would not be edifying to recount all the interpretations that have been given of this clause, for when I have established its true and natural import, it would be quite superfluous to enter upon a refutation of others" (CO 32:163).

30. WA 5:49, 56, 456, 465; WA 45:209, 246.

31. CO 31:231, 227–28. All the other references to Christ's two natures lead more to a discussion of Christ as mediator. See his comments on Ps 2:8, 22:1, and 45:6 in CO 31:47–48, 222, 454. This is much like Bucer's emphasis on the restorative work of Christ but with much less explicit attention to his two natures.

32. CO 31:450–51, 666–67, 667, and CO 31:5052. See WA 40/2: 299–302 and Bucer, 27a.

33. See CO 31:88, 91–92. Calvin sees Ps 8:3 as setting up a contrast between God's goodness and the lowliness of humanity. The remainder of the Psalm describes the goodness that God gives to humanity: namely, honor and dominion over the works of creation.

34. CO 31:149, 154.

35. CO 31:158.

36. CO 31:220, 222, 223–24; CO 32:163, 203, 206.

37. CO 31:89, 91, 94, 95. Barbara Pitkin discusses Calvin's unusual emphasis on children as preachers of God's providence in her articles "The Heritage of the Lord: Children in the Theology of John Calvin," in *The Child in Christian Thought*, ed. Marcia Bunge (Grand Rapids, MI: Eerdsman, 2001), 160–93, 479–80, there 166–67, and "Psalm 8:1–2," *Interpretation* 55 (April 2001): 177–80.

38. CO 31:155, 225–26, there 155. Psalm 22:9 reads (NRSV), "Yet it was you who took me from the womb; you kept me safe on my mother's breast." This evokes a reading concerning God's provision of care directly from birth. Indeed, the mentions of the womb (Ps 22:9–10, 45:4, 72:6, and 110:3) elicit no application to the virgin birth at all for Calvin but, rather, indicate God's providence. Of these, he interprets all but Ps 45:4 as concerning God's providential care. See CO 31:226, 667, and CO 32:163.

39. CO 31:452, 664–65. Calvin's comments on Ps 16:3 ("the saints on the earth"), 16:11 ("you show me the path of life"), 22:3–4 ("yet you are holy... our fathers trusted in you"), and 22:30 ("their seed will serve him") all point to God's providential care of

the elect. See CO 31:151, 157–58, 223, 236. Chapter 4 of Pitkin's book (*What Pure Eyes Could See*, 98–130) analyzes the providential character of Calvin's understanding of faith based on his interpretations of several Psalms.

40. CO 31: 42, 44.

41. CO 31:155.

42. Thus, Calvin concludes his interpretation of Psalm 16 with this teaching: "David, therefore, testifies that the true and solid joy in which the minds of [humans] may rest will never be found anywhere else but in God; and that, therefore, none but the faithful who are contented with his grace alone can be truly and perfectly happy." See CO 31:155–56; 158, there 158.

43. See CO 31:220–22, 224–26. Calvin writes: "It is a wonderful instance of the power of faith that he [David] not only endured his afflictions patiently, but that from the abyss of despair he arose to call upon God. Let us, therefore, particularly mark that David did not pour out his lamentations thinking them to be in vain and of no effect . . . . He does not pray in a doubting manner, but he promises himself the assistance that the eyes of sense did not as yet perceive" (CO 31:230). For other examples of David as the exemplar of faith, see CO 31:149, 154–55, 155, 156, 220–21, 223, 226, 230, 663, 672; CO 32:162, 203–204.

44. CO 31: 49–50, 150, 224; CO 32:205–206.

45. CO 31:45–46, 236–37. Through all of these preachers, Calvin argues that Christ is ultimately speaking: "As often, therefore, as we hear the gospel preached by [humans], we ought to consider that it is not so much they who speak as Christ who speaks by them. And this is a singular advantage that Christ lovingly allures us to himself by his own voice that we may not by any means doubt the majesty of his kingdom" (CO 31:45–46).

46. CO 31:221, 222, there 222.

47. See CO 31:225, 226, 230, 664, 670; CO 32:203, 209, 213. Psalm 72 as David's last prayer should, says Calvin, "stir up the church the more earnestly to pour forth before God the same prayers that David had continued to offer even with his last breath" (CO 31:672). He finds in David's prayer of Ps 118:5 ("I called upon God in my distress") a reminder that God's mercy never fails (CO 32:203). Likewise, he interprets the repetition of "we beseech you" in Ps 118:25 as a design of the Holy Spirit through the mouth of David to arouse the faithful to "earnestness and ardor in prayer" (CO 32:209).

48. CO 31:88.

49. CO 31:88–90, 91, 149–50, 155, 226, 232, there 232. Calvin's emphasis on God's beneficence echoes Bucer's emphasis. Calvin writes, "David here confines his attention to God's temporal benefits, but it is our duty to rise higher and to contemplate the invaluable treasures of the kingdom of heaven that he has unfolded in Christ and all the gifts that belong to the spiritual life. That by reflecting upon these, our hearts may be inflamed with love to God, that we may be stirred up to the practice of godliness, and that we may not suffer ourselves to become slothful and remiss in celebrating his praises" (CO 31:95).

50. CO 31:150–51, 152, 153.

51. CO 31:153.

52. CO 31:233; CO 32:208. Calvin also depicts David as the true, pious king and emphasizes the important role of the king in maintaining purity, piety, and the true religion of God. See CO 31:450–51, 663, 665–66.

53. CO 31:150–51, 232, 666–67; CO 32:208.

54. This is especially clear in Calvin's exhortation to the church in his comments on Ps 16:8–9: "We must look to [God] with other eyes than those of the flesh, for we shall seldom be able to perceive him unless we elevate our minds above the world; and faith prevents us from turning our back upon him . . . he [David] constantly depended upon the assistance of God, so that, amidst the various conflicts with which he was agitated, no fear of danger could make him turn his eyes to any other quarter than to God in search of succor. And thus we ought so to depend upon God as to continue to be fully persuaded of his being near to us, even when he seems to be removed to the greatest distance from us. When we shall have thus turned our eyes towards him, the masks and the vain illusions of the world will no longer deceive us" (CO 31:155).

55. Indeed, the opposite characteristics indicate the ungodly, says Calvin. For example, Calvin writes, "But the ungodly . . . never experience true joy or serene mental peace; rather, they feel terrible agitations within, which often come upon them and trouble them, so much as to constrain them to awake from their lethargy" (CO 31:156).

56. Thus Calvin writes, "By this manner of speaking, he [David] not only ascribes to God the beginning of faith, but acknowledges that he is continually making progress under his [God's] tuition; and, indeed, it is necessary for God, during the whole of our life, to continue to correct the vanity of our minds, to kindle the light of faith into a brighter flame, and by every means to advance us higher in the attainments of spiritual wisdom" (CO 31:155).

57. CO 31:88.

58. CO 32:162.

59. CO 31:153.

60. CO 31:233.

61. CO 32:208, 211–12. Likewise, Calvin deploys Ps 45:10 ("Hear, O daughter . . . forget your people") against the Roman Catholics (CO 31:457). Calvin writes on Psalm 118, clearly aiming his statement at the Roman Catholics, "From the first, we know that the master-builders have endeavored to subvert the kingdom of Christ. The same thing is taking place in our times, in those who are entrusted with the superin-tendence of the church having made every attempt to overturn that kingdom by directing against it all the machinery that they can devise" (CO 32:211–12).

62. CO 31:225, 227; CO 32:204–206.

63. See Calvin's comments on Ps 2:1–3 in CO 31:41–44. Here Calvin does mention the Jews. However, his point is that David speaks of two sets of enemies—domestic and foreign—in which the Jews are the domestic enemies and other nations are the foreign enemies. Calvin does not read Psalm 2 in reference to the passion of Christ (where the Jews are the crucifiers of Christ) but rather in reference to Christ's kingdom (where all nations rise up), and thus, his reading does not carry the same tone against the Jews as Luther's.

64. CO 32:161.

65. See CO 32:165–66. Again, Calvin does not mention the Jews as a specific group in this category of "enemies." In a couple of instances, he speaks of the enemies of the church more generally, such as on Ps 8:2 ("enemy and avenger") and Ps 2:12 ("lest you perish in the way"), where he interprets the enemies in these passages as the despisers of God (CO 31:51, 89).

66. These images are very few in number in these Psalms but include depictions of the Jews as stubborn, prideful, idolatrous, and wicked. The view of Jews as stubborn appears in Calvin's comments on Ps 22:16, the title of Psalm 110, and Ps 118:25–26 (CO 31:229; CO 32:159, 213). The view of Jews as prideful appears only once and may be found in Calvin's comments on Ps 22:16 (CO 31:228). The depiction of Jews as idolatrous also appears only once in Calvin's interpretation of these eight Psalms (comments on Ps 16:5–6 in CO 31:153). Depictions of Jews as wicked appear on Ps 2:1–3, 22:16, and 118:25–26 (CO 31:42, 229; CO 32:213).

67. CO 31:89, 457; CO 32:205, 210–12. Calvin read Ps 118:10 solely in reference to David and his enemies, where "bees" indicate the fury of David's enemies (CO 32:205). He does mention the "scribes and the priests in Christ's time" as the "builders" in Ps 118:22, but his emphasis is on how the religious leaders in all ages, including Calvin's own (i.e., Roman Catholics), continue to fail to recognize Christ and mislead the people (CO 32:210–12).

68. However, ultimately Calvin envisions David as a type of the church—thus, more as a *Christian* than as a Jew. The appeals to the Jewish nation as worthy of imitation should also be understood within Calvin's view of the church as the continuation and fulfillment of God's elect people, Israel.

69. CO 31:223.

70. CO 31:455–57. Similarly, in Ps 72:10, Calvin elevates the Jews as an example of keeping away from the corruptions of foreign nations (CO 31:668).

71. CO 32:213.

72. These passages are especially Ps 22:16, 45:6, 110:4, and 118:22. The criticisms are especially strong on Ps 22:16 and Ps 45:6. See CO 31:228–29, 451, 453; CO 32:162, 213. To be clear, I do not mean to argue that Calvin is not anti-Jewish, for there is plenty of evidence demonstrating that toward the Jews of his day he holds the same anti-Jewish views as his Protestant and Catholic contemporaries. For example, after expounding on the faithfulness of *biblical* Jews in his *Institutes* (II.x.7–23), he concludes this account with a negative evaluation of present-day Jews: "Nor would the obtuseness of the whole Jewish nation today in awaiting the Messiah's earthly kingdom be less monstrous, had the Scriptures not foretold long before that they would receive this punishment for having rejected the gospel. For it so pleased God in righteous judgment to strike blind the minds of those who by refusing the offered light of heaven voluntarily brought darkness upon themselves" (*Institutes* II.x.23). For studies on Calvin and the Jews, see Salo W. Baron, "John Calvin and the Jews," in *Essential Papers on Judaism and Christianity in Conflict: From Late Antiquity to the Reformation*, ed. Jeremy Cohen (New York: New York University Press, 1991), 380–400 [previously published in 1965]; Calvin Augustine Pater, "Calvin, the Jews and the Judaic Legacy," in *In Honor of John Calvin: Papers from the 1986 International Calvin Symposium*, ed. E. J. Furcha (Montreal: McGill

University Press, 1987), 256–95; Mary Sweetland Laver, "Calvin, Jews, and Intra-Christian Polemics," PhD dissertation, Temple University, 1988 (Ann Arbor, MI: University Microfilms, 1989); Hans-Joachim Kraus, "Israel in the Theology of Calvin— Towards a New Approach to the Old Testament and Judaism," *Christian Jewish Relations* 22 (1989): 75–86; Mary Potter Engel, "Calvin and the Jews: A Textual Puzzle," *Princeton Seminary Bulletin*, Supp. 1 (1990): 106–23; and Jack Hughes Robinson, *John Calvin and the Jews* (New York: Peter Lang, 1992). See also the more recent article by Achim Detmers, "Calvin, the Jews, and Judaism," in *Jews, Judaism, and the Reformation in Sixteenth-Century Germany*, ed. Dean P. Bell and Stephen G. Burnett (Leiden: Brill, 2006), 197–217; and his book *Reformation und Judentum: Israel-Lehren and Einstellungen zum Judentum von Luther bis zum frühen Calvin* (Stuttgart: Kohlhammer).

73. CO 31:228–29, 452, 453. The same may be seen in Calvin's defense of the application of Ps 110:4 and Ps 118:22 to teach the divinity of Christ, for such readings according to Calvin retain the simple and natural sense of the passage. See CO 32:163 and 213.

74. A longer version of this section on "Calvin and Jewish Exegesis" appears in an article in volume 85 of the *Dutch Review of Church History*. See "Luther, Bucer, and Calvin on Psalms 8 and 16: Confessional Formation and the Question of Jewish Exegesis," in *The Formation of Clerical and Confessional Identities in Early Modern Europe*, ed. Wim Janse and Barbara Pitkin, *Dutch Review of Church History*, Vol. 85 (Leiden: Brill, 2005), 169–86.

75. See Bucer, 56a.

76. CO 31:88. Bucer makes this point also, not by rejecting the Jewish reading, but by adding that the Name also refers to the works and properties of God. Bucer, 56a.

77. Bucer, 56b–57a.

78. CO 31:89–90.

79. Bucer, 56b.

80. CO 31:89.

81. Bucer only briefly quotes Kimhi, and he leaves out Kimhi's interpretation of this verse as concerning the providence of God in his account. Kimhi writes, after expounding on infants' ability to suck, that this verse is given "that man may be able to see that all is within the design of a Designer and not, as the enemies of the Lord say, that everything happens by nature and chance without the direction of a Director and the design of a Designer" (David Kimhi, *The Longer Commentary of R. David Kimhi on the First Book of Psalms* [trans by R. G. Finch; New York: Macmillan, 1919], 49). See the Hebrew text in *The First Book of the Psalms according to the Text of the Cambridge MS Bible with the Longer Commentary of R. David Qimchi*, ed. S. M. Schiller-Szinessy (Leipzig: F. A. Brookhaus, 1883), 26.

82. CO 31:88, 91, 95. Kimhi writes, "Such being the case, it is incumbent upon humanity to reflect and to recognize the work of God and to confess God in everything" (Kimhi in Schiller-Szinessy, 26, and in Finch, 50).

83. CO 31:88; Kimhi in Schiller-Szinessy, 25, and Finch, 48–49. Again, Bucer does not discuss the translation of the verb תְּנָה or give Kimhi's reading of it. There is one other citation of Jewish exegesis by Bucer in Psalm 8 not dealt with here. Bucer refers to Kimhi's interpretation of "whatever passes along the paths of the sea"

in Ps 8:8 as concerning humanity's ability to cross the seas by ship. Bucer rejects Kimhi's reading (Bucer, 59a). Calvin makes no reference at all to this interpretation.

84. Bucer, 91a. See the commentary of Rashi in *Rashi's Commentary on Psalms 1–89*, with English translation by Mayer I. Gruber (Atlanta: Scholars, 1998), 4, 99. Bucer gives no specifically named exegete on the translation of עֲצְבוֹתָם as "troubles," though this is how Kimhi translates it.

85. CO 31:151–52; Kimhi in Schiller-Szinessy, 42–43, and Finch, 75.

86. Bucer, 90a–91a; CO 31:150–51. Calvin writes, "David, after the sentence we have just now been considering [verse two], now adds that the only way of serving God aright is to endeavor to do good to his holy servants. And the truth is that God, as our good deeds cannot extend to Him, substitutes the saints in His place, towards whom we are to exercise charity. . . . This passage, therefore, teaches us that there is no sacrifice more acceptable to God than when we sincerely and heartily connect ourselves with the society of the righteous, and . . . cultivate and maintain with them brotherly good-will" (CO 31:150).

87. See Bucer, 90a, 92a, 93b; Kimhi in Schiller-Szinessy, 42, 43, 44, and Finch, 74–75, 76, 76–77, 77–78; CO 31:153, 155, 155–56, 158.

88. Admittedly, these elements of Calvin's exegesis of Psalms 8 and 16 can be adequately explained by factors other than that he is using David Kimhi; however, Hans-Joachim Kraus is convinced that Calvin is reading the Jewish exegetes themselves and not simply via other Christian resources that use Jewish exegesis. Kraus writes, "Calvin may have drawn on his encyclopedic *Postillen*. But he probably also knew the sources directly, or through the works of the highly respected Hebraists among the Reformation exegetes" ("Calvin's Exegetical Principles," *Interpretation* 31 [1977]: 9). Twelve years later, Kraus is even more convinced that Calvin knew the Jewish sources directly: "Calvin was not content, as for instance Luther had been, to study the great Jewish commentators . . . in the compendia of Nicholas of Lyra (1270–1340), but read them in the original and referred to them constantly" ("Israel in the Theology of Calvin—Towards a New Approach to the Old Testament and Judaism," *Christian Jewish Relations* 22 [1989]: 75).

89. In the beginning of this discussion, Calvin points out: "for we know what freedoms the apostles took in quoting texts of Scripture" (CO 31:92).

90. This, however, may be limited to Bucer's treatment of these two particular Psalms (though I have found it generally true for all eight Psalms considered here), for Hobbs argues that Bucer gives primarily historical readings of the Psalms in reference to the life of David. See "How Firm a Foundation," 485–91.

91. Indeed, this head-member reading is in keeping with the medieval and late-medieval interpretive traditions' reading of these Psalms in reference to the mystical body of Christ, the church.

92. Aegidius Hunnius, *Calvinus Iudiazans, hoc est: Iudaicae Glossae et Corruptelae, quibus Iohannes Calvinus illustrissima Scripturae sacrae Loca & Testamonia, de gloriosa Trinitate, Deitate Christi, & Spiritus Sancti, cum primis autem ascensione in caelos et sessione ad dextram Dei, detestandum in modum corrumpere no exhorruit. Addita est corruptelarum*

confutatio per Aegidium Hunnium (Wittennberg, 1593), 4–5, 126, 149, 149–50, 151, 172–73.

93. CO 31:157.

94. Bucer, 7a.

95. Irena Backus finds a shift in Bucer's use of the church fathers between 1528 and 1536 from a much less critical appropriation of them to a more cautious but more frequent use of them. See Backus, "Martin Bucer and the Patristic Tradition," in *Martin Bucer and Sixteenth-Century Europe: Actes du colloque de Strasbourg* (28–31 août 1991), ed. Christian Krieger and Marc Lienhard (Leiden: Brill, 1993), 1:64. This is important because the writing of Bucer's Psalms commentary appears before this shift.

96. Not included here is an analysis of Calvin's use of the church fathers, mostly for reasons that this venture is beyond the scope of this project. Furthermore, Calvin makes very little explicit reference to church fathers in his exegesis of these eight Psalms. In fact, there is only one overt reference to a church father: he explicitly argues against Augustine's application of "head of the corner" in Ps 118:22 to Christ as the cornerstone who unites the two different walls representing the Jews and the Gentiles (CO 32:211). All of Calvin's other references to other interpreters are very general, and he refers to the vast majority in his debates on how to translate a Hebrew word (e.g., "some translate it . . . while others translate it . . . " after which Calvin proceeds to give his preferred translation and his reasons). Thus, it is at least initially unclear in these cases whether Calvin is speaking of Jewish exegetes, Christian exegetes, or both. The handful of comments in which it is immediately clear that he is referring to Christian inter-preters all express criticism of these interpreters. These include Calvin's denunciation of the use of Ps 2:7 in reference to the Trinity (CO 31:46–47), the dismissal of the translation of Ps 2:12 as "embrace purity" (which is Jerome's; see CO 31:51), the refuta-tion of the attribution of Psalm 72 as "simply a prophecy of Christ" (CO 31:664), and rejection of the various interpretations of "from the womb of the morning" in Ps 110:3 (CO 32:163). For a study of Calvin's use of the church fathers, see the book by Anthony N. S. Lane, *John Calvin: Student of the Church Fathers* (Grand Rapids, MI: Baker Books, 1999) and his extensive bibliography. See also the article by David Steinmetz, "Calvin and Patristic Exegesis," in *Calvin in Context* (New York: Oxford University Press, 1995), 122–40.

5. THE JUDAIZING CALVIN: THE DEBATE OF HUNNIUS AND PAREUS

1. Aegidius Hunnius, *Calvinus Iudiazans, hoc est: Iudaicae Glossae et Corruptelae, quibus Iohannes Calvinus illustrissima Scripturae sacrae Loca & Testamonia, de gloriosa Trinitate, Deitate Christi, & Spiritus Sancti, cum primis autem ascensione in caelos et sessione ad dextram Dei, detestandum in modum corrumpere no exhorruit. Addita est corruptelarum confutatio per Aegidium Hunnium* (Wittennberg, 1593).

2. Hunnius, 7.

3. Hunnius, 5–7, there 6. As a pertinent historical note, just four years prior to the publication of Calvin's Psalms commentary, Michael Servetus had been executed (1553)

for his anti-Trinitarianism. Indeed, at this time Calvin was lecturing on the Psalms in Geneva. Calvin would not have imagined that he would be accused of undermining the doctrine of Trinity.

4. Interestingly enough, seven of the eight Psalms considered in this study play a central role in the case Hunnius is trying to make against Calvin. The only Psalm Hunnius does not use is Psalm 118. Two other Psalms (Ps 33:6 and Ps 68:18) are also employed in Hunnius's arguments against Calvin.

5. See the chapter by David Steinmetz, "Calvin and His Lutheran Critics," in *Calvin in Context* (New York: Oxford University Press, 1995), 172–86. Calvin is seen as a judaizer even by someone like Servetus, who accused him of creating a kind of "Jewish legalism." See Baron, "John Calvin and the Jews," in *Essential Papers on Judaism and Christianity in Conflict: From Late Antiquity to the Reformation,* ed. Jeremy Cohen (New York: New York University Press, 1991), 383–84. Lutherans also accused Calvin of judaizing because of his more positive view of the law in the Christian life. See, for example, the brief comment made by Kraus, "Israel in the Theology of Calvin—Towards a New Approach to the Old Testament and Judaism," *Christian Jewish Relations* 22 (1989): 77. Louis Israel Newman writes about charges of judaizing against Calvin from both Catholics and radical Protestants (*Jewish Influence on Christian Reform Movements,* Columbia University Oriental Studies 23 [New York: Columbia University Press, 1925], 584–96).

6. Aegidius Hunnius, *Articulus de Trinitate, per quaestiones et responsiones pertractatus solide, et indubitatis testimonies sacrarum literarum contra quavis haereticorum veterum et recentium blasphemas strophas et corruptelas firmissime communitus* (Frankfurt am Main: Johannes Spies, 1589).

7. See David Steinmetz, "The Judaizing Calvin," in *Die Patristik in der Bibelexegese des 16. Jahrhunderts,* ed. David C. Steinmetz and Robert Kolb, Wolfenbütteler Forschungen, Band 85 (Wiesbaden: Harrassowitz, 1999), 136.

8. See the reply of David Pareus in his *In Quartem Explicationum Catecheticarum Partem, De Gratitudine, Praefatio, in Miscellanea Catechetica* (Johannes Tornaesius, 1622), 177–93, esp. 181. See also Steinmetz, 136–37.

9. Specifically, Hunnius attacks Calvin's exegesis of Gen 1, Gen 19:13, Gen 35:7, Ps 2:7–8, Ps 33:6, Ps 45:6–7, Ps 68:18, Mic 5:2, Is 6:3, Jn 10: 30, Jn 14:10, Jn 17:21, 1 Jn 5:7, Col 1:15–16, Gen 3:15, Jer 31:22, Hag 2:6–7, Is 40:3, Deut 18:18–19, Is 61:1–2, Zech 9:9, Zech 13:7, Zech 11:12, Is 50:6, Ps 8:4–6, all of Psalm 22, Is 63:1–4, Is 43:25, Zech 9:11, Ps 16:8–10, Mic 2:13, Hos 6:2, Hos 13:14, Zech 14:4, and Ps 110:1. He also criticizes Calvin's exegesis of Ps 72:8 within the larger discussion of his exegesis of Zech 9:11.

10. David Pareus, *Libri Duo: I. Calvinus Orthodoxus de Sacrosancta Trinitate: et de aeterna Christi Divinitate. II. Solida Expositio XXXIIX. Difficilimorum Scripturae Locorum et Oraculorum: et de recta ratione applicandi Oracula Prophetica ad Christum. Oppositi Pseudocalvino Iudaizanti nuper a quodam emisso* (Neustadt: Matthaeus Harnisch, 1595).

11. Hunnius, 4, 5, 6.

12. Hunnius, 18, 19, 22, 23, there 22, 23.

13. Hunnius, 30–32, there 32. See CO 31:451, 452–54. After first applying Ps 45:6–7 to Solomon, Calvin clearly states that this is the literal sense of the text and then moves on to show the comparison of Christ under the type of Solomon. Hunnius points out that the apostle warns those who ignore this testimony (Heb 2:1–4) and states, "I do not doubt that this applies to Calvin when he narrates the pericope of this Psalm concerning Solomon and this in a judaizing way" (Hunnius, 31).

14. Hunnius, 32–35, there 33. Hunnius calls him an αυτοδιδακτω, a self-teacher of Scripture. For Calvin's exegesis, see CO 31:628.

15. Hunnius, 122–125, there 124. See CO 31:92. Here Hunnius cites Dan 4:35 and Is 40:17.

16. Hunnius, 125–26, there 125. Hunnius goes on to point out Calvin's further statements that the Apostle Paul drags [trahit] the meaning of Ps 8:4 to the debasement of Christ, just as the apostle also "deflects" and "accommodates" the meanings of Deut 30:12 in Rom 10:5–7 and Ps 68:18 in Eph 4:8. See CO 31:93.

17. Hunnius, 127–28.

18. Hunnius, 131, 133, 134, there 133. Calvin writes on Ps 22:16–17 and Hunnius quotes: "If they object that David was never nailed to a cross, the answer is easy, namely, that in bewailing his condition, he has made use of a metaphor, declaring that he was not less afflicted by his enemies than the man who is suspended on a cross, having his hand and feet pierced through with nails. We will meet a little after with more of the same kind of metaphors" (CO 31:229; Hunnius, 132). Likewise, Calvin comments on Ps 22:18 and Hunnius quotes: "What follows in the next verse concerning his garments is metaphorical. It is as if he [David] had said that all his goods had become a prey to his enemies, even as conquerors are accustomed to plunder the vanquished or to divide the spoil among themselves by casting lots to determine the share that belongs to each" (CO 31:229; Hunnius, 132).

19. Hunnius, 146–48. Calvin comments on Ps 16:10 (and Hunnius quotes), "David entertains the undoubted assurance of eternal salvation, which freed him from all anxiety and fear. It is as if he had said, 'There will always be ready for me a way of escape from the grave that I may not remain in corruption'" (CO 31:156).

20. Hunnius, 149–50.

21. Hunnius, 151, 164–65.

22. Hunnius, 166. He writes, "Truly in this way Calvin weakens this citation of Psalm 68 with his wicked metaphors when he believes its sense to be characteristic of the things and history encompassed under David."

23. Hunnius, 170–74, there 174.

24. See Hunnius, 175–76, 176–77, 180–81. Of course, Hunnius points to the interpretations of Ps 110:1 concerning Christ in Heb 1:13, Matt 22:41–46, Mk 12:35–37, and Lk 20:41–44.

25. Hunnius, 178–79.

26. Hunnius, 181, 182–83, 183, 186.

27. Hunnius, 185–86, 187–88.

28. Hunnius, 182–83, 183, 186.

29. Hunnius, 181.

30. Hunnius, 185–86, 187–88.

31. Pareus, 21–43. The nine passages concerning Christ's deity are Ps 45:6–7, Is 9:6, Jer 23:6, Hos 11:5, Gen 32:29, Zech 1:9–12, Zech 2:3–4, Is 25:9, and Mal 3:1. He also demonstrates Calvin's testimonies of the deity of the Holy Spirit in his *Institutes* and Old Testament commentaries on Gen 1:1–3, Gen 1:26, Gen 11:7, Gen 1:3, Gen 18:2 and 13, Gen 48:15–16, Ex 3:2, Ex 33:14, Ps 33:6, Ps 45:6–7, Is 6:1, Is 7:14, Is 8:14, Is 9:6, Is 25:9, Jer 23:5–6, Jer 33:15–16, Dan 7:13, Hos 12:4, Mic 4:3, Mic 5:4, Zech 1:19–20, Zech 2:8, Zech 3:3, Zech 11:14, Zech 12:10, Ex 8:9, Is 6:10, and Is 48:16.

32. Pareus, 43–74. The passages considered in Calvin's harmony of the Gospels are Lk 1:17, 32, 35, 43; 24:45; and Matt 1:23, 9:4, 17:5, 21:2, 22:10, 22:45, 23:37, and 28:19. The passages discussed from Calvin's commentary on John are Jn 1:1, 3, 6, 14; 2:19: 5:17; 8:58; 10:36; 15:26; 16:28; 17:3, 5; 19:37; and 20:28, 31. The passages discussed from his Acts commentary are Acts 2:33, 5:4, 7:30, 9:3, 9:14, 13:2, and 20:28. The passages covered from Calvin's commentaries on the epistles are Rom 1:3, 8:11, 9:5, 14:11, 15:12; 1 Cor 1:2, 3:16, 10:9, 12:11; Gal 4:4; Phil 2:6, 2:10; Col 2:9–10; 1 Thes 3:10; 2 Thes 2:16; 1 Tim 3:16; Tit 2:13; Heb 1:2, 1:3, 1:8, 13:21; and 1 Jn 2:22, 4:2, 5:20.

33. These are Gen 1:1, Gen 19:24, Gen 35:7, Ps 33:6, and Is 6:3.

34. These are Jn 10:30, 10:38, 14:11, 17:11, and 5:7.

35. These are Gen 41, Is 43:25, Is 63:1, Jer 31:22, Hos 6:2, Hos 13:14, Mic 2:13, Hag 2:8, Zech 9:11, and Zech 14:4.

36. These are Ps 2:7, Ps 16:8, Ps 22:1, Ps 45:8, Ps 68:19, Is 40:3, and Is 50:5.

37. These are Gen 3:15, Gen 22:18, Ps 8:5, Deut 18:15, Is 61:1, and Zech 13:7.

38. These are Ps 110:1, Mic 5:2, Zech 9:9, Zech 11:12, and Col 1:15.

39. Pareus, 76–77, there 76.

40. Pareus, 77–78, 79. Here Pareus refers to Paul's censure of Peter's behavior in Gal 2:14: "If you, though a Jew, live like a Gentile and not like a Jew, how can you compel the Gentiles to judaize, that is, to live like Jews."

41. Pareus, 80–82. Pareus provides a friendly quote from a letter of Brentz to Calvin.

42. See Pareus, 84–85.

43. Pareus, 85–86; CO 10:405.

44. Pareus, 87; CO 10:403.

45. Pareus, 86–89.

46. On the first class of passages, Pareus denies that these are all clear testimonies of the Trinity, and he points out that there is not an exegetical consensus that the Genesis passages concern Trinity. See Pareus, 91. On the second class, Pareus points out that even Luther did not read all of these in reference to the essential unity of the persons of the Trinity. See Pareus, 92. As for the third class of passages, Pareus contends that many others also read these texts according to their literal-historical sense. See Pareus, 92.

47. Pareus, 93–98. He gives examples of each of the four kinds of composite types. For example, Ps 22:1 is an example of a prophecy that is fulfilled literally in both Christ and the type, David. On the other hand, Ps 22:16 ("they pierced my hand and feet") and Ps 22:18 ("they divide my clothes among themselves") are prophecies that are fulfilled

literally in Christ and figuratively in David. Psalm 2:9 ("You shall break them with a rod of iron") is a prophecy that applies literally to David and figuratively to Christ. Finally, Ps 118:22 ("The stone that the builders rejected") is a prophecy that is fulfilled figuratively by both Christ and the type. See Pareus, 97–98.

48. Pareus, 95–96.

49. Augustine, *City of God*, xvii.3 and Pareus, 101. Pareus goes on to give specific examples of Augustine's application of this principle to Solomon in Psalm 72 (*City of God*, xvii.8) and to David in Psalm 89 (*City of God*, xvii.9). See Pareus, 101–102.

50. Pareus cites the examples of Pomeranus's and Cornerus's exegeses of Psalms 2, 16, 8, 22, 45, and 118, among others. See Pareus, 102.

51. Pareus, 103–104.

52. Pareus, 104–105, 105–106, there 106. Of course, these are reformulations of Hunnius's accusations in Pareus's language of simple and composite types—terminology that Hunnius does not use. Thus, one could say that Pareus artfully evades the simple fact that Hunnius's point is that when one does not take the apostles' or evangelists' reading of a text as authoritative, but accuses them of bending the text, this undermines the exegetical foundation of key Christian beliefs.

53. Pareus, 193–96, 198. See CO 31:42–43. He quotes a long section from Calvin, including his statement that Psalm 2 is "not violently or even allegorically twisted to apply to Christ but truly predicted concerning him."

54. Pareus, 199–202.

55. Pareus, 203–205, there 205.

56. Pareus, 206–207, there 207.

57. Pareus, 209–210.

58. Pareus, 212–13. See Calvin's comments on Acts 2:25–28 in his commentary on the Acts of the Apostles in CO 48:41–45. Thus, one should note that Pareus has not actually defended Calvin's *Psalms* commentary. Pareus also points to an anti-Jewish statement Calvin makes in his Acts commentary concerning Ps 16:8–10 to argue against Hunnius's accusation of judaizing. See Pareus, 214.

59. Pareus, 217–21, 224–25. Of course, what Pareus is either purposefully neglecting or failing to see is that Hunnius and much of the Christian tradition reads Psalm 22 as *pure* prophecy and not through the tool of typology at all. He also quotes an anti-Jewish statement of Calvin that the Jews have corrupted the translation of Ps 22:16 to prove that Calvin is not judaizing but is concerned to argue against the Jews (Pareus, 221–22).

60. Pareus, 223–24. See CO 31:229 and CO 47:415–16.

61. See CO 31:451; Hunnius, 31. Hunnius's other criticism is that this verse refers to Christ's deity and Calvin does not interpret it as such. Pareus does not address this part of Hunnius's charges.

62. Pareus, 229, 227–28, 232. Pareus cites from Luther's 1532 commentary on Psalm 45: "Here we should call to mind again what we said above that the psalm is purely allegorical and that beneath these metaphorical words like 'king' and 'kingdom' a spiritual kingdom and the church are to be understood" (WA 40/2:481–82). Thus Pareus contends, "In truth, the argument is weakened and overthrown if the psalm is

seen completely to be an allegory or a metaphor. . . . Luther labors more in vain than Calvin" (232, 233). He argues that the "literal sense" can rightly refer to both its historical and prophetic senses. Thus, just because Calvin said that the "simple and natural" sense applies to Solomon does not negate that the literal sense is also its meaning concerning Christ. Pareus also complains that the way Hunnius portrays Calvin would make one think that Calvin did not apply Psalm 45 to Christ at all, which is most certainly not the case. Thus, he accuses Hunnius of "craftily suppressing" the fuller content of Calvin's exegesis. See Pareus, 229–31.

63. Pareus, 271–73. See CO 55:22–25, quote on 23. That is, Calvin's reading of Ps 8:4–6 as concerning the excellence of humanity can be seen as the precise excellence *that is restored by Christ*. Note that Pareus does not actually deal with the fact that Calvin hardly mentions Christ at all in his interpretation of Ps 8:4–6 in the *Psalms* commentary.

64. Pareus, 273–76.

65. Pareus, 276–79. Note that Pareus leaves out Hunnius's criticism that Calvin does not use this Psalm to teach Christ's deity, passion, or ascension.

66. Pareus, 279–80.

67. Pareus, 283; CO 45:84.

68. Pareus, 296, 298, 300. Hunnius has referred to Calvin's opening statements on the first verse that it might "to some extent be applied to the person of David," inasmuch as David was a king by divine right. See Hunnius, 176–80, and CO 32:160. Pareus wants the reader to see this statement couched between Calvin's contentions against the Jews. In Calvin's discussion of the title of Psalm 110, he has already written that the Psalm "would itself admit no other interpretation" except the one in reference to Christ. Afterward, Calvin adds, "For although we should have a dispute with the Jews, the most obstinate people in the world, about the right application of it, we are able by the most irresistible arguments to compel them to admit that the truths here stated relate neither to David nor to any other person than the Mediator alone" (CO 32:159). Calvin later makes three more negative statements about Jewish exegesis. See CO 32:160, 163, 164.

69. See Jerome Friedman, *The Most Ancient Testimony: Sixteenth-Century Christian-Hebraica in the Age of Renaissance Nostalgia* (Athens: Ohio University Press, 1983), 5–6, and his article, "Protestants, Jews, and Jewish Sources," in *Piety, Politics, and Ethics: Reformation Studies in Honor of George Wolfgang Forell*, ed. Carter Lindberg, Sixteenth Century Essays and Studies 3 (Kirksville, MO: Sixteenth Century Journal Publishers, 1984), 139–56, esp 155–56.

70. Scholars, particularly those who maintain the existence of two schools of Reformation exegesis, have noted this disparity between Reformed and Lutheran views on the usefulness of Jewish exegesis for Christian biblical interpretation. Generally, Lutherans espouse the usefulness of Hebrew but not the usefulness of Jewish exegesis, and Reformed exegetes find both to be eminently useful. See Frank Rosenthal, "The Rise of Christian Hebraism in the Sixteenth Century," *Historia Judaica* 7 (1945): 173–91; Bernard Roussel, "Strasbourg et l'école rhénane d'exégèse

(1524–1540)," *Bulletin de la Société de l'Histoire du Protestantisme Française* 135 (1989): 36–41; and Friedman, *Most Ancient Testimony*, 2, 165–74.

71. This is not to say that Luther and Lutherans were not also quite critical of the previous exegetical tradition, but significantly less so in the particular area of christological interpretation and more so concerning specific doctrinal concerns, such as the teaching of justification by faith alone or the contrast between law and gospel.

CONCLUSION

1. See John W. O'Malley, *Trent and All That: Renaming Catholicism in the Early Modern Era* (Cambridge: Cambridge University Press, 2000), 138–39, and Bodo Nischan, *Prince, People, and Confession: The Second Reformation in Brandenburg* (Philadelphia: University of Pennsylvania Press, 1994), 1. See also Thomas Brady, "Confessionalization—The Career of a Concept," in *Confessionalization in Europe, 1555–1700: Essays in Honor and Memory of Bodo Nischan*, ed. John M. Headley, Hans J. Hillerbrand, and Anthony J. Papalas (Burlington, VT: Ashgate, 2004), 11, 19.

2. See Brady, 12, and Ernst Walter Zeeden, *Die Entstehung der Konfession. Grundlagen und Formen der Konfessionsbildung im Zeitalter der Glaubenskämpfe* (München: R. Oldenbourg, 1965). Likewise, in a later essay in *Confessionalization in Europe*, Mack P. Holt also appeals to the need to return to Zeeden's original definition of "confessional formation," which contains an emphasis on the religious aspects of confessional formation and the forces "from below" equal to those "from above" (i.e., the state). See Mack P. Holt, "Confessionalization beyond the Germanies: The Case of France," in *Confessionalization in Europe*, 272–73.

3. This is also one of the important goals of the recent volume edited by Wim Janse and Barbara Pitkin, *The Formation of Clerical and Confessional Identities in Early Modern Europe*, Dutch Review of Church History 85 (Leiden: Brill, 2005). The editors rightly point out the vital—and perhaps more direct—role of preaching (in addition to the biblical commentary) for formation of confessional identities. I fully concur with the significance of preaching, but the study of the preaching of the Psalms is beyond the scope of this project.

4. Markus Wriedt argues for the important role of the printing press as Luther's instrument of preaching and teaching. Wriedt specifically points to Luther's use of the biblical commentary for confessional interests and the influences of the printing press upon this process. He writes, "Even the style of biblical commentaries changed under the influence of the extensive use of the printing press by Luther and other Wittenberg professors to a continuous explanation as *lectio continua* . . . . Theology became either commenting on the Scriptures or the controversial explanation of the evangelical truth against its opponents" ("'Founding a New Church . . .': The Early Ecclesiology of Martin Luther in the Light of the Debate about Confessionalization," in *Confessionalization in Europe*, 63). Mark U. Edwards also points to Luther's creative and shrewd use of the printing press (*Printing, Propaganda, and Martin Luther* [Berkeley: University of California Press, 1994]).

5. The one thing I thought I might find, but did not find, was a contrast between Luther's emphasis on law versus gospel and Calvin's more positive use of the law. This can be seen in a few places in a study contrasting Luther's and Calvin's exegesis of the Psalms; however, Calvin's lack of maintaining the contrast between law and gospel is not a criticism Hunnius used in his arguments against Calvin's exegesis of the Psalms.

6. Thus, Luther, Bucer, and Calvin differ in their understandings of the content of the prophecies contained in these Psalms. For Luther, the content is, first and foremost, predictions of Christ's earthly life (incarnation, crucifixion, etc.). Bucer retains this content but equally emphasizes the prophecies of Christ's kingdom. Calvin keeps only the prophecies of the kingdom.

7. See, for example, Pareus, 227–28.

8. It was also a weapon used by the Roman Catholic Church to discredit the Protestants. See, for example, Louis Israel Newman's discussion of Roman Catholic charges of judaizing against Protestants in *Jewish Influence on Christian Reform Movements*, Columbia University Oriental Studies 23 (New York: Columbia University Press, 1925), 584–96.

9. Note that this *Defense* is written just two years after Bucer's first edition of his Psalms commentary. Luther writes, "We have not acted out of a misunderstanding of the languages nor out of ignorance of the rabbinical commentaries, but knowingly and deliberately" (WA 38:9). See Stephen G. Burnett's discussion in "Reassessing the 'Basel-Wittenberg Conflict': Dimensions of the Reformation-Era Discussion of Hebrew Scholarship," in *Hebraica Veritas? Christian Hebraists and the Study of Judaism in Early Modern Europe*, ed. Allison P. Coudert and Jeffrey S. Shoulson (Philadelphia: University of Pennsylvania Press, 2004), 188–89.

10. Burnett shows that fellow Reformed expositors appeared even more concerned about Bucer's use of Jewish exegesis than Luther was. This can be seen in Conrad Pellican and Ulrich Zwingli's evaluations of Bucer's commentary on the Psalms. Pellican writes in a letter concerning Bucer's Psalms commentary, "I have read almost all of your first book . . . and am compelled to approve your effort and your judgment, save that I am pained by your labors in searching out and sifting the opinions of the rabbis, which you repeat time and again while they disagree with one another both in grammar and sense" (quote taken from Burnett, 189, as quoted and translated in Hobbs, "Conrad Pellican," 97–98).

11. Burnett, 192–93.

12. See the many studies of Willem Van't Spijker on this topic: "Prädestination bei Bucer und Calvin. Ihre gegenseitige Beeinflussung und Abhängigkeit," in *Calvinus Theologus: d. Referate d. Congrès Europ. de Recherches Calviniennes vom 16.–19. September 1974 in Amsterdam*, ed. W. H. Neuser (Neukirchen-Vluyn: Neukirchener Verlag, 1976), 85–111; "The Influence of Bucer on Calvin as Becomes Evident from the *Institutes*," in *John Calvin's Institutes* (Potchefstroom, South Africa, 1986), 106–32; "Bucer und Calvin," in *Martin Bucer and Sixteenth Century Europe: Actes du colloque de Strasbourg*, ed. Christian Krieger and Marc Lienhard, 1:461–70 (Leiden: Brill, 1993), 461–70; "Bucer's Influence on Calvin: Church and Community," in *Martin Bucer: Reforming Church and*

Community, ed. D. F. Wright (Cambridge: Cambridge University Press, 1994), 32–44; and "Calvin's Friendship with Martin Bucer: Did It Make Calvin a Calvinist?" in *Calvin and His Contemporaries: Colleagues, Friends and Conflicts*, ed. David Foxgrover (Grand Rapids, MI: CRC Product Services, 1998), 169–86. See also Hasting Eells, "Martin Bucer and the Conversion of John Calvin," *Princeton Theological Review* 22 (1924): 402–19. Eells argues that Bucer was not a significant figure in Calvin's conversion.

13. Wilhelm Pauck gives a nice summary of the earlier scholarship of Seeberg, A. Lang, Scheibe, and O. Ritschl on these topics. See Pauck, "Calvin and Butzer," in his *The Heritage of the Reformation* (Glencoe, IL: Free Press, 1961), 86–87. On continuities between their doctrines of predestination, see August Lang, *Der Evangelienkommentar Martin Butzers und die Grundzüge seiner Theologie* (Leipzig: Aalen, 1900); and Willem Van't Spijker, "The Influence on Calvin as Becomes Evident from the *Institutes*," 119–22. On their shared emphasis on the crucial work of the Spirit, see Pauck, "Calvin and Butzer," 87, and Willem Van't Spijker, "The Influence on Calvin as Becomes Evident from the *Institutes*," 116–19, and "Bucer's Influence on Calvin: Church and Community," 33. With specific reference to exegetical methods and emphases, Craig Farmer's study of Reformed readings of the story of the Samaritan woman reveals their shared emphases upon proper self-knowledge as the true fruit of grace and upon the doctrine of election. See his article, "Changing Images of the Samaritan Woman in Early Reformed Commentaries on John," *Church History* 65 (1996): 365–75, esp. 374–75.

14. See his "Bucer's Influence on Calvin: Church and Community," in *Martin Bucer: Reforming Church and Community*, 34–44. Here, Spijker stresses the *mutual* influences between Bucer and Calvin. For their shared emphasis on piety, see "Calvin's Friendship with Martin Bucer: Did It Make Calvin a Calvinist?" in *Calvin and His Contemporaries*, 176.

15. They share, however, the usefulness of Jewish exegesis to support their particularly Reformed doctrinal readings (beneficence of God, election, and providence) and the use of these Psalms to encourage the cultivation of piety.

16. This is especially the argument of Jerome Friedman in his *The Most Ancient Testimony: Sixteenth-Century Christian Hebraica in the Age of Renaissance Nostalgia* (Athens: Ohio University Press, 1983), 128–35, 165–76. Earlier proponents of the theory, such as Bernard Roussel, also point to the key factors of the Rhenish School's emphases on the actual words of the biblical texts and their context, author, and audience. For a more recent summary of his views, see his "Strasbourg et l'école rhénane d'exégèse (1525–1540)," *Bulletin de la Société de l'Histoire du Protestantism Française* 135 (1989): 42–53, esp. 39–40.

17. See Barbara Pitkin's article, "Seeing and Believing in the Commentaries of John by Martin Bucer and John Calvin," *Church History* 68 (1999): 865–85, esp. 882–83, and Burnett, 189, 192.

18. See my clarification of this in footnote 72 of chapter 4.

19. Calvin Augustus Pater, "Calvin, the Jews and the Judaic Legacy," in *In Honor of John Calvin: Papers from the 1986 International Calvin Symposium*, ed. E. J. Furcha (Montreal: McGill University Press), 290–91.

20. Salo W. Baron, "John Calvin and the Jews," in *Essential Papers on Judaism and Christianity in Conflict: From Late Antiquity to the Reformation*, ed. Jeremy Cohen (New York: New York University Press, 1991), 380–400, there 394.

21. See Hans-Joachim Kraus, "Israel in the Theology of Calvin—Towards a New Approach to the Old Testament and Judaism," *Christian Jewish Relations* 22 (1989): 85. Though Kraus does recognize the distinction between Calvin's treatment of the biblical Jew (i.e., quite positive) as opposed to the post-biblical Jew (i.e., rather negative), he still makes this claim, which I find to be overstated. See Kraus, 83.

22. Mary Potter Engel, "Calvin and the Jews: A Textual Puzzle," *Princeton Seminary Bulletin* Supp 1 (1990):106–23. For example, Engel argues that Calvin simultaneously affirms that God's covenant with the Jews is eternal and also that it has been ruptured by Jewish apostasy (110).

23. Though much of Calvin's Old Testament exegesis escapes prior Christian anti-Jewish tendencies, this is not necessarily true of his New Testament exegesis. Precisely because Calvin emphasizes reading the literal sense of the text in its original historical setting, this leads him to read the Jews of the Old Testament as part of God's covenant, whereas many of the Jews of the New Testament are those who question and oppose Christ.

24. See the helpful surveys of the changing understandings of the literal sense of Scripture given by Brevard S. Childs, "The Sensus Literalis of Scripture: An Ancient and Modern Problem," in *Beitrage Zur Alttestamentlichen Theologie*, ed. Herbert Donner, Robert Hanhart, and Rudolf Smend (Göttingen: Vandenhoeck & Ruprecht, 1977), 80–87, and Richard Muller, "Biblical Interpretation in the Era of the Reformation: The View from the Middle Ages," in *Biblical Interpretation in the Era of the Reformation*, ed. Richard A. Muller and John L. Thompson (Grand Rapids, MI: Eerdmans, 1996), 8–11.

25. Childs, 86–87. See also Hans W. Frei, *The Eclipse of Biblical Narrative: A Study in Eighteenth and Nineteenth Century Hermeneutics* (New Haven: Yale University Press, 1974), 19–20, 23–24. Frei is clearer and more careful than Childs on the distinctions between Luther and Calvin, though I think Childs is still basically right; yet, I want to clarify that uniting the grammatical sense with the theological is not the same as uniting the *historical* sense with the theological. In other words, Luther and Calvin define and treat "history" in these Psalms in very significantly different ways.

26. See, for examples, August Tholuck, "Die Verdienste Calvin's als Ausleger der heiligen Schrift," in *Vermischte Schriften, großtentheils apologetischen Inhalts* (Hamburg: Friedrich Perthes, 1839), 2:330–60; Eduard Reuss, "Calvin considéré comme exegete," *Revue de Théologie* 6 (1853): 223–48; Philip Schaff, "Calvin as a Commentator," *Presbyterian and Reformed Review* 3 (1892): 462–69; Frederic W. Farrar, *History of Interpretation* (Grand Rapids, MI: Baker Book House, 1961, reprint from 1886), 342–54; and Kember Fullerton, *Prophecy and Authority: A Study in the History of the Doctrine and Interpretation of Scripture* (New York: Macmillan, 1919), 133.

27. Farrar, 346–47. See Schaff, 466–67. Though immediately after this quote Farrar admits that Calvin does not deny the reality of these messianic prophecies, he emphasizes that Calvin retains the particular, original contexts of these prophecies so

that one might better see the universal spirit within them. This identification of the meaning of the text with an external "universal spirit" is a typical Enlightenment interpretive move. See Frei, 217–21.

28. Gerhard Ebeling, *Word and Faith*, trans. James W. Leitch (Philadelphia: Fortress, 1963; original German in 1960), 55. Specifically, Ebeling relates the Protestants' doctrine of justification by faith alone with the historical critical method:

> The *sola fide* of the Reformation doctrine of justification both contains a rejection of any existing ways of ensuring present actualization, whether ontological, sacramental, or hierarchical, and also positively includes an understanding of actualization in the sense of genuinely historic, personal encounter. If this encounter with the historic revelation takes place solely in hearing the Word, then the shattering of all historical assurances that supposedly render the decision of faith superfluous is completely in line with the struggle against the saving significance of good works or against understanding the working of the sacrament in the sense of the *opus operatum*. The *sola fide* destroys all secretly docetic views of revelation which [*sic*] evade the historicalness of revelation by making it a history *sui generis*, a sacred area from which the critical historical method must be anxiously debarred. In the Reformers' view, both revelation and faith are discovered in their genuine historicalness, and that quite definitely means that faith is exposed to all the vulnerability and ambiguity of the historical. (56)

Though in the end, Ebeling is critical of the historical critical method, he still maintains an important tie between the Protestant Reformation and the "rise of the modern spirit" (see 55).

29. See David Steinmetz, "The Superiority of Pre-Critical Exegesis," *Theology Today* 37 (1980): 27–38, and "John Calvin on Isaiah 6: A Problem in the History of Exegesis," *Interpretation* 36 (1982): 156–70; Muller, 13–16; and Muller and John L. Thompson, "The Significance of Precritical Exegesis: Retrospect and Prospect," in *Biblical Interpretation in the Era of the Reformation*, 339–45.

30. Muller expresses many of these aspects of Calvin's exegesis in more detail, and he has eloquently aligned this with an echo of the fourfold sense—a move from *littera* to *credenda*, *agenda*, and *speranda*—from the letter to doctrine, morality, and hope. See Muller, 11.

31. For example, in his comments on Ps 5:10, Calvin writes that David "in his person represents both Christ as well as the whole body of the church" (CO 31:70). See also similar comments on Ps 109:1 (CO 32:147).

32. Frei uses the examples of Calvin's interpretation of Gen 3:15, where he denies a christological reading of the text, and Is 7:14, where he affirms a christological reading of the text, to argue for the "natural coherence" between literal and figurative readings for Calvin. Frei writes:

> Calvin would not have worried in the slightest about the contrasting conclusions of the literal reading of these two Old Testament passages,

rejecting a reference to Christ in the first instance but affirming it in the second. He would have denied that either this primacy of grammatical or literal procedure or any specific outcome of its application in any way softens the claim that the canon is one because the meaning of all of it is salvation in Jesus Christ. The reason for his confidence in the harmony of grammatical with pervasive Christological interpretation is his unquestioned assumption of a natural coherence between literal and figural reading, and of the need of each for supplementation by the other. That one reads specific passages in one way rather than another in no sense denies their mutual enhancement. (*The Eclipse of Biblical Narrative*, 26–27)

33. See David Pareus, *Libri Duo: I. Calvinus Orthodoxus de Sacrosancta Trinitate: et de aeterna Christi Divinitate. II. Solida Expositio XXXIIX. Difficilimorum Scripturae Locorum et Oraculorum: et de recta ratione applicandi Oracula Prophetica ad Christum. Oppositi Pseudocalvino Iudaizanti nuper a quodam emisso* (Neustadt: Matthaeus Harnisch, 1595), 103–104.

34. CR 38:403.

35. Much research has been done on Calvin's principle of accommodation. To name just a few significant sources, see Ford Lewis Battles, "God Was Accommodating Himself to Human Capacity," *Interpretation* 31 (1977): 19–38; Vincent Bru, "La notion d'accommodation divine chez Calvin: Ses implications théologiques et éxégetiques," *La Revue Réformée* 19 (1998): 79–91; and several articles by David F. Wright: "Calvin's Pentateuchal Criticism: Equity, Hardness of Heart, and Divine Accommodation in the Mosaic Harmony Commentary," *Calvin Theological Journal* 21 (1986): 33–50; "Accommodation and Barbarity in John Calvin's Old Testament Commentaries," in *Understanding Prophets and Poets: Essays in Honor of George Wishart Anderson*, ed. A. Graeme Auld (Sheffield: Journal for the Study of the Old Testament Press, 1993), 413–27; and "Calvin's Accommodating God," in *Calvinus Sincerioris Religionis Vindex*, ed. Wilhelm Neuser and Brian Armstrong (Kirksville, MO: Sixteenth Century Journal Publishers, 1997), 3–20.

36. Just to cite a few examples: "But whether God became known to the patriarchs through oracles and visions or by the work and ministry of men, [God] put into their minds what they should then hand down to their posterity" (*Institutes* I.vi.2). "Credibility of doctrine is not established until we are persuaded beyond doubt that God is its Author. Thus the highest proof of Scripture derives in general from the fact that God in person speaks in it" (*Institutes* I.vii.4). "As far as Sacred Scripture is concerned, however much forward men try to gnaw at it, nevertheless it clearly is crammed with thoughts that could not be humanly conceived" (*Institutes* I.viii.2). "Similarly, Moses foretells things, albeit obscurely, concerning the election of the Gentiles into God's covenant, which actually took place almost two thousand years later. Is this not plain proof that he spoke by divine inspiration?" (*Institutes* I.viii.7). And speaking about the humble origins of the Gospel writers, Calvin proclaims, "Yet the truth cries out openly that these men who, previously contemptible among common folk, suddenly began to discourse so gloriously of the heavenly mysteries must have been instructed by the Spirit" (*Institutes* I.viii.11).

37. See for examples CR 5: 324, CR 6:16, and *Institutes* I.iii. 1 and 21, and *Institutes* I.v.1.

38. *Institutes* II.xi.13.

39. *Institutes* I.xvii.1.

40. *Institutes* I.xviii and II.iv.

41. I should add that Luther exhibits more of this other understanding that I have identified with Calvin in his later exegeses, especially in his exegesis of Genesis. Of course, one of the clearest ways in which this contrast appears between Luther and Calvin is on their views of the law. Luther tends to emphasize the dichotomy of law and gospel, so that law is mostly a negative term for him to signify from what the Christian is now set free. For Calvin, just as he retains the historical context and content of Old Testament Scripture as precisely the avenue through which meaning is found, so also the law continues to have a continuing, vital function in the Christian life. The law is not simply abrogated by its fulfillment in Christ, but the very details of it still illumine divine teaching and will for the Christian. So also, Christ's fulfillment of Old Testament prophecies does not negate what these texts have to say within their own context; rather, meaning resides there as well, to reveal the story of divine providence and the goodness of God.

42. Calvin makes several statements against allegory in the *Institutes*, including *Institutes* I.xiii.22, II.v.19, II.xiii.3, III.iv.4–5, IV.xi.1, IV.xvi.15, IV.xvi.31, and IV.xvii.15. For an example, in his commentary, Calvin gives an extended critique of allegories in his interpretation of Gal 4:22. Scholars who have emphasized Calvin's abhorrence of allegory include Hans-Joachim Kraus, "Calvin's Exegetical Principles," *Interpretation* 31 (1977): 8–18, and Wulfert de Greef, *Calvijn en het Oude Testament* (Amsterdam: Ton Bolland, 1984), 48–52. T. H. L. Parker and Raymond A. Blacketer caution against assuming that this means Calvin does not at all employ some kind of allegory in his own exegesis. See Parker, *Calvin's Old Testament Commentaries* (1986, reprint, Louisville, KY: Westminster John Knox, 1993), 72–74. Blacketer argues that "Calvin reserves no place for allegories that lack any textual or historical connection to the text. But he does not reject allegory altogether; allegories, as well as types, may be drawn from the *sens naturel*, as long as there is a clear textual or historical connection between type and antitype" ("Smooth Stones, Teachable Hearts: Calvin's Allegorical Interpretation of Deuteronomy 10:1–2," *Calvin Theological Journal* 34 [1999]: 62). Though I agree that one needs to be more careful between what Calvin says and what he actually does in exegesis, I do wonder if when a reading retains at least a clear historical connection, whether we are talking about allegory per se anymore, but instead are really talking about *figurative* readings.

43. See my discussion of Calvin's principles of christological exegesis in the early part of chapter 4. I name three general principles: an Old Testament text may be read christologically when it is more fully completed by Christ and more appropriate to Christ, when it is cited by New Testament authors in reference to Christ, and when it maintains the "simple and natural" sense of the text.

Select Bibliography

PRIMARY SOURCES

Saint Augustine. *Expositions on the Book of Psalms*. Oxford: John Henry Parker, 1849.

Biblia Latina cum Glossa Ordinaria. Vol. 2. Adolph Rusch of Strassburg 1480/81. A facsimile of the editio princeps. Brepols, 1992.

Bucer, Martin. *Sacrorum Psalmorum libri quinque ad hebraicam veritatem versi et familiari explanatione elucidati*. Argentorati: Georgio Ulrichero Handlanus, 1529.

Calvin, John. *In Librum Psalmorum Commentarius* in *Ioannis Calvini Opera Quae Supersunt Omnia*. Vols. 31 and 32. Edited by Guilielmus Baum, Eduardus Cunitz, and Edúardus Reuss. Braunschweig: Schwetschke, 1887.

Denis the Carthusian. *Enarrationes Psalmos* in *Doctoris Ecstatici D. Dionysii Cartusiani Opera Omnia*. Vols. 5 and 6. Monstroli: Typis Cartusiae S. M. De Pratis, 1898.

Abrohom Chaim Feuer, trans. *Tehillim=Sefer Tehilim: A New Translation with Commentary Anthologized from Talmudic, Midrashic, and Rabbinic sources*. Brooklyn, NY: Mesorah Publications, 1985.

Hunnius, Aegidius. *Calvinus Iudiazans, hoc est: Iudaicae Glossae et Corruptelae, quibus Iohannes Calvinus illustrissima Scripturae sacrae Loca & Testamonia, de gloriosa Trinitate, Deitate Christi, & Spiritus Sancti, cum primis autem ascensione in caelos et sessione ad dextram Dei, detestandum in modum corrumpere no exhorruit. Addita est corruptelarum confutatio per Aegidium Hunnium*. Wittenberg, 1593.

Kimhi, David. *The First Book of Psalms According to the Text of the Cambridge MS Bible with the Longer Commentary of R. David Qimchi*. Edited by S. M. Schiller-Szinessy. Cambridge: Deighton, Bell, and Co., 1883. [Hebrew]

———. *The Longer Commentary of R. David Kimhi on the First Book of Psalms.* Translated by R. G. Finch. New York: Macmillan, 1919.

———. "The Commentary of Rabbi David Kimhi on Psalms 42–72." Edited by Sidney I. Esterson. *Hebrew Union College Annual* 10 (1935): 309–443. [Hebrew]

———. *The Commentary of David Kimhi on the Fifth Book of the Psalms.* Edited by Jacob Bosniak. New York: Bloch, 1954. [Hebrew]

Lefèvre (d'Étaples), Jacques. *Quincuplex psalterium gallicum, rhomanum, hebraicum, vetus, concilatum.* Paris: In clarissimo Parisorum Gymnasio ex calcotypa Henrici Stephani officina, 1513.

Luther, Martin. *Dictata super psalterium* (1513–1515) in *D. Martin Luthers Werke.* Vols. 3 and 4. Weimar: Hermann Böhlau, 1885, 1966.

———. *Operationes in Psalmos* (1519–1521) in *D. Martin Luthers Werke.* Vol. 5. Weimar: Hermann Böhlau, 1892, 1966.

———. *Ennarratio Psalmi secundi* (1532) in *D. Martin Luthers Werke.* Vol. 40, part 2, pp. 192–312. Weimar: Hermann Böhlau, 1914, 1962.

———. *Praelectio in psalmum 45* (1532) in *D. Martin Luthers Werke.* Vol. 40, part 2, pp. 471–610. Weimar: Hermann Böhlau, 1914, 1962.

———. *Der achte Psalm Davids gepredigt und ausgelegt* (1537) in *D. Martin Luthers Werke.* Vol. 45, pp. 204–50. Weimar: Hermann Böhlau, 1911, 1964.

———. *Der CX. Psalm, Gepredigt und ausgelegt* and *Predigt über den 110. Psalm* (eight sermons from 1535) in *D. Martin Luthers Werke.* Vol. 41, pp. 79–239. Weimar: Hermann Böhlau, 1910, 1964.

———. *Confitemini* (1530 commentary on Psalm 118) in *D. Martin Luthers Werke.* Vol. 31, part 1, pp. 65–182.

———. *Scholien zum 118. Psalm* (1529) in *D. Martin Luthers Werke.* Vol. 31, part 1, pp. 34–64. Weimar: Hermann Böhlau, 1913, 1964.

———. *Summarien über die Psalmen und Ursachen des Dolmetichens* (1531–1533) in *D. Martin Luthers Werke.* Vol. 38, pp. 1–69. Weimar: Hermann Böhlau, 1912, 1964.

Nicholas of Lyra. *In se continens glosam ordinarium cum expositione Lyre litterali et morali, necnon additionibus ac replici, super libros Job, Psalterium, Proverbiorum, Ecclesiasten, Cantica canticorum, Sapientie, Ecclesiasticum.* Basil: Froben & Petri, 1506.

Pareus, David. *Libri Duo: I. Calvinus Orthodoxus de Sacrosancta Trinitate: et de aeterna Christi Divinitate. II. Solida Expositio XXXIIX. Difficilimorum Scripturae Locorum et Oraculorum: et de recta ratione applicandi Oracula Prophetica ad Christum. Oppositi Pseudocalvino Iudaizanti nuper a quodam emisso.* Neustadt: Matthaeus Harnisch, 1595.

Solomon ben Isaac. *The Commentary of Rashi on the Prophets and Hagiographs.* Part 3: Psalms. Edited by I. Maarsen. Jerusalem: 1936. [Hebrew]

———. *Rashi's Commentary on Psalms 1–89,* with English translation by Mayer I. Gruber. Atlanta: Scholars, 1998. [Hebrew]

SECONDARY SOURCES

Ayers, Robert H. "The View of Medieval Biblical Exegesis in Calvin's Institutes." In *Calvin and Hermeneutics*, ed. Richard C. Gamble, 410–15. New York & London: Garland, 1992.

Backus, Irena. "Martin Bucer and the Patristic Tradition." In *Martin Bucer and Sixteenth-Century Europe: Actes du colloque de Strasbourg* (28–31 août 1991), ed. Christian Krieger and Marc Lienhard, 1:55–69. Leiden: Brill, 1993.

Backus, Irena, and Francis Higman, eds. *Théorie et pratique de l'exégése*. Geneva: Droz, 1990.

Baron, Salo W. "John Calvin and the Jews," in *Essential Papers in Judaism and Christianity in Conflict: From Late Antiquity to the Reformation*, ed. Jeremy Cohen, 380–400. New York: New York University Press, 1991.

Bauer, Uwe F. W. "Antijüdische Deutungen des ersten Psalms bei Luther und im neueren deutschen Protestantismus." *Communio Viatorum* 39 (1997): 101–19.

Bedouelle, Guy. *The Quincuplex Psalterium de Lefèvre d'Etaples: Un guide de lecture*. Geneva: Droz, 1979.

———. "Lefèvre d'Étaples et Luther: Une Recherche de Frontières (1517–1527)." *Revue de Théologie et de Philosophie* 63 (1983): 17–31.

———. "Lefèvre d'Étaples et ses disciples." *Bulletin de la Société de L'histoire du Protestantisme Français* 134 (1988): 669–72.

Bedouelle, Guy, and Bernard Roussel, eds. *Le temp des reformes et la Bible*. Paris: Beauchesne, 1989.

Beintker, Horst. "Gottverlassenheit und Transitus durch den Glauben [Anfechtungen des Menschen Jesus nach Luthers Auslegungen der Ps 8, 22]." *Evangelische Theologie* 45 (1985): 108–23.

———. "Christologische Gedanken Luthers zum Sterben Jesu: bei Auslegung von Ps 8 und Ps 22 im Kommentar von 1519 bis 1521." *Archiv für Reformationsgeschichte* 77 (1986): 5–30.

Bell, Dean P., and Stephen G. Burnett, eds. *Jews, Judaism, and the Reformation in Sixteenth-Century Germany*. Leiden: Brill, 2006.

Berger, David. *The Jewish-Christian Debate in the High Middle Ages*. Philadelphia: Jewish Publication Society of America, 1979.

———, ed. *History and Hate: The Dimensions of Anti-Semitism*. Philadelphia: Jewish Publication Society, 1986.

———. "Mission to the Jews and Jewish-Christian Contacts in the Polemical Literature of the High Middle Ages." *American Historical Review* 91 (1986): 576–91.

Biersack, Manfred. "Die Unschuld Davids: Zur Auslegung von Psalm 7 in Luthers Operationes in psalmos." In *Lutheriana: zum 500. Geburtstag Martin Luthers von den Mitarbeitern der Weimarer Ausgabe*, ed. Gerhard Hammer and Karl Heinz Zur Mühlen, 245–68. Köln: Böhlau Verlag, 1984.

Blaumeiser, Hubertus. *Martin Luthers Kreuzestheologie: Schlösel zu seiner Deutung von Mensch und Wirklichkeit; eine Untersuchung anhand der Operationes in Psalmos (1519–1521)*. Paderborn: Bonifatius, 1995.

Bornkamm, Heinrich. *Luther and the Old Testament*. Translated by Eric W. Gritsch and Ruth C. Gritsch. Mifflintown, PA: Sigler, 1997.

Boulding, M. Cecily. "Jacobus Faber Stapulensis, c 1460–1536—Forerunner of Vatican II." In *Opening the Scrolls: Essays in Catholic History in Honor of Godfrey Anstruther*, ed. Dominick Aidan Bellenger, 27–49. Bath, UK: Downside Abbey, 1987.

Brady, Thomas A. "Confessionalization—The Career of a Concept." In *Confessionalization in Europe, 1555–1750: Essays in Honor and Memory of Bodo Nischan*, ed. John Headley, Hans J. Hillerbrand, and Anthony J. Papalas, 1–20. Burlington, VT: Ashgate, 2004.

Brecht, Martin. *Martin Luther: His Road to Reformation, 1483–1521*. Translated by James L. Schaaf. Minneapolis: Fortress, 1985.

———. *Martin Luther: Shaping and Defining the Reformation, 1521–1532*. Translated by James L. Schaaf. Minneapolis: Fortress, 1990.

———. "Bucer und Luther." In *Martin Bucer and Sixteenth-Century Europe: Actes du Colloque de Strasbourg (28–31 août 1991)*, ed. Christian Krieger and Marc Lienhard, 1:351–67. Leiden: Brill, 1993.

———. *Martin Luther: The Preservation of the Church, 1532–1546*. Translated by James L. Schaaf, esp. chap. 13. Minneapolis: Fortress, 1993.

Bunte, Wolfgang. *Rabbinische Traditionen bei Nikolaus von Lyra: ein Beitrag zur Schriftauslegung des mittelalters*. New York: Peter Lang, 1994.

Burnett, Amy Nelson. "Church Discipline and Moral Reformation in the Thought of Martin Bucer." *Sixteenth Century Studies Journal* 22 (1991): 438–56.

———. *The Yoke of Christ: Martin Bucer and Christian Discipline*. Kirksville, MO: Sixteenth Century Journal Publishers, 1994.

Burnett, Stephen G. "Jews and Anti-Semitism in Early Modern Germany," *Sixteenth Century Journal* 27 (1996): 1057–64.

———. "Reassessing the 'Basel-Wittenberg Conflict': Dimensions of the Reformation-Era Discussion of Hebrew Scholarship." In *Hebraica Veritas? Christian Hebraists and the Study of Judaism in Early Modern Europe*, 181–201. Philadelphia: University of Pennsylvania Press, 2004.

Bush, John Woolman. "Lefèvre d'Étaples: Three Phases of His Life and Work." In *Reformation Studies: Essays in Honor of Roland H. Bainton*, ed. Franklin Littell, 117–28. Richmond, VA: John Knox, 1962.

Cameron, Richard M. "The Charges of Lutheranism Brought against Jacques Lefèvre D'Étaples (1520–1529)." *Harvard Theological Review* 63 (1970): 119–49.

Chazan, Robert. *Church, State, and the Jew in the Middle Ages*. New York: Behrman House, 1980.

———. "A Medieval Hebrew Polemical Mélange." *Hebrew Union College Annual* 51 (1980): 89–110.

———. "An Ashkenazic Anti-Christian Treatise." *Journal of Jewish Studies* 34 (1983): 63–72.

———. "Joseph Kimhi's Sefer Ha-Berit: Pathbreaking Medieval Jewish Apologetics." *Harvard Theological Review* 85 (1992): 417–32.

Childs, Brevard S. "The Sensus Literalis of Scripture: An Ancient and Modern Problem." In *Beitrage Zur Alttestamentlichen Theologie*, ed. Herbert Donner, Robert Hanhart, and Rudolf Smend, 80–87. Göttingen: Vandenhoeck & Ruprecht, 1977.

Cohen, Jeremy. *The Friars and the Jews: The Evolution of Medieval Anti-Judaism*. Ithaca, NY: Cornell University Press, 1982.

———. "Scholarship and Intolerance in the Medieval Academy: The Study and Evaluation of Judaism in European Christendom." *American Historical Review* 91 (1986): 592–613. And response by Gavin Langmuir, 614–24.

———, ed. *Essential Papers on Judaism and Christianity in Conflict: From Late Antiquity to the Reformation*. New York: New York University Press, 1991.

———. "Traditional Prejudice and Religious Reform: The Theological and Historical Foundations of Luther's Anti-Judaism." In *Anti-Semitism in Times of Crisis*, ed. Sander L. Gilman and Steven T. Katz, 81–102. New York: New York University Press, 1991.

———. *Living Letters of the Law: Ideas of the Jew in Medieval Christianity*. Berkeley: University of California Press, 1999.

Copenhaver, Brian P. "Lefèvre D'Étaples, Symphorien Champier, and the Secret Names of God." *Warburg and Courtauld Institutes Journal* 40 (1977): 189–211.

Coudert, Allison P., and Jeffrey S. Shoulson, eds. *Hebraica Veritas? Christian Hebraists and the Study of Judaism in Early Modern Europe*. Philadelphia: University of Pennsylvania Press, 2004.

Dagens, A. "Humanisme et Evangélisme chez Lefèvre d'Étaples." In *Courants Religieux et humanisme à la fin du xvie Siècle*, 121–34. Paris: Presses Universitaires de France, 1959.

Demonet-Launay, Marie-Luce. "La Désacralisation de l'hébreu au XVIe Siècle." In *L'Hébreu au temps de la Renaissance*, ed. Ilana Zinguer, 154–71. Leiden: Brill, 1992.

Detmers, Achim. *Reformation und Judentum: Israel-Lehren und Einstellungen zum Judentum von Luther bis zum fraühen Calvin*. Stuttgart: Kohlhammer, 2001.

Ebeling, Gerhard. "Luthers Psalterdruck vom Jahre 1513." *Zeitschrift für Theologie und Kirche* 50 (1953): 43–99.

———. "The New Hermeneutics and the Early Luther." *Theology Today* 21 (1964): 34–46.

———. "The Beginnings of Luther's Hermeneutics." *Lutheran Quarterly* 7 (1993): 129–58, 315–38, 451–68.

Eckardt, Alice L. "The Reformation and the Jews." In *Interwoven Destinies: Jews and Christians through the Ages*, ed. Eugene J. Fisher, 111–33. New York: Paulist Press, 1993.

Edwards, Mark U. "Against the Jews." In *Essential Papers on Judaism and Christianity in Conflict: From Late Antiquity to the Reformation*, ed. Jeremy Cohen, 345–79. New York: New York University Press, 1991.

Eells, Hasting. "Martin Bucer and the Conversion of John Calvin." *Princeton Theological Review* 22 (1924): 402–19.

———. *Martin Bucer*. New Haven: Yale University Press, 1931.

———. "Bucer's Plan for the Jews." *Church History* 6 (1937): 127–35.

Emery, Kent, Jr. "Denys the Carthusian and the Doxography of Scholastic Theology." In *Ad litteram: Authoritative Texts and Their Medieval Readers*, ed. Mark D. Jordan and Kent Emery, Jr., 327–59. Notre Dame Conferences in Medieval Studies 3. Notre Dame, IN: University of Notre Dame Press, 1992.

———. "Denys the Carthusian and the Invention of Preaching Materials." *Viator* 25 (1994): 377–409.

———. "Monastic 'Collectaria' from the Abbey of St. Trudo (Limburg) and the Reception of Writings by Denys the Carthusian." In *Literature and Religion in the Later Middle Ages: Philological Studies in Honor of Siegfried Wenzel*, ed. Richard G. Newhauser and John A. Alford, 237–61. Medieval and Renaissance Texts 113. Binghamton, NY: Medieval and Renaissance Texts and Studies, 1995.

———. "The Matter and Order of Philosophy according to Denys the Carthusian." In *Was ist Philosophie im Mittelalter?* ed. Jan A. Aertsen and Andreas Speer, 667–79. Miscellanea Mediaevalia 26. Berlin: Walter de Gruyter, 1998.

Engammare, Max. "Olivetan et les Commentaires Rabbiniques Historiographie et recherché d'une utilization de la literature rabbinique par un hébraïsant chrétien du premier tiers du XVIème siècle." In *L'Hébreu au temps de la Renaissance*, ed. Ilana Zinguer, 27–64. Leiden: Brill, 1992.

Engel, Mary Potter. "Calvin and the Jews: A Textual Puzzle." *Princeton Seminary Bulletin*, supplement 1 (1990): 106–23.

Farrar, Frederic W. *History of Interpretation*, 342–54. 1886. Reprint, Grand Rapids, MI: Baker Book House, 1961.

Fatio, Olivier, and Pierre Fraenkel, eds. *Histoire de l' exégése au XVIe siécle: Textes du colloque international tenu*. Droz, 1978.

Fishbane, Michael, ed. *The Midrashic Imagination: Jewish Exegesis, Thought, and History*. Albany: State University of New York Press, 1993.

Floor, L. "The Hermeneutics of Calvin." In *Calvin and Hermeneutics*, ed. Richard C. Gamble, 163–173. New York: Garland, 1992.

Forde, Gerhard O. "Law and Gospel in Luther's Hermeneutic." *Interpretation* 37 (1983): 240–52.

Frei, Hans W. *The Eclipse of Biblical Narrative: A Study in Eighteenth and Nineteenth Century Hermeneutics*. New Haven: Yale University Press, 1974.

Friedman, Jerome. *The Most Ancient Testimony: Sixteenth-Century Christian Hebraica in the Age of Renaissance Nostalgia*. Athens: Ohio University Press, 1983.

———. "The Reformation in Alien Eyes: Jewish Perceptions of Christian Troubles." *Sixteenth Century Journal* 14 (1983): 23–40.

———. "Protestants, Jews, and Jewish Sources." In *Piety, Politics, and Ethics: Reformation Studies in Honor of George Wolfgang Forell*, ed. Carter Lindberg, 139–56. Sixteenth Century Essays and Studies 3. Kirksville, MO: Sixteenth Century Journal Publishers, 1984.

Fuhrmann, Paul Traugott. "Calvin, the Expositor of Scripture." *Interpretation* 6 (1952): 188–209.

Fullerton, Kemper. *Prophecy and Authority*, esp. 139–163. New York: Macmillan, 1919.

Gamble, Richard C., ed. "*Brevitas et Facilitas*: Towards an Understanding of Calvin's Hermeneutic." *Westminster Theological Journal* 47 (1985): 1–17.

———. *Calvin and Hermeneutics*. Articles on Calvin and Calvinism 6. New York: Garland, 1992.

————. "The Sources of Calvin's Genesis Commentary: A Preliminary Report." *Archiv für Reformationsgeschichte* 84 (1999): 206–21.

Gilman, Sander L. "Martin Luther and the Self-hating Jews." In *The Martin Luther Quincentennial*, ed. Gerhard Dünnhaupt, 79–97. Detroit: Wayne State University Press, 1985.

Gow, Andrew Colin. "Christian Colonialism: Luther's Exegesis of Hebrew Scripture." In *Continuity and Change: The Harvest of Late Medieval and Reformation History: Essays presented to Heiko A. Oberman on his 70th Birthday*, ed. J. Bast and Andrew C. Gow, 229–52. Leiden: Brill, 2000.

Greschat, Martin. "The Relation between Church and Civil Community in Bucer's Reforming Work." In *Martin Bucer: Reforming Church and Community*, ed. D. F. Wright, 17–31. Cambridge: Cambridge University Press, 1994.

————. *Martin Bucer: A Reformer and His Times*. Translated by Stephen E. Buckwalter. Louisville, KY: Westminster John Knox, 2004.

Gritsch, Eric W. "The Cultural Context of Luther's Interpretation." *Interpretation* 37 (1983): 266–76.

————. "The Jews in Reformation Theology." In *Jewish-Christian Encounters over the Centuries: Symbiosis, Prejudice, Holocaust, Dialogue*, ed. Marvin Perry and Frederick M. Schweitzer, 197–212. New York: Peter Lang, 1994.

Gross-Diaz, Theresa. "What's a Good Soldier to Do? Scholarship and Revelation in the Postills on the Psalms." In *Nicholas of Lyra: The Senses of Scripture*, ed. Philip Krey and Lesley Smith, 111–28. Leiden: Brill, 2000.

Hailperin, Herman. *Rashi and the Christian Scholars*. Pittsburgh: University of Pittsburgh Press, 1963.

Haire, J. L. M. "John Calvin as Expositor." *Irish Biblical Studies* 4 (1982): 2–16.

Hallo, Rudolf. "Christian Hebraists." *Modern Judaism* 3 (1983): 95–116.

Hammann, Gottfried. "Ecclesiological Motifs behind the Creation of the 'Christlichen Gemeinschaften.'" In *Martin Bucer: Reforming Church and Community*, ed. D. F. Wright, 129–43. Cambridge: Cambridge University Press, 1994.

Hasler, Richard A. "The Influence of David and the Psalms upon John Calvin's Life and Thought." *Hartford Quarterly* 5 (1964–65) 7–18.

Headley, John, Hans J. Hillerbrand, and Anthony J. Papalas, eds. *Confessionalization in Europe, 1555–1750: Essays in Honor and Memory of Bodo Nischan*. Burlington, VT: Ashgate, 2004.

Hendrix, Scott H. *Ecclesia in Via: Ecclesiological Developments in the Medieval Psalms Exegesis and the Dictata super Psalterium (1513–1515) of Martin Luther*. Leiden: Brill, 1974.

————. "The Authority of Scripture at Work: Luther's Exegesis of the Psalms." In *Encounters with Luther*, ed. Eric W. Gritsch, 2:144–59. Gettysburg, PA: Lutheran Theological Seminary, 1982.

————. "Luther against the Background of the History of Biblical Interpretation." *Interpretation* 37 (1983): 229–39.

————. "Toleration of the Jews in the German Reformation: Urbanus Rhegius and Braunschweig." *Archiv für Reformationsgeschichte* 81 (1990): 189–209.

Hesselink, John. "Calvin's Understanding of the Relation of the Church and Israel Based Largely on His Interpretation of Romans 9–11." *Ex Auditu* 4 (1988): 38–69.

———. "John Calvin on the Law and Christian Freedom." *Ex Auditu* 11 (1995): 77–89.

Hobbs, Gerald R. "An Introduction to the Psalms Commentary of Martin Bucer." PhD diss., University of Strasbourg, 1971.

———. "Martin Bucer on Psalm 22: A Study in the Application of Rabbinic Exegesis by a Christian Hebraist." In *Histoire de l'exégèse au XVIe siècle*, ed. Olivier Fatio and Pierre Fraenkel, 144–63. Genève: Librairie Droz, 1978.

———. "Exegetical Projects and Problems: A New Look at an Undated Letter from Bucer to Zwingli." In *Prophet, Pastor, Protestant: The Work of Huldrych Zwingli after Five Hundred Years*, ed. E. J. Furcha and H. Wayne Pipkin, 89–107. Pittsburgh Theological Monographs 11. Allison Park, PA: Pickwick, 1984.

———. "How Firm a Foundation: Martin Bucer's Historical Exegesis of the Psalms." *Church History* 53 (1984): 477–91.

———. "L'Hébreu, le Judaïsme et la Théologie." *Bulletin de la Société de l'Histoire Français* 135 (1989): 42–53.

———. "Martin Bucer et les Juifs." In *Martin Bucer and Sixteenth-Century Europe: Actes due colloque de Strasbourg* (28–31 August 1991), ed. Christian Krieger and Marc Lienhard, 2:681–89. Leiden: Brill, 1993.

———. "Martin Bucer and the Englishing of the Psalms: Pseudonymity in the Service of Early English Protestant Piety." In *Martin Bucer: Reforming Church and Community*, ed. D. F. Wright, 161–75. Cambridge: Cambridge University Press, 1994.

———. "Bucer's Use of King David as Mirror of the Christian Prince." *Reformation and Renaissance Review* 5 (2003): 102–28.

Holmio, Armas K. E. *Martin Luther: Friend or Foe of the Jews*. Chicago: National Lutheran Council, 1949.

Hopf, Constantin. *Martin Bucer and the English Reformation*. Oxford: Basil Blackwell, 1946.

Hotson, Howard. "Irenicism and Dogmatics in the Confessional Age: Pareus and Comenius in Heidelberg, 1614." *Journal of Ecclesiastical History* 46 (1995): 432–56.

Hughes, Philip Edcumbe. *Lefevre: Pioneer of Ecclesiastical Renewal in France*. Grand Rapids, MI: Eerdmans, 1984.

Jacobs, Louis. *Jewish Biblical Exegesis*. New York: Behrman House, 1973.

Janse, Wim, and Barbara Pitkin, eds. *The Formation of Clerical and Confessional Identities in Early Modern Europe*. Dutch Review of Church History 85. Leiden: Brill, 2005.

Jong, James A. de. "'An Anatomy of All Parts of the Soul': Insights into Calvin's Spirituality from His Psalms Commentary." In *Calvinus Sacrae Scripturae Professor: Calvin as Confessor of Holy Scripture*, ed. Wilhelm Neusner, 1–14. Grand Rapids, MI: Eerdmans, 1994.

Jordan, James. "Jacques Lefèvre d'Étaples: Principles and Practice of Reform at Meaux." In *Contemporary Reflections on the Medieval Christian Tradition: Essays in Honor of Ray C. Petry*, ed. George H. Shriver, 95–115. Durham, NC: Duke University Press, 1974.

Judah, ha-Levi. *The Kuzari: In Defense of the Despised Faith*. Northvale, NJ: Jason Aronson, 1998.

Kalita, Thomas M. "The Influence of Nicholas of Lyra on Martin Luther's Commentary on Genesis." PhD diss., Catholic University of America, 1985.

Kiecker, James George. *The Postilla of Nicholas of Lyra on the Song of Songs*. Milwaukee, WI: Marquette University Press, 1998.

Kleiner, John W. "The Attitudes of Martin Bucer and Landgrave Philipp toward the Jews of Hesse." In *Faith and Freedom: A Tribute to Franklin H. Littel*, ed. Richard Libowitz, 221–30. Oxford: Pergamon, 1987.

Klepper, Deeana Copeland. "Nicholas of Lyra and Franciscan Interest in Hebrew Scholarship." In *Nicholas of Lyra: The Senses of Scripture*, ed. Philip Krey and Lesley Smith, 289–311. Leiden: Brill, 2000.

———. *The Insight of Unbelievers: Nicholas of Lyra and Christian Reading of Jewish Text in the Later Middle Ages*. Philadelphia: University of Pennsylvania Press, 2007.

Kort, Wesley A. *"Take, Read": Scripture, Textuality, and Cultural Practice*, 14–36. University Park, PA: Pennsylvania State University Press, 1996.

Kraeling, Emil. *The Old Testament since the Reformation*. New York: Harper and Brothers, 1955.

Kraus, Hans-Joachim. "Calvin's Exegetical Principles." *Interpretation* 31 (1977): 8–18.

———. "Israel in the Theology of Calvin—Towards a New Approach to the Old Testament and Judaism." *Christian Jewish Relations* 22 (1989): 75–86.

Krey, Philip. "Many Readers but Few Followers: The Fate of Nicholas of Lyra's 'Apocalypse Commentary' in the Hands of His Late-Medieval Admirers." *Church History* 64 (1995): 185–201.

———. "'The Old Law Prohibits the Hand and Not the Spirit': The Law and the Jews in Nicholas of Lyra's Romans Commentary of 1329." In *Nicholas of Lyra: The Senses of Scripture*, ed. Philip Krey and Lesley Smith, 251–66. Leiden: Brill, 2000.

Kroon, Marijn de. *Martin Bucer und Johannes Calvin: Reformatorische Perspektiven*. Göttingen: Vandenhoeck & Ruprecht, 1991.

Lane, Anthony S. *John Calvin: Student of the Church Fathers*. Grand Rapids, MI: Baker Books, 1999.

Lange van Revenswaay, J. Marius J. "Calvin und die Juden: eine offene Frage?" *Reformiertes Erbe* 2 (1993): 183–94.

Lasker, Daniel J. *Jewish Philosophical Polemics against Christianity in the Middle Ages*. New York: Ktav, 1977.

———, trans., with introduction and notes. *The Refutation of Christian Principles* by Hasdai Crescas. New York: State University of New York Press, 1992.

———. "Jewish Philosophical Polemics in Ashkenaz." In *Contra Iudaeos: Ancient and Medieval Polemics between Christians and Jews*, ed. Ora Limoi and Guy G. Strousma, 195–213. Tübingen: J. C. B. Mohr, 1996.

Laver, Mary Sweetland. "Calvin, the Jews, and Intra-Christian Polemics." PhD diss., Temple University, 1988.

Lee, Sou-Young. "Calvin's Understanding of *Pietas*." In *Calvinus Sincerioris Religionis Vindex: Calvin as Protector of the Purer Religion*, ed. Wilhelm H. Neuser and Brian G. Armstrong, 225–39. Sixteenth Century Essays and Studies 36. Kirksville, MO: Sixteenth Century Journal Publishers.

Locher, Gottfried W. "Calvin spricht zu den Juden." *Theologische Zeitschrift* 23 (1967): 180–96.

Loewe, Raphael. "The Medieval Christian Hebraists of England." *Hebrew Union College Annual* 28 (1957): 205–52.

Lohse, Bernhard. *Martin Luther's Theology: Its Historical and Systematic Development.* Translated and edited by Roy A. Harrisville, 336–45. Minneapolis: Fortress, 1999.

Lubac, Henri de. *Medieval Exegesis: The Four Senses of Scripture,* Vol. 1. Translated by Mark Sebanc. Grand Rapids, MI: William B. Eerdmans, 1998; Vol. 2. Translated by E. M. Macierowsci. Grand Rapids, MI: William B. Eerdmans, 2000.

Marius, Richard. "On the Jews." In *Martin Luther: The Christian between God and Death,* 372–80. Cambridge: Harvard University Press, 1999.

Markish, Shimon. *Erasmus and the Jews.* Translated by Anthony Olcott. 1974. Reprint, Chicago: University of Chicago Press, 1986.

Matthias, Markus. *Theologie und Konfession. Der Beitrag von Ägidius Hunnius (1550–1603) zur Entstehung einer lutherischen Religionskultur.* Leucoreastudien zur Geschichte der Reformation und der Lutherischen Orthodoxie 4. Leipzig: Evangelische Verlagsanstalt, 2004.

Mays, James Luther. "Calvin's Commentary on the Psalms: The Preface as Introduction." In *John Calvin and the Church,* ed. Timothy George, 195–204. Louisville, KY: Westminster John Knox, 1990.

McGuire, Brian P. "Denys of Ryckel's Debt to Bernard of Clairvaux." In *Ausbreitung kartüsischen Lebens und Giestes im Mittelalter,* Bd. 1, 13–34. Analecta Cartusiana 63. Salzburg: Institute für Anglistik und Amerikanistik, 1990.

McKane, William. *Selected Christian Hebraists.* Cambridge: Cambridge University Press, 1989.

———. "Calvin as an Old Testament Commentator." In *Calvin and Hermeneutics,* ed. Richard C. Gamble, 250–59. New York: Garland, 1992.

McKim, Donald K. *Calvin and the Bible.* Cambridge: Cambridge University Press, 2006.

Mentzer, Raymond A. "Fashioning Reformed Identity in Early Modern France." In *Confessionalization in Europe, 1555–1750: Essays in Honor and Memory of Bodo Nischan,* ed. John Headley, Hans J. Hillerbrand, and Anthony J. Papalas, 243–55. Burlington, VT: Ashgate, 2004.

Mentzer, Raymond A. "Fashioning Reformed Identity in Early Modern France." In *Confessionalization in Europe, 1555–1750: Essays in Honor and Memory of Bodo Nischan,* ed. John Headley, Hans J. Hillerbrand, and Anthony J. Papalas, 243–55. Burlington, VT: Ashgate, 2004.

Merrill, Eugene H. "Rashi, Nicholas de Lyra, and Christian Exegesis." *Westminster Theological Journal* 38 (1976): 66–79.

Mevora, Barouh. "Christian Hebraists in the Post-Medieval Period." *Immanuel* 14 (1982): 114–23.

Morel, Maxine B. "Jacques Lefèvre d'Étaples: A Review Article," *Iliff Review* 42 (1985): 43–48.

Muller, Richard. "Biblical Interpretation in the Era of the Reformation: The View from the Middle Ages." In *Biblical Interpretation in the Era of the Reformation,* ed. Richard A. Muller and John L. Thompson, 3–22. Grand Rapids, MI: Eerdmans, 1996.

———. *The Unaccommodated Calvin: Studies in the Foundation of a Theological Tradition.* Oxford Studies in Historical Theology. New York: Oxford University Press, 2000.

Muller, Richard A., and Thompson, John L., eds. *Biblical Interpretation in the Era of the Reformation.* Grand Rapids, MI: Eerdmans, 1996.

———. "The Significance of Precritical Exegesis: Retrospect and Prospect." In *Biblical Interpretation in the Era of the Reformation,* ed. Richard A. Muller and John L. Thompson, 335–45. Grand Rapids, MI: Eerdmans, 1996.

Neuser, Wilhelm H. "Calvins Verständnis der Heiligen Schrift." In *Calvinus Sacrae Scripturae Professor: Calvin as Confessor of Holy Scripture,* ed. Wilhelm H. Neuser, 6–71. Grand Rapids, MI: Eerdmans, 1994.

Nijenhuis, W. "A Remarkable Historical Argumentation in Bucer's 'Judenratschlag'" and "Bucer and the Jews." In *Ecclesia Reformata: Studies on the Reformation,* 23–72. Leiden: Brill, 1972.

Oberman, Heiko A. "Biblical Exegesis: The Literal and Spiritual Sense of Scripture." In *Forerunners of the Reformation: The Shape of Late Medieval Thought,* trans. Paul L. Nyhus, 281–96. New York: Holt, Rinehart, and Winston, 1966.

———. *The Roots of Antisemitism: In the Age of the Renaissance and Reformation,* trans. James I. Porter. Philadelphia: Fortress, 1984.

———. "Darkness at Noon." In *Luther: Man between God and the Devil,* trans. Eileen Walliser-Schwarzbart, 292–97. New York: Doubleday, 1989.

———. "Discovery of Hebrew and Discrimination against the Jews: The *Veritas Hebraica* as Double-Edged Sword in Renaissance and Reformation." In *Germania Illustrata: Essays on Early Modern Germany Presented to Gerald Strauss,* ed. Andrew Fix and Susan Karant-Nunn, 19–34. Sixteenth Century Essays and Studies 18. Kirksville, MO: Sixteenth Century Journal, 1992.

———. "Reuchlin and the Jews: Obstacles on the Path to Emancipation." In *The Impact of the Reformation,* 141–70. Grand Rapids, MI: Eerdmans, 1994.

———. "The Stubborn Jews: Timing and Escalation of Antisemitism in Late Medieval Europe." In *The Impact of the Reformation,* 122–40. Grand Rapids, MI: Eerdmans, 1994.

———. "Three Sixteenth-Century Attitudes toward Judaism: Reuchlin, Erasmus, and Luther." In *The Impact of the Reformation,* 81–121. Grand Rapids, MI: Eerdmans, 1994.

Parker, T. H. L. "Calvin the Biblical Expositor." *Churchman* 78 (1964): 23–31.

———. *Calvin's Old Testament Commentaries.* Louisville, KY: Westminster John Knox, 1986.

———. "Calvin's Commentary on Hebrews." In *Church, Word and Spirit: Historical and Theological Essays in Honor of Geoffrey W. Bromiley,* ed. James E. Bradley and Richard A. Muller, 135–40. Grand Rapids, MI: Eerdmans, 1987.

———. *Calvin's New Testament Commentaries.* 2nd ed. Louisville, KY: Westminster John Knox, 1993.

Pater, Calvin Augustine. "Calvin, the Jews, and the Judaic Legacy." In *Papers from the 1986 International Calvin Symposium,* ed. E. J. Furcha, 256–95. Montreal: McGill University Press, 1986.

Pauck, Wilhelm. "Luther and Butzer." In *The Heritage of the Reformation,* 73–99. Glencoe, IL: Free Press, 1961.

Pelikan, Jaroslav, ed. *Interpreters of Luther: Essays in Honor of Wilhelm Pauck.* Philadelphia: Fortress, 1968.

———. *The Reformation of the Bible: The Bible of the Reformation.* New Haven: Yale University Press, 1996.

Pitkin, Barbara. "David as Paradigm for Faith in Calvin's Psalm Exegesis." *Sixteenth Century Journal* 24 (1993): 843–63.

———. "Seeing and Believing in the Commentaries on John by Martin Bucer and John Calvin." *Church History* 68 (1999): 865–85.

———. *What Pure Eyes Could See: Calvin's Doctrine of Faith in Its Exegetical Context.* New York: Oxford University Press, 1999.

———. "The Heritage of the Lord: Children in the Theology of John Calvin." In *The Child in Christian Thought*, ed. Marcia Bunge, 160–93, 479–80. Grand Rapids, MI: Eerdmans, 2001.

———. "Psalm 8:1–2." *Interpretation* 55 (2001): 177–80.

Preus, James S. "Old Testament *Promissio* and Luther's New Hermeneutic." *Harvard Theological Review* 60 (1967): 145–61.

———. *From Shadow to Promise: Old Testament Interpretation from Augustine to the Young Luther.* Cambridge: Harvard University Press, 1969.

Puckett, David. *John Calvin's Exegesis of the Old Testament.* Louisville, KY: Westminster John Knox, 1995.

Raeder, Siegfried. *Das Hebräische bei Luther, untersucht bis zum Ende der ersten Psalmenforlesung.* Tübingen: J. C. B. Mohr, 1961.

———. *Die Benutzung des masoretischen Textes bei Luther in der Zeit zwischen der ersten und zweiten Psalmenvorlesung (1515–1518).* Tübingen: Mohr, 1967.

———. *Grammatica theological: Studien zu Luthers Operationes in Psalmos.* Tübingen: Mohr, 1977.

———. "Die Auslegung des 50 (51) Psalms in Augustins Enarrationes in psalmos und in Luthers Dictata super psalterium." In *Lutheriana: zum 500. Geburtstag Martin Luthers von den Mitarbeitern der Weimarer Ausgabe*, ed. Gerhard Hammer and Karl Heinz Zur Mühlen, 153–92. Köln: Böhlau Verlag, 1984.

Reid, W. Stanford. "The Battle Hymns of the Lord: Calvinist Psalmody of the Sixteenth Century." In *Sixteenth Century Essays and Studies*, ed. Carl S. Meyer, 2:36–54. St. Louis, MO: Foundation for Reformation Research, 1971.

Reinhard, Klaus. "Das Werk des Nikolaus von Lyra im mittelalterlichen Spanien." *Traditio* 43 (1987): 321–58.

Reinhard, Wolfgang. "Zwang zur Konfessionalisierung? Prolegomena zu einer Theorie des konfessionellen Zeitalters." *Zeitschrift für historische Forschung* 10 (1983): 257–77.

Rice, Eugene F., Jr. "The Humanist Idea of Christian Antiquity: Lefèvre d'Étaples and His Circle." *Studies in the Renaissance* 9 (1962): 126–60.

Robinson, Jack Hughes. *John Calvin and the Jews.* American University Studies. Series 7, Vol. 123. New York: Peter Lang, 1992.

Rosenthal, Frank. "The Rise of Christian Hebraism in the Sixteenth Century." *Historia Judaica* 7 (1945): 167–91.

Roussel, Bernard. "Bucer Exegete." In *Martin Bucer and Sixteenth-Century Europe: Actes du Colloque de Strasbourg (28–31 août 1991)*, ed. Christian Krieger and Marc Lienhard, 1:39–54. Leiden: Brill, 1993.

Rowan, Steven. "Luther, Bucer, and Eck on the Jews." *Sixteenth Century Journal* 16 (1985): 79–90.

Roynesdal, Olaf. "Martin Luther and the Jews." PhD diss., Marquette University, 1986.

Ruderman, David B. "A Jewish Apologetic Treatise from Sixteenth Century Bologna." *Hebrew Union College Annual* 50 (1979): 253–76.

Russell, S. H. "Calvin and the Messianic Interpretation of the Psalms." *Scottish Journal of Theology* 21 (1968): 37–47.

Schaff, Philip. "Calvin as a Commentator." *Presbyterian and Reformed Review* 3 (1892): 462–69.

Schilling, Heinz. "Die zweite Reformation." In *Die reformierte Konfessionalisierung in Deutschland—Das Problem der "Zweiten Reformation,"* 387–438. Gütersloh: Gütersloher Verlagshaus, 1986.

———. "Die Konfessionalisierung im Reich: Religiöser und gesellschaftlicher Wandel in Deutschland zwischen 1555 und 1620." *Historisch Zeitschrift* 246 (1988): 1–45.

———. "Confessional Europe." In *Handbook of European History 1400–1600: Late Middle Ages, Renaissance and Reformation.* Vol. 2: *Visions, Programs and Outcomes,* ed. Thomas A. Brady Jr., Heiko A. Oberman, and James D. Tracy, 641–81. Leiden: Brill, 1996.

———. "Confessionalization: Historical and Scholarly Perspectives of a Comparative and Interdisciplinary Paradigm." In *Confessionalization in Europe, 1555–1750: Essays in Honor and Memory of Bodo Nischan,* ed. John Headley, Hans J. Hillerbrand, and Anthony J. Papalas, 21–35. Burlington, VT: Ashgate, 2004.

Schreiner, Susan E. *Theater of His Glory: Nature and the Natural Order in the Thought of John Calvin.* Grand Rapids, MI: Baker Books, 1991.

———. *Where Shall Wisdom Be Found? Calvin's Exegesis of Job from Medieval and Modern Perspectives.* Chicago: University of Chicago Press, 1994.

Schulze, L. F. "Calvin and Biblical Inspiration—A Case Study." In *Calvin's Books: Festschrift Dedicated to Peter De Klerk on the Occasion of His 70th Birthday,* ed. Wilhelm N. Neuser, Herman J. Selderhuis, and Willem van Spijker, 189–95. Heerenveen: J. J. Groen, 1997.

Schurb, Ken. "Sixteenth-Century Lutheran-Calvinist Conflict on the Protevangelium." *Concordia Theological Quarterly* 54 (1990): 25–47.

Signer, Michael A. "King/Messiah: Rashi's Exegesis of Psalm 2." *Prooftexts* 3 (1983): 273–78.

———. "Polemic and Exegesis: The Varieties of Twelfth-Century Hebraism." In *Hebraica Veritas? Christian Hebraists and the Study of Judaism in Early Modern Europe,* ed. Allison P. Coudert and Jeffrey S. Shoulson, 21–32. Philadelphia: University of Pennsylvania Press, 2004.

Simon, Uriel. *Four Approaches to the Book of Psalms: From Saadiah Gaon to Abraham Ibn Ezra.* New York: State University of New York Press, 1991.

Smalley, Beryl. *The Study of the Bible in the Middle Ages.* Notre Dame, IN: University of Notre Dame Press, 1964.

Smolinsky, H. "The Bible and Its Exegesis in the Controversies about Reform and Reformation." In *Creative Biblical Exegesis: Christian and Jewish Hermeneutics through the Centuries*, ed. Benjamin Uffenheimer and Henning Graf Reventlow, 115–30. JSOT Supplemental Series 59. Sheffield: JSOT Press, 1988.

Spijker, Willem Van't. "Prädestination bei Bucer und Calvin. Ihre gegenseitige Beeinflussung und Abhängigkeit." In *Calvinus Theologus: d. Referate d. Congrès Europ. de Recherches Calviniennes . . . vom 16.–19. September 1974 in Amsterdam*, ed. W. H. Neuser, 85–111. Neukirchen-Vluyn: Neukirchener Verlag, 1976.

———. "The Influence of Bucer on Calvin as Becomes Evident from the *Institutes*." In *John Calvin's Institutes: His Opus Magnum: Proceedings of the Second South African Congress for Calvin Research, July 31–August 3, 1984*, 106–32. Potchefstroom, South Africa: Potchefstroom University for Higher Education, 1986.

———. "Die Lehre vom Heiligen Geist bei Bucer und Calvin." In *Calvinus Servus Christi: Die Referate des Congrès International des Recherches Calviniennes . . . vom 25. bis 28. August 1986 in Debrecen*, ed. W. H. Neuser, 73–106. Budapest: Presseabteilung des Ráday-Kollegiums, 1988.

———. "Bucer und Calvin." In *Martin Bucer and Sixteenth Century Europe: Actes du colloque de Strasbourg*, ed. Christian Krieger and Marc Lienhard, 1:461–70. Leiden: Brill, 1993.

———. "Bucer's Influence on Calvin: Church and Community." In *Martin Bucer: Reforming Church and Community*, ed. D. F. Wright, 32–44. Cambridge: Cambridge University Press, 1994.

Steinmetz, David C. *Luther and Staupitz: An Essay in the Intellectual Origins of the Protestant Reformation*. Durham, NC: Duke University Press, 1980.

———. "The Superiority of Pre-Critical Exegesis." *Theology Today* 37 (1980): 27–38.

———. "John Calvin on Isaiah 6: A Problem of Historical Exegesis." *Interpretation* 36 (1982): 156–70.

———. "Luther and the Ascent of Jacob's Ladder." *Church History* 55 (1986): 179–92.

———, ed. *The Bible in the Sixteenth Century.* Durham, NC: Duke University Press, 1990.

———. "Calvin and His Lutheran Critics." In *Calvin in Context*, 172–86. New York: Oxford University Press, 1995.

———. "Calvin and Patristic Exegesis." In *Calvin in Context*, 122–40. New York: Oxford University Press, 1995.

———. *Luther in Context.* Grand Rapids, MI: Baker Books, 1995.

———. "Calvin as Interpreter of Genesis." In *Calvinus Sincerious Religionis Vindex: Calvin as Protector of the Purer Religion*, ed. Wilhelm H. Neuser and Brian G. Armstrong, 53–66. Sixteenth Century Essays and Studies 36. Kirksville, MO: Sixteenth Century Journal, 1997.

———. "The Judaizing Calvin." In *Die Patristik in der Bibelexegese des 16. Jahrhunderts*, ed. David Steinmetz and Robert Kolb, 135–45. Band 85. Wiesbaden: Harrassowitz, 1999.

Stephens, W. P. *The Holy Spirit in the Theology of Martin Bucer.* Cambridge: Cambridge University Press, 1970.

———, ed. *The Bible, the Reformation, and the Church: Essays in Honor of James Atkinson.* Sheffield: Sheffield Academic, 1995.

Stow, Kenneth R. "Conversion, Christian Hebraism, and Hebrew Prayer in the Sixteenth Century." *Hebrew Union College Annual* 47 (1976): 217–36.

———. *Catholic Thought and Papal Jewry Policy, 1555–1593*. New York: Jewish Theological Seminary of America, 1977.

Stuehrenberg, Paul. "The Medieval Commentary Tradition: The Glossa Ordinaria, Hugh of St. Cher and Nicholas of Lyra and the Study of the Bible in the Middle Ages." *Journal of Religion and Theology Info* 1, no. 2 (1993): 91–101.

Stupperich, Robert, ed. *Bucers Deutsche Schriften*, Vol. 7: *Schriften der Jahre 1538–1539*, 336–37. Gütersloh: Gütersloher Verlagshaus Gerd Mohn, 1964.

Talmage, Frank E. "Hebrew Polemical Treatise: Anti-Cathar and Anti-Orthodox." *Harvard Theological Review* 60 (1967): 323–48.

———. "R. David Kimhi as Polemicist." *Hebrew Union College Annual* 38 (1967): 213–58.

———. "David Kimhi and the Rationalist Tradition." *Hebrew Union College Annual* 39 (1968): 177–218.

———. "David Kimhi and the Rationalist Tradition II," in *Studies in Jewish Bibliography, History, and Literature in Honor of I. Edward Kiev*, ed. Charles Berlin, 453–78. New York: Ktav, 1972.

———. *David Kimhi: The Man and the Commentaries*. Cambridge: Harvard University Press, 1975.

———. "Kimhi's Polemics with Christianity." *Immanuel* 8 (1978): 80–87.

Talmage, Frank E., and Barry Walfish, eds. *Apples of Gold in Settings of Silver: Studies in Medieval Jewish Exegesis and Polemics*. Toronto: Pontifical Institute of Mediaeval Studies, 1999.

Thoma, Clemens, and Michael Wyschogrod, eds. *Understanding Scripture: Explorations of Jewish and Christian Traditions of Interpretation*. Studies in Judaism and Christianity. New York: Paulist, 1987.

Timmer, David E. "The Bible between Church and Synagogue: Thoughts on the Interpretation of the Hebrew Scriptures." *Reformed Review* 39 (1985–86): 94–103.

———. "Biblical Exegesis and the Jewish-Christian Controversy in the Early Twelfth Century." *Church History* 58 (1989): 309–21.

Tjernagel, Neelak S. *Martin Luther and the Jewish People*. Milwaukee, WI: Northwestern Publishing House, 1985.

Torrance, Thomas F. "Kingdom and Church in the Thought of Martin Butzer." *Journal of Ecclesiastical History* 6 (1955): 48–59.

———. *The Hermeneutics of John Calvin*. Edinburgh: Scottish Academic, 1988.

Van Deusen, Nancy. *The Place of the Psalms in the Intellectual Culture of the Middle Ages*. SUNY Series in Medieval Studies. Albany: State University of New York Press, 1999.

Vogelsang, Erich. *Die Anfänge Luthers Christologie nach der ersten Psalmenvorlesang, insbesondere in ihren exegetischen und systematischen Zusammenhägen mit Augustin und der Scholastik dargestellt*. Leipzig: de Gruyter, 1929.

Wallman, J. "Luther on Jews and Islam." In *Creative Biblical Exegesis: Christian and Jewish Hermeneutics through the Centuries*, ed. Benjamin Uffenheimer and Henning Graf Reventlow, 149–60. JSOT Supplemental Series 59. Sheffield: JSOT Press, 1988.

Walton, Michael T., and Phyllis J. Walton. "In Defense of the Church Militant: The Censorship of the Rashi Commentary in the Magna Biblia Rabbinica." *Sixteenth Century Journal* 21 (1990): 385–400.

Wassermann, Dirk. *Dionysius der Kartüser: Einfürung in Werk und Gedankenwelt.* Salzburg: Institut für Anglistik und Amerikanistik, 1996.

Wendel, François. *Calvin et l'humanisme.* Paris: Presses Universitairies de France, 1976.

———. *Calvin: Origins and Development of His Religious Thought.* Translated by Philip Mairet. 1950. Reprint, Grand Rapids, MI: Baker Books, 1997.

Witvliet, John. "Spirituality of the Psalter: Metrical Psalms in Liturgy and Life in Calvin's Geneva." In *Calvin and Spirituality: Papers Presented at the 10th Colloquium of the Calvin Studies Society,* ed. David L. Foxgrover, 93–117. Grand Rapids, MI: Calvin Studies Society, 1998.

Wood, Arthur Skevington. "Nicolaus of Lyra." *Evangelical Quarterly* 33 (1961): 196–206.

Wood, Rega. "Nicholas of Lyra and Lutheran Views on Ecclesiastical Office." *Journal of Ecclesiastical History* 29 (1978): 451–62.

Zimmer, Eric. "Jewish and Christian Hebraist Collaboration in Sixteenth Century Germany." *Jewish Quarterly Review* 71 (1980): 69–88.

Index